Civil Procedure in Sweden

Civil Procedure in Sweden

Bengt Lindell

This book was originally published as a monograph in the International Encyclopaedia of Laws/Civil Procedure.

Founding Editor: Roger Blanpain
General Editor: Frank Hendrickx
Volume Editor: Piet Taelman

Wolters Kluwer

Published by:
Kluwer Law International B.V.
PO Box 316
2400 AH Alphen aan den Rijn
The Netherlands
E-mail: international-sales@wolterskluwer.com
Website: lrus.wolterskluwer.com

Sold and distributed by:
Wolters Kluwer Legal & Regulatory U.S.
7201 McKinney Circle
Frederick, MD 21704
United States of America
Email: customer.service@wolterskluwer.com

ISBN 978-94-035-2571-6

e-Book: ISBN 978-94-035-2572-3
web-PDF: ISBN 978-94-035-2573-0

The Author

Professor Dr Bengt Lindell is Professor of Civil and Criminal Procedure at Uppsala University in Sweden since 1990. His research and teaching interests include theories on evidence, general principles of civil procedure and problem-solving analysis, national and international arbitration and alternative dispute resolution with an emphasis on mediation and negotiation. Professor Lindell has been a visiting professor at Minnesota Law School, a Guest Researcher at the Chicago Kent School of Law and several times at Bond University, Mediation Centre in Queensland, Australia. He is currently a member of *Wissenschaftlichen Vereinigung für Internationales Verfarensrecht* e.V and *Tagung für Deutscher Prozessrechtslehrer* and the International Association Procedural Law. Professor Lindell received his LLD in 1987 from the Faculty of Law in Uppsala.

The Author

Table of Contents

List of Abbreviations

ADR	Alternative Dispute Resolution
ÄktB	The Marriage Code (*Äktenskapsbalken*)
ÄL	The Act on Processing of Court Matters (*Lag om handläggning av domstolsärenden*)
BRB	The Criminal Code (*Brottsbalken*)
DF	The Decree on Service (*Delgivningsförordningen*)
Dir	Terms of Reference to a Committee, etc. (*Direktiv*)
EC	European Commission
EEA	European Economic Area
EU	European Union
FB	Code Relating to Parents, Guardians and Children (*Föräldrabalken*)
JB	The Land Code (*Jordabalken*)
JK	Chancellor of Justice (*Justitiekanslern*)
JO	The Parliamentary Ombudsman (*Justitieombudsmannen*)
Ds Ju	Ministry of Justice (*Justitiedepartementet*)
KL	The Bankruptcy Act (*Konkurslagen*)
LBH	The Act on Summary Proceedings (*Lag om betalningsföreläggande och handräckning*)
OSL	Public Access to Information and Secrecy Act (*Lag om offentlighet och sekretess*)
LOA	The Public Employment Act (*Lag om offentlig anställning*)
LRA	The Act on Litigation in Labour Disputes (*Lag om rättegången i arbetstvister*)
LSF	The Arbitration Act (*Skiljemannalagen*)
NJA	New Legal Archive (*Nytt juridiskt arkiv*)
Prop.	Proposal from the Government Concerning a New Act (*proposition*)
RB	Code of Judicial Procedure (*Rättegångsbalken*)
RF	Instrument of Government (*Regeringsformen*)
RhL	The Legal Aid Act (*Rättshjälpslagen*)
SFS	Official Publication of Statutes, etc. (*Svensk författningssamling*)

List of Abbreviations

SEK	Swedish Krona (Unit of Currency)
SOU	Government Official Investigations (*Statens Offentliga Utredningar*)
SCC	Stockholm Chamber of Commerce
UB	The Execution Code (*Utsökningsbalken*)
UNCITRAL	United Nations Commission on International Trade Law

References are made in accordance with Swedish standards. Legislation is cited by chapter, section and sometimes subsection, for example, RB 42:2 paragraph 2 (Chapter 42, section 2, subsection 2). The provisions are cited pursuant to the wording in force on 1 January 2020 with due account to later amendments.

General Introduction

Chapter 1. Sweden: A General Background

§1. Geography, Population, Climate and Economic Life

1. The population in Sweden amounts to 10.3 million inhabitants over a surface of 449,965 sq. mi. (twenty-one inhabitants for each sq. mi.), of which approximately 83.4% live in urban areas and 16.6% in the countryside. The length of the coast is 7,624 km; the land border with Finland is 586 km long and with Norway 1,619 km long. The capital city is Stockholm, which has 680,000 inhabitants. In spite of its location in the northern latitudes, Sweden has a mild climate. This is mainly a result of its proximity to the Atlantic and the warm air coming in over the country from the west during the winter.

2. In February 2020 the unemployment rate was 7.2% or 453,000 individuals. The total number of employed people aged between 15 and 74 in 2019 reported to be 5.1 million of which 2 million 694,000 were men and 2 million 438 were women.

3. In the early 1990s, Sweden experienced a deep economic recession caused by a macroeconomic imbalance, which began more than a decade earlier. A far-reaching programme has reversed the deficit in the general government finances. The budget consolidation has been followed by a significant improvement in all macroeconomic indicators. Sweden managed the 2008–2009 international financial crisis relatively well, by comparison.

4. Sweden is divided into eighteen county councils (municipalities on a regional level), two regions (Skåne Region and Västra Götaland Region) and one local authority (Gotland Local Authority). In addition, there are 286 municipalities. Above these levels, we have the Government and the Parliament. The differences between municipalities and county councils are considerable, with regard to both surface area and inhabitants. The county councils cover the same areas as the counties, with the exception of Gotland, which does not belong to any particular county council.

5. The public sector in Sweden is thus organized in the three levels mentioned above. The county councils are mainly responsible for health and medical care. The municipalities have a large area of responsibility. This covers, *inter alia*, social care, planning and protection of the physical environment, civil defence and communications. Foreign policy, defence, housing and labour-market policy, national economy and the judicial system, are examples of central government areas.

§2. The Political Parties

6. There are six established political parties in Sweden: the Moderates (*Moderata Samlingspartiet*) a conservative, centre-right-wing party; the Liberal Party (*Folkpartiet Liberalerna*), a social-liberal party; the Social Democrats (*Socialdemokratiska Arbetarpartiet*), the oldest and largest of the political parties with roots in the working class and the trade unions; the Centre Party (*Centerpartiet*), supported primarily by farmers, but also by sections of the middle-class; the Left Party (*Vänsterpartiet*), a former communist party; and finally the Christian Democratic Party (*Kristen Demokratisk Samling*), a guardian of Christian ethical values. Two new political parties have been established during the last decade: the Environment Party, the Greens in 1981 (*Miljöpartiet, De Gröna*) and New Democracy (*Ny Demokrati*) in 1990. New Democracy has been characterized as a right-wing 'protest' party. Today (2003) it does not exist any longer.

7. With the Parliamentary elections of 1976, a forty-five-year-long period of Social Democratic government was broken. During the period between 1976 and 1982, different coalitions of Liberals and Moderates ruled the country. The Social Democrats returned to power in the 1982 election, but in the 1991 election, Liberals and Conservatives returned to Government. The Environment Party, the Greens, entered the Parliament with the election of 1988, when they achieved 5.5% of the votes and thus passed the 4% minimum limit stipulated in the Constitution for a party to be represented in Parliament. However, in the 1991 election, they did not reach the 4% limit and consequently could not enter Parliament. In the 1991 election, New Democracy, as well as the Christian Democratic Party, did enter the Parliament. The latter, although well established, had never passed the 4% limit in any earlier election. These developments in the 1980s and 1990s introduced an element of instability into Swedish politics. In the 1994 election, the Social Democrats, as well as the Left Party and the Environment Party, strengthened their positions considerably. At the same time, New Democracy did not enter Parliament. In this situation, the Social Democrats decided to rule in minority. After the 1998 and 2002 elections, the Social Democratic Party formed a minority government. Before the 2006 election, the Centre Party, the Christian Democratic Party, the Liberal Party and the Moderates had formed an alliance for Sweden. The Alliance won the election against the Social Democrats, which were supported by the Green Party and the Left Party. At the same election, a new nationalistic and conservative party, The Sweden Democrats, entered the Parliament by securing 5.6% of the votes. The Alliance also won the election in 2010. In the 2014 election, the Alliance got fewer votes than the Social Democrats, the Green and the Left Party. With the support of the Left Party, the Social Democrats and the Green Party formed the Government. In this election, the Sweden Democrats became the third-largest political party. After the 2018 election, it took 131 days until Sweden got a Government. After the election, the difference between the blocks was only two mandates. Although the red-green had two mandates more than the Alliance, the Alliance claimed to form a government and, therefore, together with the Sweden Democrats, forced the Prime Minister to resign. However, eventually the Alliance came to rupture and the Liberals and the Center Party became supporting parties to the Social Democrats who formed the Government.

§3. THE CONSTITUTION

8. Sweden is a constitutional monarchy with a parliamentary form of government. The King, Carl XVI Gustaf, has only ceremonial functions as Head of State. Parliament consists of one chamber whose members since the 1 January 1995 are elected for a four-year term (before it was three years). Sweden has universal suffrage from the age of 18. The Swedish Constitution is composed of four fundamental laws: the Instrument of Government (*Regeringsformen* or RF), the Act of Succession, the Freedom of the Press Act and the Freedom of Expression Act.[1]

9. The RF,[2] which contains fundamental rules about the Government's organization and competence, entered into force on 1 January 1975, replacing the Constitution of 1809, which at that time was the oldest written European Constitution. The Act of Succession is, however, much older than the present RF (1810), but it was fundamentally changed in 1979 when female and male descendants of the ruling king, Carl XVI Gustaf, became equal with respect to succession. The Freedom of the Press Act regulates the use of the printed word. Sweden is unusual in providing for detailed regulation of the freedom of the press in the Constitution.

10. According to the fundamental rule in the Constitution, all power stems from the people.[3] The Constitution is thus based on the principle of sovereignty of the people, which presupposes freedom of opinion and a public and equal right to vote. These rights are secured by a representative and parliamentary Constitution and by municipal autonomy. The fundamental rule in question also expresses the principle of legality: all public power must be lawfully executed.

11. Freedom of opinion is guaranteed by regulations containing certain basic freedoms and rights, for example, freedom of information, assembly, demonstration, association and religion.[4] In addition, there is freedom of the press and the principle of public access to official records. The latter principle means that citizens are ensured access to official records, kept by state or local authorities, in so far as they are not classified secret.[5] The rules regarding the public and equal right to vote

1. Furthermore there is the Parliament Act, although this is not a fundamental law. However, its amendment is subject to special provisions.
2. Extensive changes were made to the RF in 2011. *See* Prop. 2009/10:80.
3. RF 1:1 para. 1.
4. RF Ch. 2.
5. Whether an official record is classified secret or not appears from Public Access to Information and Secrecy Act (OSL).

contain far-reaching regulations in order to guarantee that each political party obtains parliamentary mandates in proportion to the votes it received.[6] However, as was previously mentioned, a political party that does not obtain at least 4% of the vote does not participate in the distribution of the mandates.[7]

12. The principle of representative government means that the people in Sweden indirectly rule the country via the Parliament, which is the peoples' foremost representative. The Parliament, which has 349 members, introduces laws, determines state taxes and how the state income shall be used, and also examines state government and administration.[8] These four central functions are set out in the Constitution and will be described in the following paragraphs.

13. According to the Constitution, the Parliament basically possesses all legislative power. In accordance with this basic principle, the concept of 'law' in the Constitution means 'a rule decided by the Parliament'. Some rules must be enacted as laws, while others can have lower priority (decrees). However, Parliament can delegate parts of its rule-making competence to the Government.[9] In addition, the making, changing or withdrawing of the provisions of the Constitution requires two identical parliamentary decisions, separated by an intervening election to the Parliament.

14. Concerning the financial power, it is stipulated that the use of public funds must be decided by Parliament.[10] Furthermore, there are regulations to determine the state budget, for raising public loans – which is possible only with Parliament's permission – and regulations concerning the National Department Office (*Riksgäldskontoret*) and the Central Bank (*Riksbanken*), institutions which have responsibility for handling questions concerning public loans and the monetary system.

15. The Swedish Parliamentary Standing Committee on the Constitution examines how ministers discharge their duties and whether governmental issues have been handled in a proper way. Interpellations and questions are two other instruments of control.[11] These instruments, of which the former addresses more important questions, can be addressed to a minister of the cabinet, if they are related to the performance of his or her duty. The ultimate review is a vote of censure, which is a declaration that a minister no longer has Parliament's confidence. Another element of the power to review is that courts and administrative organs must exercise public power in accordance with the laws. A consequence of this principle of legality is that incorrect decisions, including governmental ones, can be set aside by way of review. Furthermore, the RF contains provisions about the legal responsibility of the highest judges and contains also regulations concerning the examination of laws,

6. RF Ch. 3.
7. There is, however, an exception to this rule stating that if a party obtains 12% of the votes in a constituency, that district will be represented in the Parliament.
8. RF 1:4 para. 2.
9. RF Ch. 8.
10. RF Ch. 9.
11. The control power is regulated in RF Ch. 13.

that is to say the right and duty of all public organs to refuse to apply a rule which contradicts a rule with a higher constitutional value. Finally, indirect control is performed by the Parliament's Ombudsman – *Justitieombudsmannen* (JO) – and by the Parliaments accountants.[12]

16. Although the Government, according to a fundamental provision in the Constitution, is responsible for governing the country, its powers are residual, that is to say the Government decides issues that neither the Parliament nor any other authority decides. The Constitution gives the Government the independent power to enact subordinate legislation on certain matters, for example regulations concerning the implementation of an Act of Parliament.[13] It is also true that public funds are at the disposal of the Government,[14] but how far these powers extend depends on the extent to which the Parliament itself wishes to exercise them. However, in practice, the Government uses a considerable amount of the rule-making power. Furthermore, by drafting budget proposals and legislative bills, the Government controls the substance and agenda of much of Parliament's work.

17. The Constitution provides that elected assemblies govern the municipalities, and that the municipalities are entitled to impose taxes in order to perform their tasks.[15]

18. Courts are for the administration of justice. There are also national and municipal administration authorities to deal with public sector matters.[16] These and other authorities, which perform tasks within the public administration, take into consideration the fact that everyone is equal under the law. They must also be objective and impartial. As far as the courts are concerned, there are ordinary courts, which include the district courts, the courts of appeal and the Supreme Court, and administrative courts, which include the county courts, the fiscal courts and the Supreme Administrative Court. In addition, there are special courts, for example the Labour Court and the Patent and Market Court.[17]

19. The Constitution does not define the concept of 'administration of justice' or the concept of 'administration'. This causes some problems in determining what belongs to civil procedure. This issue will be discussed in the following section.

12. About Justitieombudsmannen, *see* paras 154–155 *infra*. *See also* J. Ekroth, *Jo –ämbetet* (Stockholm 2001).
13. RF 8:13.
14. RF 9:8.
15. RF 1:7.
16. RF 1:8 and Ch. 11-12 RF.
17. For a detailed discussion of the special courts, *see* Part I *infra*.

Chapter 2. Definition of the Term 'Civil Procedure'

20. The definition of the term civil procedure is connected with the division of tasks between the courts and the public administration. Since the administration of justice is a task for the courts, the concept of civil procedure thus presupposes that it is possible to distinguish between tasks involving the administration of justice and tasks involving public administration.

21. In the older Swedish legal system, no distinction was made between public administration and the administration of justice. The King was the highest administrative authority and had jurisdiction over all judges. In the beginning of the seventeenth century, five corporate bodies were established, but any distinction between them with respect to public administration and the administration of justice was not made. Around 1670, the closest advisers to the King were separated into two departments, the Council of the Realm (*Riksrådet*) and the Department of Justice (*Justitierevisionen*). The latter, which functioned as a court, was abolished in 1789 and was transformed into the Supreme Court of Justice. The Constitution enacted in 1809 was influenced by Montesquieu's doctrine on the separation of powers, and consequently the power of administering justice increasingly became regarded as a separate and independent power. However, outwardly the governmental power and the power of administering justice remained formally united until the present Constitution was enacted in 1974. Nonetheless, in practice, there was a division since the Supreme Administrative Court was established in 1909 in order to relieve the Government from examination of administrative appeals.

22. Although it is stipulated in the Constitution that there are courts for the administration of justice and national and communal administration authorities for the public administration, unfortunately the Constitution is silent when it comes to the meaning of the crucial concepts 'administering justice' and 'public administration'. In the preparatory legislative works (*travaux préparatoires*) to the Constitution, there are some statements of interest. The Constitution Committee suggested the following definition:

> The Courts resolve adversary contests, apply criminal law and resolve other questions of law … national and communal administration authorities execute instructions made by the decision-making authorities.[18]
> However, the minister responsible for introducing the draft constitution did not like the idea of characterizing the functions at issue in the Constitution. He meant that, on the whole, it was not possible to give a fair description of the similarities and differences that exist between courts and administrative authorities in such brief definitions.[19]

23. The division in the Constitution between public administration and the administration of justice is thus purely formal. If a task is handled by a court, it is

18. SOU 1991:106, p. 47.
19. Prop. 1973:90, 233.

called administration of justice, and if an administration authority handles it, it is called administration.[20] The division of work that nevertheless exists, and in practice works satisfactorily, is based on a rule prescribing that legal disputes between individuals may not be resolved by any authority other than a court.[21] The reasoning behind this rule is the principle of legal security (*Rechtssicherheit*). It is the right of an individual to have important questions handled and decided by well-qualified institutions in a carefully regulated proceeding.

24. It is thus obvious that the concept 'legal dispute' is crucial in this context. As stated above, the main borderline between administering justice and administration is that the resolution of legal disputes is a task for the courts, while the administrative authorities generally do not handle such tasks.[22] This borderline works well in most cases. Many issues of a public service character, in which the juridical features are minimal, are handled by the administrative authorities, for example those concerning education, research, defence and communications.[23] Furthermore, when an administrative authority handles an issue, it is not characterized by a conflict between two persons, which is typical of litigation. Thus, if a person makes an application for social welfare benefits, for example social assistance or housing allowance, only one legal subject exists, namely the applicant versus the authority.[24] In addition, typical administrative operations regulate concrete cases in advance, while courts apply legal rules to past events.[25]

25. The principal business for the ordinary courts is the resolution of adversarial disputes in civil and criminal cases. Besides this task they also – customarily and because of purely historical reasons – handle some matters which, with a literal English translation, would be called 'legal care' (*jurisdictio voluntaria*), for example appointment of a property division executor.[26]

26. It was proposed in a report entitled 'The Courts facing the twenty-first century' that a large number of the so-called ancillary functions (e.g., certain registration matters) imposed on the ordinary courts ought to be removed to the administrative authorities. The background to this proposal can be found in the Government directives to the investigation in question.[27] The directive points out that

20. G. Petrén & H. Ragnemalm, *Sveriges grundlagar och tillhörande författningar med förklaringar*, 34 (Stockholm 1980).
21. RF 11:5.
22. SOU 1991:106, p. 47.
23. *Ibid.*, p. 48. However, the content of law application is considerable, *inter alia*, in matters concerning taxation and treatment of drug abusers.
24. P.O. Ekelöf, H. Edelstam, L. Heuman & M. Pauli, *Rättegång I*, 32 (9th ed., 2016). However, there might be a dispute whether the applicant is entitled to welfare. As has already been noted, administrative authorities sometimes must resolve disputes between individuals, for example, neighbours might have opinions on the suitability of a building permit.
25. *Ibid.* It should, however, be mentioned that courts sometimes make prognostic judgments.
26. Notice that adversary disputes presented to the courts for resolution in RB are called 'cases' while civil matters referred to the courts in contrast to other matters are called 'court matters'. These are regulated in the Act on Processing of Court Matters, *see* paras 735–736 *infra*.
27. Dir. 1989:56.

the number of cases and other matters dealt with by the courts have increased, and simultaneously have become more complicated in recent years. Consequently, it has not been possible to handle the situation satisfactorily in spite of a continued rationalization of labour. Therefore, the Committee was assigned to investigate and put forward proposals designed to ensure that the courts only handle tasks that really demand judicial examination. Hence, according to the directives, a matter should be removed from the courts to an administrative authority, provided the latter can handle it in a satisfactory way. In 2011, the legislator moved a large number of court matters to different administrative authorities.[28]

28. *See* Prop. 2010/11:119 p. 36.

Chapter 3. Sources of Civil Procedure Law

§1. Brief History

27. During the Great Migration (AD 400–900), German tribes invaded the Roman Empire and occupied the western part of it.[29] Two German tribes settled down in Sweden. The oldest of them, the Goths, occupied two large counties, Östergötland and Västergötland. The other tribe, Svearna, occupied mainly the counties of Uppland, Västmanland, Södermanland and some areas north of Uppland.[30] Our knowledge about administration of justice during this period is limited. However, we do know that the family was the primary social unit and thus handled all necessary lawmaking in its domain. Our knowledge about the Swedish judicial system during the Early Middle Ages increases considerably thanks to the unique Provincial Codes, most of which date from the fourteenth century.

28. In the Early Middle Ages, the plaintiff's case focused on the legal right in itself, and the defendant contradicted this right. The evidentiary theme corresponded to the claim and its denial presented in this form, hence, the legal relationship in itself became subject to proof taking.[31] This proceeding implies that neither the claim nor the denial was founded on factual circumstances. Although, it is probable that the parties presented the facts in controversy, these facts lacked legal relevance and thus cannot have been necessary for the process.[32]

29. The formalism in the judiciary of the Early Middle Ages was caused by the limited power of the judges and a simultaneous need for a trial, which was easy to follow and understand. Procedures that were easy to watch and control from the outside thus became the criteria for fair treatment.[33]

30. As far as the means of evidence are concerned, these were purely formal. Most common among the means of evidence was the party's oath, generally strengthened by a helping oath from twelve 'oath helpers', who, at the trial, swore that the party had stated the truth. It was never inquired if, and in such a case, how, the 'oath helpers' had obtained knowledge of the evidentiary theme.[34]

31. Thus, the means of evidence was regarded as a means of defence, to protect against a personal attack on the defendant, who generally had an exclusive right to

29. E. Anners, *Den europeiska rättens historia, del I* 11 et seq. (1974).
30. G. Hafström, *De svenska rättskällornas historia*, 12 f.
31. T. Engströmer, *Vittnesbeviset* 32 (1911); W. Sjögren, *Om den fornsvenska skuldprocessens grundformer*, 43 f., in TfR 1898; E. Carlquist, *Studier i den äldre svenska bevisrättens utveckling med särskild hänsyn till institutet erkännande* 11 f. (1918). Concerning the concept 'evidentiary theme', *see* para. 596 *infra*.
32. Sjögren, *supra*, 44.
33. Carlquist, *supra*, 6 et seq.
34. J.E. Almquist, *Processrättens historia* 42 (6th ed., Stockholm 1975).

present evidence to avoid this attack.[35] Exceptions from this principal rule were sometimes made; *inter alia*, if someone had been apprehended while committing a crime.[36] It was carefully stated in the law, which one of the parties, in different situations, was obliged to present evidence, and what kind of evidence that had to be in order to be brought to trial.[37] If the party who had to present evidence according to these rules succeeded with his proof taking, he won the case; otherwise he lost it. As the substantial right, in itself, was possible to be obtained directly by using evidentiary means, their function was to realize rights (or duties).[38] Because of this function, the case was conditionally resolved when the duty to proof had been determined. It is thus obvious that the central point of the procedure was to obtain this decision, which was rendered by a so-called evidentiary judgment.[39]

32. Eventually the defendant brought substantive grounds into the procedure.[40] While a plaintiff who did not claim a right would not be taken seriously in the old legal system, a defendant could be suspected of perjury if he made a non-motivated denial concerning a debt that was known by others. Such an empty denial could also make it difficult for the defendant to get 'oath helpers'.[41] Thus, the defendant could choose between a motivated and a non-motivated denial. If he motivated his denial by, for example, stating that he had paid the debt, the object for the proof taking would be this fact. This marked a progression, and divergence, from the older law. This progression was particularly notable in the evidentiary area, since most substantive testimonial evidence was used to prove an objection presented by the defendant that he had paid the debt.[42]

33. The Provincial Codes also offer examples showing that the plaintiff alleged grounds for his right. If, for example, the defendant in a case concerning ownership to real estate alleged that he had bought the land, *Östgötalagen* required him to prove this statement with fifteen oath helpers on his side. If he succeeded, he won the case, unless the defendant contested this and presented evidence that contradicted the plaintiff's statement in the form of two oaths each supported by fourteen persons. One of these oaths was to affirm that the defendant was still the owner of the real estate and the other to affirm that he had legally obtained possession of it. If the defendant successfully performed this task, the case was brought before the *Nämnd* (a kind of jury).[43]

---

35. I. Afzelius, *Om parts ed såsom processuellt institut* 51 (2nd ed., 1915); R.A. Wrede, *Grunddragen av bevisrätten enligt gällande lag* 126 (1894).
36. H. Hjärne, *Om den fornsvenska nämnden enligt landskaps-, stadsoch landskapslagarne* 10 (1872).
37. Engströmer, *supra*, 25.
38. Sjögren, *supra*, 78.
39. S. Bergendal, *Bidrag till de svenska rättsmedlens historia* 26 (1916); Carlquist, *supra*, 18.
40. Sjögren, *supra*, 75.
41. *Ibid.*
42. *Ibid.*, 68. Cf. Engströmer *supra*, 60.
43. Engströmer, *supra*, 66.

34. In the *Nämnd*, which is mentioned in the Provincial Codes, the examination of evidence was substantial and not formal.[44] The establishment of the *Nämnd* was thus an essential prerequisite to the breakthrough of the principle of free evaluation of evidence, but very little is known about why it was established, its members, competence and way of working.[45] However, one widely accepted theory is that it grew out of, and eventually superseded, the Oath-Helper Procedure, since the Oath-Helper Procedure was clumsy and difficult to handle in practice. Sometimes as many as 156 oath helpers were required to make an oath at trial.[46] Another reason to get rid of the Oath-Helper Procedure emerged for legal security reasons and the fact that the Oath-Helper Procedure did not reveal the truth in the case.[47]

35. Eventually the *Nämnd* became a permanent element of the court, and more and more cases were successively brought over from the Oath-Helper Procedure to the *Nämnd* Procedure.[48] However, this development was progressive. The Oath-Helper Procedure was not abolished until 1695 and, consequently, two forms of procedure existed side by side for a long period. In addition, there were two other forms of procedure, the Ecclesiastical Inquisitorial procedure and the King's adjudication. These forms of procedure were, like the *Nämnd* procedure, investigative.[49]

36. The adoption of the first National Legal Codes was a milestone in the progress towards unification of the different Provincial Codes. These were the General Country or Rural Code and the General Urban Code, both modelled after the Provincial Codes and put into effect by the end of the fifteenth century. A revised version of the Rural Code was adopted in 1442, but was not generally accepted until the seventeenth century.

37. When the Code of 1734 was enacted, it replaced both the Rural and Urban Codes. It included two procedural sections. One regulated litigation in both civil and criminal proceedings, and the other preliminary enforcement measures and modes of execution following final judgment.

38. According to the Code of 1734, the procedure was written and was strongly influenced by the legal theory of evidence, which was adopted from Romano-German law and became predominant during the Middle Ages and subsequently. The legal theory of evidence must have been easy to adopt, as it, like earlier formal rules on evidence, was based on the idea that a certain kind and a certain amount of evidence was both sufficient and necessary. An example of a formal evidence rule

---

44. *Ibid.*, 94; Hjärne, *supra*, 13; K.G. Westman, *Den svenska nämnden* 4 (1912).
45. *See* Westman, *supra* and Hjärne, *supra*.
46. J.J. Nordström, *Bidrag till den svenska samhällsförfattningens historia. Efter de äldre lagarne till senare hälften av sjuttonde seklet*, 780 (1840); Afzelius, *supra*, 55; Almquist, *supra*, 42. According to Å. Holmbäck & E. Wéssen, *Svenska landskapslagar. Tolkade och förklarade för nutidens svenskar* part (1) p. XXVI (1933), the required number of oath-helpers sometimes amounted to 195 men.
47. Holmbäck & Wessén, *supra*, XXVII and Part 5 of the same work, LXVIII (1946).
48. Hjärne, *supra*, 37.
49. Engströmer, *supra*, 88.

in the Code of 1734 is the rule stating that one witness was regarded as half evidence, which was not sufficient, but that two witnesses represented full evidence if their testimony corresponded.[50] In addition, many people were deemed incompetent to be witnesses.[51]

39. There are different explanations as to why the legal theory of evidence was adopted. One important reason was that it was considered to benefit legal security by preventing arbitrariness.[52] Furthermore, the judges' lack of competence during this period made it risky to entrust to them the task of freely evaluating evidence.[53] Another aspect, which is also connected with legal security, is that the procedure during the Middle Ages was inquisitorial in character. The judge thus participated actively in the procedure in order to find the truth. Under these circumstances, the evidentiary rules could protect the parties from the judge's abuse of power.[54]

40. A further explanation as to why the legal theory of evidence was adopted might have been the scientific ideal that was prevailing during the Middle Ages. This ideal, the scholastic school, tried to formulate abstract principles for all human behaviour and the legal theory of evidence can certainly be regarded as a product of this ideal.[55] Finally, there is a connection between the evidentiary system in force and the form of procedure. According to the Code of 1734, the procedure was mainly written. A purely written procedure is difficult to harmonize with the principle of free evaluation of evidence, since the former prevents all relevant factors from being taken into consideration. For example, the judge cannot observe how the parties and their witnesses will behave (in court). However, this is not necessary if the evaluation is performed according to legal rules made in advance, stating the value of different kinds of evidence.[56] This explains why free evaluation of evidence and oral procedure most often appear together.[57]

41. The legislation technique in the Code of 1734 is casuistic, that is to say enumerating and descriptive. It has been said that clarity in the description of the actual circumstances relevant to the rules is characteristic of the Code in question and inherited from its predecessors.[58]

42. In many ways, the Code of 1734 was already outmoded when enacted. However, in practice, the courts tried to liberate themselves from the straitjacket imposed on them by the legal theory of evidence. Hence, the courts eventually found themselves competent to decide a case only on the basis of circumstantial evidence, or

50. 17:29, RB from 1734.
51. Disqualified as witnesses were, *inter alia*, members of a party's family or household, atheists, children and women. A testimony of a qualified witness could not be rejected by the court as unreliable.
52. N. Gärde, *Bevisteori och förhandlingsform*, SvJT 143 (1940).
53. Almquist, *supra*, 44.
54. SOU 1926:32, s. 32.
55. P.O. Ekelöf & R. Boman, *Rättegång IV* 20 (6th ed., 1992.
56. Kungl. Maj:ts Prop. 1931 No. 80, p. 94.
57. Gärde, *supra*, 146.
58. E. Wéssen, *Svenskt lagspråk*, 37 (1965).

to use this evidence to supplement witness evidence in order to reach full evidence. Furthermore, they permitted counter-evidence to be submitted against the main evidence. As far as the disqualification of witnesses was concerned, however, the legal theory of evidence was decisive until the new Code of Legal Procedure came into force.[59]

43. During the latter part of the nineteenth century, some attempts were made to work out a new Code of Procedure, but these attempts did not lead to any legislation.[60]

44. Hence, the Code of 1734 remained in force until 1 January 1948, the effective date of the present Code of Judicial Procedure (RB).

45. The new Code introduced the principle of free evaluation of evidence. The preparatory legislative works give as the main reason for this the fact that the legal theory of evidence counteracts one important task for the administration of justice: to reach the truth in the case.[61] The Code of 1734 was, however, also defective in other respects. One of the main faults with its oral and formal system was its slowness.[62] The principles of oral testimony, immediacy and concentration were intended to cure these defects and thus lead to a faster, more reliable and cheaper administration of justice, and at the same time, they were intended to pave the way for the principle of free evaluation of evidence.[63]

46. The present Code has been changed in many important respects since it was enacted. Other important changes in legislation outside the Code have also been made. One important procedural innovation, introduced in 1973, was the Small Claims Act. As the name implies, cases concerning small sums of money were handled according to this Act.[64] Attorneys did thereby not represent the parties, and the procedure was not strictly divided into preparation and trial as in ordinary proceedings. The Small Claims Act ceased to exist in 1987 when it was included in the Code.

47. Another important reform dates back to 1971, when the provisions concerning appeal to the Supreme Court were changed. These now provide that, in principle, only questions of law can be tried by the court. During the last decade, the Code has also been reformed in many other aspects.

---

59. *See* SOU 1926:31, p. 25 f. and E. Kallenberg, *Svensk Civilprocessrätt, andra bandet* 674 (1927–1939).
60. *See* the Law Committees proposal for a Code of Procedure in 1849; The New Law Committee's proposal concerning reconstruction of the judiciary system in 1884 and the Law Committee's proposal concerning the main principles for a new Code of Procedure in 1887.
61. SOU 1926:32, p. 26.
62. SOU 1926:31, p. 17.
63. These principles are explained in para. 71 *infra*.
64. Claims not increasing half of the basic amount, i.e., Swedish Krona (SEK) 22,500 in 2013.

48. The main reason underlying the reforms in question is that the Code has become regarded as inflexible in its rigorous adherence to the principles of concentration, oral testimony and immediacy. Hence, a more flexible mode of procedure has been deemed desirable, which, *inter alia*, has led to increasing possibilities to settle dispositive actions on the merits.[65] Moreover, affidavits are accepted largely than before and the provisions regulating interruption and postponement have been extended.[66]

49. Other examples of reforms that have recently been undertaken have improved administrative efficiency. Examples of such reforms are the increase in the competence of the single judge and a sharpening of the rules that make it possible to reject new circumstances and new evidence submitted by the parties.[67]

§2. Preparatory Legislative Works (*Travaux Préparatoires*)

50. Preparatory legislative works are of great importance in Swedish jurisprudence when it comes to interpretation and application of legal rules. It is, therefore, necessary to know something about the lawmaking process.

51. If the head of a department finds that there is a need for legislation or a change of legislation relating to an area for which he is responsible, he will set up a committee (at least if it is a large and complicated issue).[68] This committee consists of a chairperson and a number of Members of Parliament and, in most cases, of experts. The Government gives the committee a directive for its work. In these directives, published in a special series called *The Committee Directive* (abbreviated dir, with year and number), the objects and motives for the investigation are formulated. The Committee Report (*betänkandet*) is generally published in a series, Government Official Investigations (*Statens Offentliga Utredningar*, abbreviated SOU, with a name, year and a number, for example, SOU 1982:26 'The Procedure in the District Courts').

52. The Committee Report is subsequently circulated among authorities, organizations etc. and sometimes individuals, for comments (*remiss*). These comments are collected and can be found in the legislative proposal (*proposition*) from the Government, which usually follows. Sometimes the Council on Legislation (*lagrådet*) examines the Committee Report. This examination is not obligatory, but ought to take place when the legislative issue concerns important rules, for example a

65. Concerning the difference between dispositive and indispositive case, *see* s. 64 *infra*.
66. *See also* para. 26 *supra* and paras 76–77 *infra*.
67. *See also* para. 71 *supra*.
68. Sometimes legislation is based on preparatory work in the department. Such investigations are published in the departmental series. There is a series for each governmental department. The series of the Ministry of Justice is abbreviated *Ds Ju*.

change in the Freedom of the Press Act.[69] If the Council of Legislation comments on the proposal, their remarks can be found in the Minutes from the Council of Legislation (*lagrådsprotokollet*).

53. A legislative proposal contains a compilation of all material relevant to the issue and is referred to by year of the parliamentary session and a number (abbreviated Prop., for example, Prop. 1986/87:89). The next step is the debate in the Parliamentary Committee, which usually proposes that the Parliament accept the proposal. If the law is accepted, it must be enacted immediately, which is done by a Government decision. The publication generally takes place in the Statute Book (*Svensk Författningssamling*, abbreviated SFS with a statute number, for example, SFS 1991:375). Preparatory works to a law can be found in a compiled form in the annual reporter *Nytt juridiskt arkiv*, Part II (literally translated 'New Legal Archive', abbreviated NJA), which is published yearly.[70]

54. The original preparatory legislative works to the Code consist of the proposals of the Expert Investigation Commission, concerning the main features for a reform of the procedure (*Processkommissionens betänkande angående rättegångsväsendets ombildning*, SOU 1926 31–33) are: the 1928 Opinion of the Law Council thereon (*Lagrådets utlåtande*, SOU 1928:19); the 1931 Cabinet proposition requesting the Parliament's approval of the essential features of the proposed reform (*Kungl. Maj:ts* Prop. 1931 No. 80) and the commentaries of the Expert Drafting Committee (*Processlagberedningens betänkande*, SOU 1938:43–44).

55. Preparatory legislative works to important later reforms of the Code can be found in SOU 1982:26, 'The Procedure in the District Courts' (*Processen i tingsrätt*) and the subsequent proposal 1986/87:89, 'A Reformed Procedure in the District Courts' (*Ett reformerat tingsrättsförfarande*) and, with respect to the procedure in the courts of appeal, Prop. 1988/89:95, 'Questions Concerning the Court of Appeals, Composition of the Bench etc.' (*Hovrättsfrågor, sammansättningsfrågor m.m.*) The latest important report can be found in SOU 2001:103 'A More Modern Procedure' (*En modernare rättegång*). The most important Government Bill in the last decade is probably Prop. 2004/2005:131, A Modernized Procedure (*En modernare rättegång*). The new proposed legislation took effect in November 2008. It introduced audio and picture recording technique in all courts. Since it took years to build up this technique in the courthouses, the new legislation started to operate four years after the Bill. This technique is still often called 'video technique' in the legal language in Sweden. Other words such as 'videoconferencing', which sometimes is used in this book, means audio- and picture recording.

69. *See* RF 8:15.
70. *See also* para. 56 *infra*.

§3. CASE MATERIALS

56. Since 1874, cases from the Supreme Court have been published annually in *Nytt Juridiskt Arkiv*, Part I.[71] It is cited NJA to distinguish it from the above-mentioned NJA II, which contains extracts from the principal legislative reports. NJA is divided into two sections. The first section contains extensive reports on cases, which are considered to have value as precedents. They are referred to by column, year and page (e.g., NJA 1988 section 766). The second division is subdivided into three groups: section A contains judgments in civil cases, section B contains judgments in criminal cases and section C contains decisions that do not constitute judgments, but, for example, concern procedural questions. Volume-year, note group and number cite the notes. In each yearly volume, which contains more than one hundred cases, there is both a statutory and subject matter index to the precedent cases. Cases reported only as notes are not indexed. In addition, there are indexes covering ten-year periods.

57. From 1916 to 1981, decisions rendered by the Court of Appeals were published in *Svensk Juristtidning* (SvJT). Since 1981, they have been published in an annual series of their own, *Rättsfall från hovrätterna*, containing judgments in civil and criminal cases. Between 100 and 200 cases are published annually. These judgments are not regarded as precedent cases, but are considered as a valuable source of information, mainly with respect to questions of law.

58. There are also annual reports from some of the special courts. Decisions of the Labour Court (*Arbetsdomstolens domar*) have been published annually since the court was established in 1929. Decisions from The Housing Court (*Rättsfall från Bostadsdomstolen*) have been yearly published since 1975 and decisions from the Market Court (*Marknadsdomstolens avgöranden*) since 1971.[72] In the annual report from the Parliamentary Ombudsman (JO, *Justitieombudsmannens ämbetsberättelse*), interesting statements concerning legal issues (including procedural issues) can be found. The same applies to the series containing decisions of the Chancellor of Justice (*JK- beslut*). The last-mentioned annual report mainly contains questions concerning the freedom of the press and the right of individuals to obtain damages from the state.

59. Judgments from the European Court of Human Rights and the European Union (EU) Court are regularly described and commented in SvJT and in various electronic databases.

71. NJA I and NJA II are private publications edited by members of the Supreme Court. Both are authoritative sources frequently used by judges and lawyers.

72. The Housing Court ceased to exist as of 1 Jul. 1994. The Market Court has been merged with the Patent Court, *see infra* para. 94.

§4. Other Sources

60. In spite of modern electronic databases, the book *Rättspraxis i litteraturen*, edited by Nils Regner et al., can be helpful in finding literature which comments upon judgments from the courts, mainly precedent-setting cases. An older index to legal publications (books and periodicals) can be found in *Svensk juridisk litteratur*, edited by Göran and Hans Regner.

61. Databases on the net are a growing industry and today a necessary source for every lawyer. The Parliament has its own site on the Web www.rikdagen.se, which contains *inter alia* legislative proposals from the Government, the Statute Book (SFS) and Committee Directives. Info Torg is the largest Swedish database. From InfoTorg it is possible to reach 100 a large number of Swedish and international databases. Amongst the Swedish databases which can be reached from Info Torg, the so-called *Rättsbanken* gives access to forty databases with decisions and judgments from the courts, reference to literature etc. and, in addition, it gives access to Communitatis Europae Lex (CELEX) a European Law database.

62. As far as periodicals are concerned, *Svensk Juristtidning* has already been mentioned. A rather new periodical is *Juridisk Tidskrift*, issued by the faculty of law at the University of Stockholm. The periodical of the Swedish Advocates Association – *Advokaten*– (formerly called *Tidskrift för Sveriges Advokatsamfund*) has been published since 1935. A couple of periodicals not published in Sweden, but with a large Swedish readership should also be mentioned, namely *Tidskrift for Rettsvitenskap* (TfR, published in Denmark) and *Tidskrift utgiven av juridiska föreningen i Finland* (TjFF).

Chapter 4. General Features of the Administration of Justice in Civil Matters

§1. The Principle of Party Disposition and the Ex Officio Competence of the Court

63. If a procedural rule is dispositive for the parties, the court shall undertake procedural acts in accordance with the requests from the parties. Thus, under the principle of party disposition the court may undertake a procedural measure only in accordance with a claim by one or both of the parties.[73] This means, *inter alia*, that in cases amenable to out-of-court settlement, the judgment may not be based upon circumstances not alleged by a party as the foundation of his case. According to *Ekelöf*, the principle of disposition is a special form of the principle of negotiation (*Verhandlungsmaxime*), since these are rules that are permissive but not dispositive. For example, the parties in their closing arguments can touch upon questions concerning the application of law and the evaluation of evidence, but such questions are decided exclusively by the court, independent of what the parties might have said.[74] The principle of party disposition is in this context defined in a formal way since it does not say when a party may make a disposition. In order to find the answer to this question the relevant civil law provision must be examined.[75]

64. It is the responsibility of the parties to present evidence relevant to the case.[76] Since 2005, the court may not on its own motion supplement the evidence in a dispositive case.[77] In cases, which are non-dispositive, for example cases concerning custody of children, the court may collect all kinds of evidence on its own motion, but in dispositive cases the possibilities for the court to supplement the evidence submitted by the parties is limited. In such cases, the court may not examine a witness unless a party proposes that the witness be heard or the witness was previously examined on request of a party. Nor may the court in dispositive cases direct the production of documentary evidence, except on request of a party.

65. Certain cases are mixed in the sense that they contain both dispositive and non-dispositive elements. For example, in a case concerning custody of a child, the issue of custody is non-dispositive while the issue concerning maintenance is dispositive. In mixed cases, the principle of party disposition and the principle of the ex officio competence of the court are applied depending upon which part of the case is involved. However, with respect to the procedure, non-dispositive rules are applied.

66. In practice, it almost never occurs that the court on its own motion completes the evidentiary material in non-dispositive cases.

73. Ekelöf et al., *Rättegång I*, 73.
74. *Ibid.*, 61.
75. B. Lindell, *Civilprocessen* 134 (4th ed. 2017).
76. RB 35:6.
77. Prop. 2004/05:131, p. 230.

67. A rule addressed to the court stating its power of action can be either obligatory or optional. An obligatory rule states that the court 'shall' act in a certain way under certain conditions. However, if a rule is optional, it states that the court 'may' or 'can' perform a procedural act. An example of an obligatory rule is that which concerns joinder of claims, stating that claims instituted by a plaintiff at the same time against the same defendant 'shall' be joined in a single action if they are supported on essentially the same ground.[78] It is obvious that the court cannot refuse to join the claims if the conditions stated are fulfilled. If there are several claims joined in an action, which are possible to sever, the court 'may' enter judgment upon any of them.[79] Obviously, this is an optional rule.

68. The parties must obey a mandatory rule. For example, the court decides if the preparatory part of the proceedings shall be oral or written.[80] If a rule, however, is dispositive, a party can by his procedural acts influence the course of the proceedings. Obviously, it depends on how the party wishes to use his options. An example of a dispositive rule is one that states that the judgment may not be based upon circumstances not alleged by a party as the basis of his cause.[81] The party can thus choose not to allege a particular circumstance.

69. It follows from what has been stated above that a procedural rule can be classified as, for example, mandatory and obligatory or as optional and dispositive. This terminology is important in order to describe and systematize a procedural rule in an easy manner. However, it should be underlined that the borderline between obligatory and optional rules is vague. In addition, it is sometimes difficult to separate or confine the parties' influence from the ex officio examination of the court.[82]

§2. The Principles of Oral Testimony, Immediacy, Concentration and Publicity

70. The leading basic ideas in the Code are embodied in the principles of oral testimony, immediacy, concentration and publicity.

71. The meaning of the principle of oral testimony is that the material on which the court bases its judgment shall be orally presented at the proceedings. Furthermore, the case must be decided directly based on this material. This presupposes that the proceedings can be completed in a single session or at least in sessions that are so closely related in time that the court can proceed with its judgment with a clear recollection of the entire proceedings. It is, thus, obvious that the meaning of the concentration principle is that a main hearing, when started, should continue

78. RB 14:1.
79. RB 17:4.
80. Although it is unusual for a party to be forced to perform a procedural measure, *see* Ekelöf et al., *Rättegång I*, 61.
81. RB 17:3, p. 2.
82. B. Lindell, *Civilprocessen*, 91.

without interruptions and delay until the case is ready for judgment.[83] However, the modern technique, which means that oral testimonies are recorded by the court, makes the principles in question less important. Furthermore, in 2016 new legislation made it possible to take up oral evidence through audio- and picture recording from witnesses who appeared to testify in the main hearing, which for some reason is cancelled.[84] However, pursuant to the new legislation a witness who has appeared will be heard, if the court deems it suitable and the parties have been serviced. Thus, if the witness is heard even though the main hearing is cancelled, the audio- and picture recording will subsequently be played when the main hearing later on takes place. Of course, the advantage is that the witness may not have to attend the main hearing again. However, on the very early stage of the procedure when the testimony is given it could be difficult to which relevance it will have later on, if any. The rule is therefore optional. However, in spite of the new technique the legislator upholds the borderline between preparation and main hearing, even though the importance of a main hearing has decreased.

72. Court hearings are generally open to the public.[85] However, for reasons of secrecy the court may direct that the hearing be held behind closed doors.[86] Examination of anyone under the age of 15 years, of anyone who is insane or 'feeble-minded', or of anyone who suffers from any other mental disturbance, may also be held behind closed doors. Furthermore, there are some special provisions outside the Code that permit closed hearings. Deliberations on judgments or orders shall occur *in camera*, unless the court decides that they can take place in public.[87]

73. There are a number of other exceptions to the principle of public court hearings, which are focused on special situations. If there is cause to believe that, in the presence of a party or the public, a witness, through fear or otherwise, is likely to be inhibited from telling the truth unreservedly, or if a party or a member of the public hinders the witness from testifying by interrupting the witness or otherwise, the court may exclude the party or the member of the public from the courtroom during the examination. Upon the return of the party, the testimony shall be read to him; thereafter the party may question the witness.[88]

74. In order for the court to exclude a party or a member of the public from the courtroom, special reasons ought to exist suggesting that the witness will not give complete and truthful testimony in the presence of the party or member of the public.[89] In practice, it will rarely, if ever, be necessary to exclude the press from the

83. *See Underrättsförfarandet enligt nya rättegångsbalken. Utgiven av processnämnden* 20 (1947). This work will be cited as 'PN'. PN points out that the principle of concentration has a particular meaning in connection with the principles of oral testimony and immediacy. The concept concentration refers more to the reliability of the proceedings than to their speed.
84. RB 43:3 para. 2.
85. RB 5:1. *See also* RF 1:9 and 2:11.
86. *See* RB 5:1 para. 2 and OSL.
87. RB 5:5.
88. RB 36:18.
89. NJA II 1987, p. 206.

hearing according to this rule.[90] Through the 2004/2005 reform, which was implemented in November 2008, a new rule was introduced in 36:18 of the Code. This rule makes it possible for a person, who has been excluded from the courtroom because of fear from a witness, to follow the hearing from another room on a video screen or through sound transmission. At the same time, another rule was inserted in 5:12 of the Code, stating that other participants may follow the hearing through video technique from a side courtroom. This option may be useful in cases where many people are expected to attend the hearing.

75. It is a responsibility for the chairperson of the court to maintain order at the court hearing. He has the discretion to expel any person who disturbs a hearing or otherwise behaves in an unseemly manner.[91] A fine can also punish anyone who disturbs the hearing.[92] Regarding the relation between this rule of order and the rule mentioned above, under which the court may expel a party or a member of the public, the rule of order is meant to be applied when more manifest means are used to disturb the hearings.

76. Until 1987, the Code contained an absolute prohibition against the parties submitting or reading any written statement of position or other written address. However, this prohibition eventually became regarded as too strict and it was, therefore, softened by legislation. The content of the present rule is that the parties may submit or read a written statement if the court finds that it would facilitate the understanding of an oral statement or in some other way would benefit the proceedings.[93]

77. The rules in the Code on documentary evidence were earlier seldom interpreted to require documents to be read aloud by the party wishing to submit the document in evidence. The present provision states that the court may order that documentary evidence shall be deemed to have been taken at the main hearing without actually having been read at that hearing. However, this is permitted only where the parties admit it, where the members of the court have taken part in it, and where it is not considered inappropriate under the circumstances.[94] With regard to the last-mentioned condition, it should be emphasized that the principle that court hearings shall be open to the public must not be neglected. If the possibilities for observers to follow the trial would be substantially diminished if the evidence is not read, this is a reason to read the material.[95] As will be described in Chapter Four, the general possibility to refer to documents in the case was introduced through the 2004/2005 reform.

78. With respect to the right to trial by court (*domstolsprövning*), the Constitution contains certain provisions in order to protect individuals. Courts and administrative authorities, which perform tasks within the domain of the public

90. *Ibid.*
91. RB 5:9.
92. RB 9:5.
93. RB 42:13, 43:5; *see* NJA II 1987, p. 247 and para. 352 *infra*.
94. RB 43:8, para. 2.
95. NJA II 1987, p. 249.

administration, shall take into consideration the principle of equality before the law and, furthermore, observe the principles of objectivity and impartiality. In addition, courts may not be established for a crime that has already taken place or for a particular dispute or case.

79. The only courts that are mentioned in the Constitution are the Supreme Court and the Supreme Administrative Court. The Constitution lays down that these courts are the highest courts and that the right to appeal to them can be limited by law. The Constitution also declares that only those who have been appointed as tenured judges may act as judges in these courts. Furthermore, it is stated that the law can establish other courts. As far as other courts are concerned, the Constitution only says that tenured judges shall exist. The legislator has not demanded that at least one tenured judge shall participate in every decision and, thus, made exceptions with respect to some special courts that have been established defined group or groups of cases. It has thus been possible to appoint the chairpersons of the Labour Court and the Patent and Market Court for a certain fixed period.[96]

80. A tenured judge is, in principle, irremovable.[97]

81. The purpose of the provisions in the Constitution concerning the courts' composition and tenure of the judges is obviously to maintain the independence of the judiciary. The rule stating that neither a public authority nor the Parliament may decide in which way a court shall judge an individual case or apply a legal rule in a specific case has the same purpose.[98]

82. Of great importance for individuals' rights and public obligations are Sweden's international commitments, in the first place to the European Convention on Human Rights. When Sweden ratified the Convention, the Parliament deemed Swedish laws to be in accordance with the Convention, and so legislative incorporation was not necessary.[99] To this extent Swedish rules have been changed to be in harmony with the Convention, and have been carried out by means of national legislation.

83. The European Convention has been incorporated in the Swedish law by an ordinary law (and not by changing the Constitution) effective as of 1 January 1995. The incorporation clarifies the status of the Convention and creates an explicit base to apply the Convention in our courts and other administrative authorities. In addition, the protection of freedom and rights in the Convention is part of the general principles of European Commission (EC) law and today Sweden is a member of the EU. The membership has strengthened the Convention's internal position and probably resulted in fewer cases going to Strasbourg.

---

96. RF 11:1 para. 3.
97. RF 11:5, para. 3. *See also* paras 150–152 *infra*.
98. RF 11:2.
99. Prop. 1951:165, p. 11.

84. Sweden was found to be in breach of the Convention for the first time in 1982. The judgment concerned the application of expropriation rules. The second time Sweden was found to have violated the Convention was in 1984, by failing to provide for access to a court within a reasonable time following the arrest of a suspect. The Swedish rules concerning arrest and detention were subsequently changed. Sweden has been found to be in violation of the Convention on a number of other occasions. One of these concerned the right to oral hearing in appeal proceedings, and another concerned the lack of impartiality of the Housing Court. The Swedish legislator obviously wishes to avoid being found in violation of the Convention, and the Swedish courts have become observant regarding how our legislation corresponds to the rules in the Convention.

Part I. Judicial Organization

Chapter 1. The Courts and Their Members

§1. Courts

I. The Structure of the Court System

85. The ordinary courts are the district courts (*Tingsrätt*), the appellate courts (*Hovrätt*) and the Supreme Court (*Högsta domstolen*). The district court is the Court of First Instance unless otherwise prescribed.[100] Until 1971, there was a difference between city and county courts for historical reasons. In the larger cities, there were city courts (*Rådhusrätt*) composed of a chief judge (*borgmästare*) and a panel of associate judges as ordinary members. In the country and in medium-sized cities, there were district courts with a *Häradshövding* as Chief Judge. The city courts were nationalized in 1965. This started the uniform organization of the lower courts, which was completed in 1971 when city and district courts were transformed into district courts. There are presently forty-eight district courts, six courts of appeal and the Supreme Court.

86. The administrative courts consist of twelve county administrative courts (*Förvaltningsrätt*), four administrative courts of appeal (*Kammarrätt*) and the Supreme Administrative Court (*Högsta förvaltningsdomstolen*).

87. The size of the courts varies greatly. However, the smallest courts have disappeared because of the reduction of the number of district courts. Furthermore, some county courts and district courts have a common administration and even a common chief judge. The largest geographical judicial districts are situated in the counties of Norrland, while the smallest – as far as area is concerned – are to be found in the cities.

88. The courts of appeal have jurisdiction over appeals from the lower courts. Each Court of Appeal also has supervisory authority over the lower courts within its circuit.[101]

100. RB 1:1.
101. RB 2:1.

89. The ordinary courts of appeal are the Court of Appeals for Upper Norrland, in Umeå; the Court of Appeals for Lower Norrland, in Sundsvall; the Svea Court of Appeals, in Stockholm; the Göta Court of Appeal, in Jönköping; the Court of Appeals for Western Sweden, in Göteborg; and the Court of Appeals for Skåne and Blekinge, in Malmö. In actions, concerning crimes committed in office by a judge in an ordinary lower court, or by a court registrar, or other official directed to handle land registration cases, the courts of appeal function as Courts of First Instance. The same applies to civil claims related to such offences committed in office. The reason for this regulation is that it would not be satisfactory if the judge's own court had jurisdiction over him. In cases where the law so prescribes, the courts of appeal also sit as Courts of First Instance.[102]

90. The Supreme Court has jurisdiction over appeals from the courts of appeal and functions as first instance in actions to impose criminal or civil sanctions because of an offence committed in the exercise of his office by a cabinet minister, a Justice of the Supreme Court, a Justice of the Supreme Administrative Court, a JO, and the Attorney General. It shall also act as a Court of First Instance to determine whether a Justice of the Supreme Administrative Court should be removed from, or suspended from, his or her office, or be obliged to submit to a medical examination. The Supreme Court also sits as a Court of First Instance whenever this function is specially prescribed.[103]

A. *Special Courts and Boards*

91. The Labour Court (*Arbetsdomstolen*), the Defence Intelligence Court (Försvarsunderrättelsedomstolen) are special courts which are wholly independent from the ordinary court system and final courts in their domains. Other special courts (*see* below) are more or less organizationally linked to the ordinary lower courts.

1. The Labour Court

92. Labour disputes are regulated in a special Act (SFS 1974:371) applicable in disputes concerning collective labour contracts and other labour disputes.[104] Such disputes are handled by the Labour Court, which is the oldest special court in Sweden, established in 1929. It is composed of three categories of members: officials, employers and employees, up to a maximum of twenty-five. These are divided into four chairmen, four vice-chairmen, three other officials and fourteen members from the social partners. The social partners appoint members in the last-mentioned group upon nomination. The chairman and the vice-chairman must be legally qualified and

102. RB 2:2.
103. RB 3:1 and 3:3.
104. LRA s. 1.

have judging experience. Other official members must have insight into the conditions of the labour market. The bench in the Labour Court is composed of a chairperson and between four and six other members.

93. In certain cases, labour disputes will be handled by a district court as the Court of First Instance. This is primarily relevant when the dispute is not directly related to a collective labour agreement.[105]

2. The Patent and Market Court

94. The Market Court handled previously matters according to the Competition Act as the final court (SFS 2008:579), as well as matters according to, e.g., the Act on Contract Conditions in Consumer Relations (SFS 1994:512), the Act on Contract Conditions Between Tradesmen (SFS 1984:292), and the Act on Standing for Certain Foreign Consumer Authorities and Consumer Organizations (SFS 2000:1175).

95. Members of the Market Court included a chairperson, a vice-chairman and five special members. The chairperson and the vice-chairman had to be legally qualified and have had judging experience. The other members were economic experts. The Market Court was competent to judge with a chairperson and three other members. The chairperson was competent to act alone to prepare the case and to try simpler questions.[106]

3. Patent Cases

96. Certain patent cases fell in the first instance within the exclusive jurisdiction of the District Court in Stockholm. There was also the Patent Appeal Court, which was an administrative court established in 1978.

97. The Patent Appeal Court, which was organized in divisions, consisted of patent law councilors (*Patenträttsråd*) legally qualified or knowledgeable in technical matters. These judges were appointed by the Government. The court had a quorum with three members. On 1 September 2016, new provisions on the Patent and Market Court came into force. At the same time, the Patent Court, the Patent Appeals Court and the Market Court ceased to exist and merged into the same court, the Patent and Market Court. The purpose of the reform was to avoid splitting up issues in different courts and instead collecting them in one court for a uniform and concentrated court trial. This leads to a faster, more efficient and cheaper process. The proposal emphasizes that the intellectual property, marketing and competition cases are relatively few in number, which means vulnerability and poor resource utilization, that differences can arise with recruitment, and skills supply. In view of the

105. *See* LRA 1:2.
106. MDL s. 3.

fact that the goals and issues in the field in question are among the most complex and comprehensives ones being dealt with in court, a reform was also important in this respect. This is also the reason why the Government or Government authority determines which of the judges of the Stockholm District Court and Svea Court of Appeal shall serve as judges in the Patent and Market Court. Thus, these judges do not circulate between different tasks in the same way as judges in the ordinary courts, but remain for a long time in the same court. The Patent and Market Court shall also have jurisdiction to review objectives for better patent application. It may also investigate questions of information concerning infringement proceedings. Furthermore, it has jurisdiction to investigate another dispute (e.g., criminal cases) related to an intellectual property law, marketing or competition law dispute. In the latter case, the bench shall normally be composed of four members in the main proceedings, two ordinary judges and two with technical and financial expertise. There is room for increasing the number of members, as well as the right in simple cases to decide about a smaller composition.[107]

4. Land and Environmental Courts

98. The Environmental Code (SFS 1998:808), which came into force on 1 January 1999, coordinates the Swedish legislation in the environmental area. In addition, the Environmental Code has a broad scope because it aims to unify social and economic development with the effective protection of the environment. In order to reach this goal many laws have been incorporated in the Environmental Code, e.g., the Water Act, the Health protection Act and the Nature Conservation Act.

99. Regulations about land courts were earlier to be found in the Act on Courts in Cases Concerning Real Estate Property. Each county had a land court, which was constituted by an ordinary court in a special composition.

100. Through legislation in 2011, the environmental courts and the land courts merged into Land and Environmental Courts. The same courts, which were earlier Environmental Courts, are now Land and Environmental Courts. On 1 June 2017, some changes were made by the legislator with the aim of achieving more effective handling of goals and cases in the land and environmental process.

5. Rent and Tenancy Tribunals

101. These tribunals were established in 1969, when they took over the issues handled by the rental tribunals in the municipalities. They were initially established to settle disputes between landlords and tenants, but their area of competence has

107. Prop. 2015/16:57.

successively increased. The differences between ordinary proceedings in court and the proceedings at the rent and tenancy tribunals are, thus, no longer very significant.

102. There are eight rent and tenancies tribunals spread over the country, and with few exceptions they are located in the county cities.

103. A rent tribunal is generally composed of a legally qualified member and two other members. One of these must be well experienced in the administration of apartment buildings and another should have experience of the tenant's perspective in a housing dispute. If it is a tenancy dispute one member must be experienced in tenancy relations, e.g., as the owner of a farm or in a similar way and the other must be a tenant of a farm.

6. Maritime Law Courts

104. In Chapter 21 of the Sea Act (SFS 1994:1009), there are regulations about the maritime courts. The Government decides which district courts shall be maritime courts. At present, there are seven: the district courts of Luleå, Sundsvall, Stockholm, Kalmar, Malmö, Göteborg and Karlstad. The maritime courts handle disputes enumerated in the Sea Act, for example disputes concerning damages caused by collisions between ships or by shipwreck.

7. Cases Concerning Freedom of the Press and Freedom of Expression

105. The basic rules on these issues are to be found in the Freedom of the Press Act. Jurisdiction in such cases is assigned to the district court in which circuit the County Administrative Board is located. However, the Government has also authorized the district courts in Eskilstuna, Norrköping and Helsingborg to handle cases concerning freedom of the press and freedom of expression. The cases in question are subjected to trial by jury.

8. Tribunals

106. There are also boards, which handle matters similar to those dealt with in the courts. The biggest board is The National Board for Consumer Complaint (*Allmänna reklamationsnämnden*). It acts as a court with disputes concerning consumer law, but its decisions are not legally enforceable. The Board for Health and Medical treatment (*Hälso och sjukvårdsnämndens ansvarsnämnd*) examines claims concerning malpractice by doctors and nurses. Another tribunal is the Higher Education Board (*Överklagandenämnden för högskolan*), which examines appeals from high schools and universities. Recently dispute resolution boards have seen the light of the day as a result of the European Parliament Directive 2013/11/EU on Dispute Resolution in Consumer Disputes and amending Regulation (EC) No. 2006/2004 and Directive 200/22/EC – Dispute Resolution Directive – which were adopted on 21 May 2013. At the same time, Regulation (EU) No. 524/2013 was adopted on Dispute Resolution online in consumer disputes and amending Regulation (EC) No. 2006/2004 and Directive 2009/22/ EC – Dispute Resolution. The purpose of the directive and regulation is to create a high level of consumer protection, which will contribute to a well-functioning consumer market through the establishment of fast, inexpensive, impartial and effective out-of-court dispute settlement. The Directive applies to procedures aimed at resolving domestic and cross-border disputes concerning contractual obligations arising from purchase contracts or service contracts between a trader who is a member of the Union and a consumer resident in the Union. Because of these acts, the Parliament adopted a law on alternative dispute settlement in consumer relations, which entered into force on 1 January 2016. By this act it was decided that the competent authority in Sweden for approval of dispute resolution boards should be the Legal, Financial and Administrative Services Agency (*Kammarkollegiet*). Currently, there are six approved dispute resolution boards: the General Complaints Board, the Personal Insurance Committee, the Swedish Property Complaints Board, the Legal Affairs Committee, the Swedish Lawyers Association's Consumer Affairs Board, the Trafficking Board and the Funeral Board.

107. During 1960–1970, the legislature had a great belief in the special courts. The Market Court and the Housing Court were established during this period. Today, there has been a turnaround of policy; the Government wants to reduce the number of special courts and move more disputes to the ordinary courts, e.g., the Housing Court ceased to exist on 30 June 1994 and the Supreme Insurance Court on 30 June 1995. The reason for this change of policy can be found *inter alia* in a desire to ensure that ordinary courts will not be regarded as a poor alternative, to relieve judges from dealing with purely expedition matters, to make administration of justice cheaper and to avoid competence conflicts.[108] However, the Land and Environmental Courts are new special courts as well as the Migration Courts from 2006.

II. Administration of the Courts

108. Before 1971, the courts handled their own administration directly under the *Ds Ju*. However, the administration of the district courts was mainly a task for the Court of Appeals. This system with two parallel administrative units caused bureaucratic delays and difficulties in coordinating the work. In addition, the *Ds Ju* had to spend a lot of time on questions concerning appropriation and administration of the courts. Because of these problems, the National Courts Administration Committee was assigned to investigate these issues in 1970. It also investigated the tasks that ought to be handled by a central administrative authority for the courts, and how such an authority should be organized. The general opinion was that the time had come for effective planning, coordination and following-up of the activities of the

108. Cf. para. 26 *supra*.

courts. For these reasons, the legislator proposed that a court administration board should be established to lead and plan the administration of the courts.[109] On 1 July 1971, the Parliament decided to establish a central administration authority office for the courts. This authority eventually came into being on 1 July 1975.

109. The National Court Administration Office (*Domstolsverket*, www.dom.se), which was reorganized in 1995 and thereafter in 1999, is today a central administrative authority for court service. The National Courts Administration, is headed by a Director General (*Generaldirektör*) and a Board appointed by the Government. Responsible for the education and training of judges is the Court Academy, installed in 2009 in Jönköping.

110. The National Courts Administration also performs secretarial work for the Appointment Board for Judges (*Domarnämnden*) and the Notary Board (*Notarienämnden*). The main task of the Appointment Board is to give proposals to the Government concerning the appointment of judges. Today a person interested in such a top position can apply for it. At the same time, there is still room for an informal calling of a suitable person for the highest positions.[110]

111. According to the existing division of departmental responsibilities, the Labour Court deals with issues falling within the area of the Labour-Market Department and the Defence Intelligence Court under the Ministry of Defence. Other courts belong to the Department of Justice.

112. With regard to administration within the courts, the provisions are contained partly in the Code and partly in certain decrees.[111]

113. A district court must have one chief judge (*Lagman*), who is the administrative head of the court. There are also senior judges (*Chefsrådman*) and judges (*Rådman*).

114. In the instructions for the district courts, it is provided that there can also be technical councils (*Tekniska råd*), deputy district judges (*Tingsfiskal*), law clerks (*Tingsnotarier*), law secretaries (*Beredningsjurister*) and others. There must also be lay judges (*Nämndemän*) in each circuit.

115. Each Court of Appeal has a president, one or more division heads (*Hovrättslagman*) and judges of appeal (*Hovrättsråd*), all of whom must be legally qualified. In addition, there are associate judges of appeal (*Hovrättsassessor*), reporting

109. *See* the report of the National Court Administration Board, SOU 1971:41.
110. Prop. 2009/10:181, p. 80.
111. *See* decree (SFS 1996:381) with instruction for the district courts; decree (SFS 1996:379) with instruction for the Court of Appeals; and decree (SFS 1996:377) with instruction for the Supreme Court.

clerks (*Hovrättsfiskal*) and technical councils. Each division consists of the president or a division head as the chairperson and other judges, one of whom shall be the deputy chairperson. Associate judges of appeal (*Hovrättsassessor*) can function as co-opted members.[112]

116. Cases in a Court of Appeal are distributed to sections. Each legally trained member of a division normally has his own section. The section head is responsible for the preparation of the cases allocated to the section and is normally the reporter (*rapporteur*) of the case. The president is the administrative head of the Court of Appeal. He can refer a matter to a collegium or plenum.

117. Today the Supreme Court consists of fourteen justices (*Justitieråd*). Pursuant to the law there must be at least fourteen judges. One of the justices is appointed by the Government as president of the court and thereby becomes the administrative head of the court. The Supreme Court decides if it shall be divided into divisions, which it is. Each division has a chairperson. A secretary of justice (Justitiesekreterare) prepares cases. A Supreme Court judge acts as a referee.[113]

III. The Bench

118. In the district courts, three legally qualified judges constitute the bench at main hearings, unless otherwise prescribed.[114] If three legally qualified judges constitute the bench, it is still competent to judge with two legally qualified judges in the event one of them drops out after commencement of the main hearing.[115] Family law cases, in particular, are exceptions to this general rule. At the main hearing in cases concerning divorce, support to a spouse, paternity, custody and access to children, the principal rule is that the district court must be composed of a legally qualified member and three lay judges.[116]

119. If the main hearing is held in simplified form, one legally qualified judge is sufficient.[117] Moreover, the court is competent to judge with one legally qualified judge if the court deems it sufficient that one judge constitutes the bench and the parties agree to this, or if the case is of a simple nature.[118] One judge normally is not enough in cases with comprehensive oral evidence and cases involving difficult legal issues.[119] If the parties should, nonetheless, wish that the case be handled and decided by a single judge, in principle this requires agreement between the parties

112. RB 2:4.
113. RB 3:4.
114. RB 1:3 a para. 1.
115. RB 1:3 a para. 4.
116. *See* ÄktB 14:17 and FB 20:1. This composition applies unless the exceptions in RB 1:3 a para. 2 or 3 are applicable.
117. RB 1:3 a para. 2. Concerning the main hearing in simplified form, *see* paras 375–378 *infra*.
118. RB 1:3 a para. 3.
119. Prop. 1986/87:89, p. 75.

and the court. It is essential that it be noted in the court record that the parties have given their approval according to the rule in question.[120]

120. As mentioned above the court is competent to judge with a single legally qualified judge if the case is of a simple nature, irrespective of the parties' consent. Concerning the background to this rule, which was enacted in 1989, it is stated in the preparatory legislative works that in certain simple cases it can be difficult to get information from the parties about their opinion on the composition issue, and that one of the parties might oppose a single judge in order to delay the judgment.[121] Of course, it is difficult to specify criteria on what constitutes simple cases. In dubious situations, the stronger composition was recommended.

121. However, since the general requirement for review dispensation was introduced in 2008, it became more common for the parties to request that the court should be composed of three judges. By the amendment to the Code of 1 July 2016, the provision in question was changed by the legislator so that the parties' decision-making power over the composition of the bench has been completely removed.[122] Regarding the scope of the new rule, the preparatory works state that a rule of thumb may be three judges, if the court expects the main hearing to last for several days or if the investigation is otherwise complicated. The degree of difficulty refers not only to legal complexity but also to the complexity of the alleged ground of action. The aim for the court is to make an overall assessment of the extent and complexity of the case, but according to the preparatory works, this assessment by the court should be separated from the question of how the rules of review dispensation in the Court of Appeal are applied. However, the questions are in substance interlinked with each other. Obviously, the guarantees of quality of the judgment from the district court will increase with three judges instead of one.

122. In an action amenable to an out-of-court settlement, the bench is always quorate with one legally qualified judge if it is obvious that the value of the claim does not amount to half of the 'basic amount' in accordance with the National Insurance Act.[123] If the plaintiff claims a fixed sum, this sum is directly decisive of the question of whether a single judge is competent.[124] Whether the plaintiff has substantial grounds for his calculations is not examined, nor shall the court take into account the fact that the claimed amount is totally or partly disputed by the parties.[125] Sometimes it is possible to determine the value of the claim even though the plaintiff has instituted a declaratory claim.[126] This might also be possible if the plaintiff institutes an action about something else than money.[127] When different

120. RH 1986:90.
121. Prop. 1989/89:95, p. 60.
122. Prop. 2015/16:56.
123. RB 1:3 d para. 1. This limit (SEK 23,650 in 2020) is adjusted annually in accordance with inflation.
124. *See* NJA 1976, p. 470.
125. Cf. RH 1982:131.
126. *See, e.g.*, NJA 1979, p. 591.
127. Lindell, *Civilprocessen*, 170.

claims instituted by a plaintiff against the same defendant are joined, the cases are regarded as a unit, which means that the different values are added together. The preparatory legislative works are silent regarding the question of how the value ought to be calculated when a plaintiff against more than one defendant has instituted claims.[128] In the doctrine, the opinion has been put forward that the decisive circumstance in those cases is the total value of the different claims. This opinion has later on become praxis.

123. The rule regarding the competence of a single judge is, however, not applicable if a party requests that ordinary rules be applied at his first appearance in court and gives reason to believe that the underlying dispute concerns a higher value, or that the outcome is of extraordinary importance with respect to the examination of other existing legal relationships between the parties.[129] This rule is aimed both at cases where a party has an interest in getting the case tried in an ordinary way and in cases where there is public interest in such a trial.

124. When the rule about competence of a single judge is applied, the court must, when the summons application is filed with the court, decide if the rule in question applies, *inter alia* because of the importance of legal costs and for the possibilities of appeal. In addition, if a party applies for legal aid, the court must decide whether an attorney is to be appointed. An attorney may not be appointed if the action is disposed of as a small claim action. If a case has been dealt with in ordinary proceedings in a district court, it should not be handled in a simplified form in an appellate court, unless a party has appealed the decision concerning the form of proceeding.[130] The reason for this state of affairs is to be found in certain differences between the two forms of procedure, which apply especially to legal costs.[131] Changing the form of proceedings from the simplified procedure in the district court to the ordinary procedure in the appellate court does not meet the same standards.[132]

125. When cases are decided without a main hearing and when procedural issues are tried, the court may have the composition that is prescribed for the main hearing if there are particular reasons with regard to the nature of the case or matter.[133] An officer at the court may prepare a case, although he or she is not legally qualified, if the measures are of a simple nature.[134]

126. Three judges constitute the bench in an appellate court. However, in appeal cases from district courts, at least four legally qualified judges must sit in the court – but not more than five – when a case is decided, if the district court consisted of three legally qualified judges. If one of the legally qualified judges is prevented from

128. Joinder of claims is described further in paras 296–305 *infra*.
129. RB 1:3 d para. 2. *See* NJA 1990, p. 152.
130. NJA 1982, p. 723.
131. *See* para. 560 *infra*.
132. KRB 1:23.
133. RB 1:3 c.
134. Rules about this are to be found in the instructions for the district courts.

adjudicating after the commencement of the main hearing, the bench nevertheless constitutes a quorum. When an appellate court deals with the question of whether to grant leave to appeal, it shall consist of three legally qualified judges. When rendering a decision whether to remove a case from the court's agenda after withdrawal of a claim, an appellate court is properly constituted with one legally qualified judge. One legally qualified judge may carry out preparatory measures or, if they are of a simple nature, by some other officer.[135]

127. Knowledge of particular fields is required in some cases. Thus, in addition, to the members mentioned above, an appellate court could also contain an economist and/or tax law expert.[136]

128. According to 3:5 of the Code, five members of a division of the Supreme Court constitute a *quorum*. No more than seven members may sit in court. However, the rules on the composition of the bench of the Supreme Court were changed in 2009 in order to make sure that the court uses five members only for qualified legal issues. Otherwise, in cases enumerated in the law, the Supreme Court, pursuant to 3:5a of the Code, itself decides the number of judges required.[137] Extended cooperation between the Supreme Courts became possible through new legislation in 2017.[138] A member of the Supreme Administrative Court may be ordered by the Supreme Court to serve in the Supreme Court and the Supreme Administrative Court may order correspondingly. The purpose of this reform is to contravene complex conflicts of competence between these courts.

129. If a division of the Supreme Court finds that the opinion prevailing in the division diverges from a legal principle or construction of law previously adopted by the Supreme Court, the division may direct that the Supreme Court by nine members or en banc shall adjudicate the case in its entirety.[139] This provision is seldom used. In addition, it may be used in other situations in which it is of special importance for the application of law.

IV. Appointment of Judges

130. After completing the four and a half year law-degree programme and graduating from one of the five law schools in Sweden, many of the graduates apply for a post as a law clerk. Clerking can be performed in a district court or a county court. The required period of practice is two years. A candidate who is interested in becoming a judge may apply, after serving as a law clerk, for an appointment as a reporting clerk trainee at an appellate court or appellate administrative court.

135. RB 2:4.
136. RB 2:4 a.
137. Prop. 2008/09:117, 23–26.
138. Prop. 2016/17:174, RB 3:4 para. 5.
139. RB 3:5.

131. A person who is appointed as a reporting clerk trainee normally becomes a reporting clerk after six months. The reporting clerk then serves for a number of years in this capacity and is competent to deal with all cases apart from the most complicated. The next step is practise as an 'adjunct' member in a Court of Appeal for a period of approximately one year, and after this the candidate follows an appointment as an associate judge of appeal. After working six to eight years as an associate judge of appeal, a person can count on becoming a district judge, for most the final appointment in one's career. Today it is possible to reach this final step at the age of about 40. However, the career path has become more open. Today any Swedish citizen with a law degree can apply to be a judge when a position is advertised. Thus, the career path does not any longer exclusively go through the court system. This is true also with respect to the highest positions.

132. The Government appoints all tenured judges. In the Act Appointment of Ordinary Judges (2010:1390) there are rules about the appointment of judges and about the task and composition of the Appointment Board for judges. For many years, the ambition has been to make the recruitment basis for judges wider. This objective also includes the highest positions, that is to say Supreme Court judges, which before 2010 were appointed after an informal contact between the Department of Justice and the person approached. Today, these offices are also advertised.

133. Lay judges are elected. If a court district covers more than one local district, the court divides the number of lay judges among the local districts in proportion to their population. The Government, or an authority determined by the Government, shall prescribe the number of lay judges to be elected to an appellate court for every county in its circuit or, if its circuit includes part of a county, for that part of the county.[140]

134. The Government appoints those who shall serve as economic experts for three years at the time.[141] During this period, further persons may be appointed for the remaining part of the period. In the event that an economic expert's appointment must cease, while a case is pending the appointment shall nonetheless be deemed to have continued validity with regard to the pending case.

§2. Members of the Judiciary

I. Incompatibilities

135. In the Code, there are general competence rules for judges and lay judges and, in addition, particular rules concerning disqualification.

136. With respect to the rules of general competence, the legally qualified judges shall be Swedish citizens and must have passed the tests prescribed for qualification

140. RB 4:5.
141. *See* RB 4:10 a, 1:8 and 2:4 a.

to the judiciary.[142] Tests here refer to graduation from a Swedish law school. Graduation from law school in another Scandinavian country is, under certain circumstances, regarded as equivalent to a Swedish graduation.

137. A person who is under age, bankrupt or who has a guardian appointed under the Parental Code may not qualify to be a judge.[143]

138. The Government has the right to issue other regulations regarding the discharge of a judge's duties, including appropriate tests of knowledge and conditions other than those mentioned above. Such conditions can be found in the decree with instructions for the Supreme Court (SFS 1996:337), the decree with instructions for the courts of appeal (SFS 1996:379) and the decree with instruction for the district courts (SFS 1996:381).

139. Every Swedish citizen who is registered in the municipality or, in the case of a lay judge in a Court of Appeals in the county or the part thereof which is under the jurisdiction of the Court of Appeals, is eligible to be a lay judge. The county councils assemblies carry out elections for lay judges for the district courts by the municipal councils and for the courts of appeal. The elections must be proportional. Legally qualified judges, court officers and employees, public prosecutors, police officers, advocates and all other persons who are professionally engaged in the representation of litigants in judicial proceedings are ineligible for service as lay judges. No person may, at the same time, be a lay judge in a Court of Appeals and in a district court. Lay judges are elected for a period of four years.[144] In electing lay judges, diversity with regard to age, sex and occupation shall be sought. To be elected as a lay judge the candidate must show good judgment, independence and compliance with the law in order to be deemed suitable for the assignment. The court shall dismiss a lay judge who is not suitable.

140. Individuals who are or have been married to each other, who are related by blood or marriage in lineal ascent, or descent, who are brothers or sisters or who are so related by affinity, or others who are similarly related may not sit together as judges on the bench.[145] This general competence rule embraces legally qualified judges as well as lay judges, technical members and other special members. It has been claimed that the purpose of this rule is not to ensure the court's reputation for impartiality, but rather to avoid the situation where an individual judge, in discharging his duty, may be influenced by some close relative.[146] If the rule in question applies, the court is not competent to judge. This competence requirement must be

---

142. RB 4:1.
143. The rule in FB (11:7) refers to a person who has a guardian appointed because of illness, mental retardation or bad health and who, therefore, needs help to ensure his rights. This general rule of competence is also applicable to lay judges and economic experts, as well as to members of the special courts.
144. RB 4:6 paras 4 and 4:8.
145. RB 4:12.
146. Prop. 1973:30, p. 68.

observed by a higher court ex officio should the case be appealed (i.e., irrespective of whether or not a party raises this point on appeal).

141. The rule concerning disqualification of judges enumerates ten different situations, which result in disqualification, and is applicable to all kinds of judges. Disqualifications apply on a case-by-case basis.[147]

142. A judge shall be disqualified from hearing a case if he is a party thereto or otherwise has an interest in its subject matter, or when he can expect special advantage or injury from the outcome of the action. Whether or not the judge himself is a party is easy to establish. It is more difficult to decide if he has an interest in its subject matter. The Expert Drafting Committee has, with regard to this condition, only stated that it must be an interest of a legal nature.[148] Hence, a judge is deemed to be disqualified if he can appear as a party or an intervening party.[149] Moreover, it has been suggested that a judge shall be deemed to have an interest in the subject matter of the case if he could have been a party in the proceedings and thereby would have been able to proceed on the same grounds or essentially the same grounds as one of the parties in the pending action.[150] However, the borderline between the 'interest in its subject' and 'special advantage or injury' might be hard to determine. If the judge does not have an interest in its subject in the way that has been mentioned, but can expect special advantage or injury, he is disqualified. An example of the latter is where the judge is a shareholder in a company, which is a party in the case, provided that his share of the stocks as well as the economic value of the dispute are significant.[151]

143. The judge is similarly disqualified if he and one of the parties are or have been married, are related by blood or marriage in lineal ascent or descent, are brothers or sisters, are so related by marriage that one of them is or has been married to a brother or sister of the other, or if he is similarly related to one of the parties (RB 4:13 p. 2). Disqualification because of family relationship is thus the same as in 4:12 of the Code.[152]

144. Furthermore, a judge will be disqualified if he is related, as specified in RB 4:13 para 2, to anyone who has an interest in the subject-matter or who can expect special advantage or injury from the outcome of the case. The disqualification rule also applies if he, or anyone related to him as specified in RB 4:13 p. 2, is a guardian of or otherwise serves as a representative of a party, or is a member of the board of a corporation, partnership, cooperative, association or similar society, foundation or similar institution which is a party. The same rule applies when a municipality or

147. RB 4:13.
148. NJA II 1943, p. 52.
149. NJA II 1943, 52. Å. Hassler, *Svensk Civilprocessrätt* 49 (1963). Kallenberg, *supra*, 249–256.
150. Ekelöf et al., *Rättegång I*, 165.
151. P. Fitger, *Rättegångsbalken I*, 4:27 (1984, hereafter 'KRB').
152. *See* para. 140 *supra*.

similar community is a party, and the judge, or anyone related to him as specified in RB 4:13 p. 2, is a member of the board in charge of administration of the subject area within which the case falls.

145. In addition, a judge is disqualified if he, or anyone related to him as specified in RB 4:13 p. 2, is related in the way specified in RB 4:13 p. 4 to anyone who has an interest in the subject-matter or can expect special advantage or injury from the outcome of the case. There is a similar disqualification if he is the adversary of a party, though not if the party has cast him in that role in order to disqualify him. The meaning of the word 'adversary' is that the judge and a party have opposite interests in another pending proceeding. Clearly, the rule does not mean that a judge who is on trial for a minor offence shall be deemed disqualified in all cases where a public prosecutor has instituted an action, or that a judge who is, for example, in dispute with the state over the amount of tax he is to pay in one particular year shall be hindered from dealing with all sorts of cases where the state is a party. The crucial factor in cases like these is, instead, the relationship the judge has to the individual case.[153]

146. Furthermore, a judge is disqualified if he, acting as a judge or officer of another court, has rendered a decision concerning the matter or if he, before an adjudicative body other than a court or as an arbitrator, has dealt with the matter. However, not every decision results in disqualification. The word 'decision' in this rule shall be read as final decision on the matter.[154] The condition 'dealt with the matter' should be interpreted in a restrictive way.

147. In addition, a judge is disqualified if, in a criminal case before the main hearing, he has previously tried the issue of the defendant's guilt or innocence or if he has served in the case as attorney for or assistant to one of the parties, or if he has been a witness or expert therein. Finally, he is disqualified if some other circumstance exists that is likely to undermine the confidence in his impartiality. Obviously, this is a general clause. It might apply, for example, where the judge obtains his salary or support from one of the parties, is economically dependent on a party or a party in a related action in another court, or if he is clearly hostile to a party.[155]

II. End of Function

148. Ordinarily, a legally qualified judge is, in principle, irremovable.[156] This means that he remains in office until he decides to resign or until his death. Of

153. KRB 4:26.
154. Ekelöf et al., *Rättegång I*, 168.
155. SOU 1938:44, p. 107. *See, e.g.*, NJA 2008, p. 893 and NJA 2010, p. 274. In NJA 2010 p. 482, a prosecutor who was on leave from the Public Prosecutor's Office and served as a member of the Court of Appeal was disqualified pursuant to RB 4:13, as the permanent employment as a prosecutor was deemed to be such a special circumstance that could cause reasonable doubt about the impartiality of her as a judge.
156. *See* para. 80 *supra*.

course, a judge's personal circumstances may change. For example, a guardianship or declaration of bankruptcy may result in a lack of general competence, because of which he can no longer function as a judge. Obviously, the same applies when something occurs that is related to the individual case leading to disqualification.

149. If a lay judge establishes a valid excuse, the court may relieve him. He may also resign at the age of 60, and his appointment automatically ends when he or she is no longer competent.

III. Discipline

150. It is provided in the Constitution (RF 11:2) that neither any authority nor the Government may decide how a court shall rule in an individual case. In order to implement this principle it is necessary to safeguard the independence of the judiciary. Thus, it is laid down in the Constitution that an ordinary legally trained tenured judge may be removed from his office only if he:

(1) through a crime or severe or repeated negligence in the discharge of his duties has been shown to be obviously unsuitable for the office; or
(2) has reached the prescribed age for retirement with pension or otherwise according to the law is obliged to resign with pension.[157]

To guarantee the constitutional position of the judge a special form of employment is required. Thus, a judge has a tenured position, which means that the employment agreement cannot terminate or be limited in time. Before 1994 there where special provisions about this special kind of employment in the Public Employment Act, which applies to state and municipal employees (LOA, SFS 1994:260). However, when this Act was reviewed the special provisions in question were moved to a new Act (the Act SFS 1994:261 on Tenured Positions). This Act confirms the grounds for removal of a judge stated in the Constitution (§7). It should be observed that LOA applies also to judges if nothing else is prescribed in the Act on Tenured Positions.

151. The Public Liability Board (*Statens ansvarsnämnd*) decides on dismissal, suspension or medical examination of a judge. The judge can demand court review of such decisions.

152. It is provided in LOA that if a judge intentionally or negligently sets aside his duties and the wrongdoing is not minor in nature, sanctions may be imposed on him. The sanctions can be either a warning and/or a salary reduction.[158]

157. RF 11:5.
158. LOA § 15.

IV. Supervision

153. The Chancellor of Justice (JK, *Justitiekanslern*) is the Government's own advocate, who presents the Government's cases and watches over its interests. Amongst his more important tasks the following should be mentioned: He supervises those who are working in the public administration to ensure that they correctly apply laws and in other aspects carry out their duties. As a special prosecutor he may prosecute a public officer who has committed a crime, and he can also initiate proceedings for disciplinary sanctions and dismissal. In addition, he has the authority to institute an action against a member of the Supreme Court or the Supreme Administrative Court. Moreover, he is entitled to be present at court deliberations, although he may not give his opinion. Court and administrative authorities and employees of the state or municipalities are obliged to give the JK any information he requests.[159]

154. Sweden has had an Ombudsman Institution (*Justitieombusmannen* or JO) since 1809 (www.jo.se). Today there are four ombudsmen, each with his or her own area of responsibility. They are elected by the Parliament to supervise the application of laws in public administration in accordance with instructions decided by the Parliament.[160] In particular, the Parliamentary Ombudsmen must ensure that the courts and the administrative authorities observe the constitutional requirements of objectivity, impartiality and basic human rights in the performance of their functions. Furthermore, JO is authorized to bring defects in legislation to the attention of the Parliament.

155. The JO is helped in carrying out his supervision through complaints from the public, inspections and other investigations. The JO reviews decisions made by government authorities or by a public employee to determine whether they are unlawful or in some other way unsuitable. The JO is also entitled to make statements, which are intended to support a harmonious and logical application of the law. In addition, JO may, as a special prosecutor, institute a criminal action against a public employee, who, by setting aside his official duties or assignment, has committed some criminal act other than a crime under the Freedom of the Press Act. Furthermore, JO may request the initiation of disciplinary proceedings and the dismissal of a civil servant. JO may also institute criminal actions against Supreme Court judges and Supreme Administrative Court judges. JO submits an annual written report to the Parliament containing a description of the matters dealt with during the year and of the measures, he has undertaken to deal with these matters.[161]

---

159. *See* the Act (SFS 1975:1339) on the Supervision of the JK and his instruction (SFS 1975:1345).
160. RF 12:6.
161. *See* para. 58 *supra*.

Chapter 2. The Bar

§1. Conditions of Admission

156. The parties may have an attorney to present their cases.[162] However, they are not obliged to be represented by an advocate in a legal dispute, in contrast to many other European countries. However, advocates hold a unique position in Sweden. They belong to the Swedish Bar Association, (*Sveriges advokatsamfund*, www.advokatsamfundet.se) which was founded in 1887, initially as a voluntary society of academically educated advocates. In 1947, i.e., around the same time as the Judicial Code of Procedure came into force, the Association became a kind of public law body, since the Government then approved the charter of the Association. The Government supervises the Association also via the JK. The purpose of the Association is to maintain just and skilled corps of advocates for the benefit of a good administration of justice, to follow the development of law and to work for the experience of the Association benefiting this development, to safeguard the advocates' general professional interests, and to work for concord and unison between advocates.

157. A person who appears as an advocate without authorization may be punished with a fine.[163] Furthermore, in principle only an advocate can be appointed as a public defence council.[164]

158. There is an explicit rule in the Code (RB 12:1) declaring that an attorney must master the Swedish language.[165]

159. When the Code came into force in 1948, the requirements were both Swedish citizenship and domicile in Sweden. Adjustments were made in 1993, due to the adoption of the European Economic Area (EEA) treaty, and the requirement in this treaty concerning free movement of persons and services. Today, membership of the Bar Association is open to any person who is a Swedish citizen or a citizen in another state within the EU, the EEA or Switzerland. In the provision, residence in these states is given equal right to membership as residence.

160. In order to become a member of the Swedish Bar Association, the applicant must have completed the practical and theoretical education prescribed for practising advocates (a Master of Laws degree) and must have passed the test prescribed for qualification to the judiciary.[166] The charter of the Swedish Bar Association further requires that an applicant shall have acquired practical juridical training over a period of three years after completion of the Master of Laws.

162. RB 12:1.
163. BrB 17:5.
164. RB 21:5.
165. RB 8:2 para. 1, 1–2.
166. RB 8:2 para. 1, 3–4.

161. The educational requirements are also fulfilled by anyone who has passed an education required to become an advocate within the EU or the EEA or Switzerland. This is true also with respect to a person who is authorized as an advocate in a state within the EU other than Sweden and who practises Swedish law or otherwise meets the requirements to be a member of the Swedish Bar Association.[167]

162. In individual cases, the board of the Bar Association may dispense with the admission requirements in respect of citizenship and domicile and may dispense with the education requirements for those who have been authorized as advocates in another state.

163. Another requirement for admission to the bar as an advocate is that the applicant shall have 'a reputation for honesty' and 'in all other respects' must be qualified to practise as an advocate.[168]

164. Anyone who has been admitted as an advocate in Denmark, Norway, Iceland or Finland, in accordance with these countries' requirements, and thereafter has practised for at least three years as an assistant lawyer in an advocate's office in Sweden, shall be deemed to have fulfilled the requirements of education, honesty and suitability.[169] A person who is authorized as an advocate in another state within the EU and permanently practises in Sweden under the professional designation used in his state shall, pursuant to RB 8:2 a, be registered at the Swedish Bar Association.

165. A person who is bankrupt, who has a guardian or who has been forbidden to perform a profession as a legal or economic adviser, according to the Act on Prohibition Against Professional Advising (SFS 1985:354), may not be admitted as a member of the Association of Advocates. Neither may legally qualified judges, officers and employees at the ordinary courts, public prosecutors and enforcement officers be accepted as members. Nor, without special dispensation of the Board of the Swedish Bar Association, may membership be extended to any person employed by the state or a municipality or to a person employed by a private enterprise or individual other than an advocate.

§2. Rights and Duties

166. An advocate's position is, to a considerable extent, privileged. The obligations of an advocate stem partly from a general rule in the Code (RB 8:4), the Charters of the Association of Advocates and the Directives on good advocate praxis.[170]

167. RB 8:2 paras 3 and 8:2a.
168. RB 8:2 para. 1, 5–6.
169. RB 8:2 para. 4.
170. The Charters was instituted 1962. The latest version of the Directives is from 2016.

167. According to the Code, an advocate shall carry out the tasks entrusted to him honestly and diligently and shall always observe good advocatory ethics. Advocates are bound, when good advocate ethics so require, not revealing what they learn during the exercising of their profession.

168. Activities as an advocate may not, without special dispensation of the Board of the Bar Association, be carried out in corporation or in partnership with any person other than another advocate. Advocates are obliged to keep their own property segregated from the money and other assets of their clients.

169. The Directives contain rules about the activities of an advocate, in particular with regard to declining, and retirement from, assignments, and his relationship with clients, the opposing parties, the court, other authorities, colleagues and the Swedish Bar Association.

§3. Discipline

170. The board of the Swedish Bar Association and the Disciplinary Committee supervises the activities of advocates.[171] An advocate who, while exercising his profession, deliberately acts incorrectly or otherwise dishonestly shall be expelled from the association. In addition, if an advocate in other ways, by having committed crimes, has shown to be not suitable for the profession, he or she shall be expelled.[172] If there are extenuating circumstances, the Disciplinary Committee may instead give him a warning. If an advocate in any other respect disregards his professional duties, he may receive a warning or a reminder from the Disciplinary Committee; however, if the circumstances are particularly serious, he may also be expelled from the Association. Additionally, if an advocate has been warned, he may be ordered to pay a monetary penalty to the Association for a special cause, amounting to at least SEK 1,000 and at most SEK 50,000.[173] If it is considered sufficient, the Disciplinary Committee may express an opinion that the advocate's action is wrong or inappropriate, instead of issuing a reminder to the advocate. If a circumstance occurs that would make an advocate ineligible for acceptance according to RB 8:2 paragraph 5 or 6, he is bound to resign from membership immediately. Otherwise, the board may make an order for exclusion. The same applies to an advocate who no longer fulfils the requirements on citizenship or residence.

171. Matters of expulsion, warning, penalty reminder and opinion are reviewed by the Board of the Association or, to the extent prescribed in the charter, by another organ of the Association. The charter establishes a Disciplinary Committee consisting of a chairperson, a vice-chairman and nine other members. As indicated above

171. RB 8:6.
172. RB 8:7 a.
173. RB 8:7.

the charter authorizes the Disciplinary Committee to handle matters concerning disciplinary actions against a member of the Association, in accordance with certain rules in the charter, and to decide about expulsion, warning, penalty reminder and opinion.

172. Matters concerning disciplinary responsibility for a member shall initially be brought to the Disciplinary Committee, after notification from an individual or after intervention from the JK.[174]

173. A person who has been denied membership to the Bar Association, or who has been expelled from it, has the right to appeal the decision. The same applies to a person who has been refused registration in accordance to RB 8:2 a or lost his registration because of the provision in RB 8:7. The JK has the right to appeal decisions rendered under section RB 8:7 and 8: 7 a by the board or the Disciplinary Committee. Such appeals shall be taken to the Supreme Court. What is prescribed in the Code or any other statute about advocates shall also govern, to the extent applicable, a person authorized as an advocate in another state within the EU, the EEA or Switzerland when he practises in Sweden.

174. Concerning the supervision of the Chancellor of Government, *see* RB 8:6, paras 3 and 8:8.

Chapter 3. The Enforcement Service

174. The Enforcement Service enforces judgments if a debtor does not freely abide by a judgment. Earlier, these activities were carried out by, *inter alia*, District Police Superintendents, who also handled police and public prosecutor tasks. However, when the police and prosecutor activities were nationalized in 1965, the Enforcement Service was established.

175. In 1988, there was one Enforcement Service in each county (i.e., to say 24). However, in 1997 the Enforcement Service was reorganized and ten regional enforcement authorities (*Regionkronofogdemyndigheten*) were created, each headed by a Regional Enforcement Director (*Regionkronodirektör*). In 2006, these offices merged into one authority headed by the National Tax Board. In 2008, the Enforcement Service became an independent authority.

176. The main legal source for enforcement is the Execution Code (UB), which came into force on 1 January 1982. Since that year, the National Tax Board (*Riksskatteverket*, www.rsv.se) is the central authority for the enforcement administration with a special department for administration of the Enforcement Service.

177. Besides dealing with, e.g., payment injunctions the Enforcement Service has some duties not related to enforcement. The Enforcement Authorities have a supervisory function over the management of bankruptcies. They ensure that the management of the bankruptcy estate is carried out in an appropriate way in accordance with the Bankruptcy Act (KL) and other statutes. In 1994, a Debt Relief Act was introduced which made it possible to relieve natural persons completely or partly from the responsibility to pay their debts. If the debtor fails to make a voluntary agreement with his creditors, he can apply for voluntary debt relief in a procedure at the Enforcement Service. If a creditor does not agree, the case can be referred to the district court, which may force the creditors to accept debt relief.

178. In 2019, 1,272,080 public cases and 657,080 individual cases were registered by the Enforcement Service. In addition 1,334,352 cases were filed in summary proceedings, 8,695 in bankruptcy supervision matters and 21,603 with regard to debt relief matters.

179. As far as the disqualification of an enforcement officer is concerned, the same provisions apply as those for a judge in ordinary proceedings.[175] However, disqualification may not be based on a measure by the enforcement officer in his profession or because of an action committed against him while performing his profession.[176] If an enforcement officer has knowledge about a circumstance that is likely to establish disqualification, he shall, on his or her own motion, give notice about it. If a question concerning disqualification has already been raised and nobody has replaced the enforcement officer, the Enforcement Service shall render

175. *See* RB 4:13, commented in paras 142–147 *supra*.
176. UB 1:4.

a decision with regard to the disqualification issue as soon as possible. The enforcement officer himself may decide upon the disqualification issue only if another enforcement officer cannot replace him immediately. An enforcement officer who is disqualified may take measures that cannot be postponed without inconvenience.[177]

177. UB 1:5.

Part II. Jurisdiction

Chapter 1. Domestic Jurisdiction

§1. Subject-Matter Jurisdiction

I. Factors to Be Taken Into Account

180. In the Code, there is a central subject-matter forum rule regulating the relation between competence rules in the Code – which can be found in Chapter 10 – and competence rules in other laws.[178] A forum that can be found in the enumeration in 10:17 of the Code excludes an application of the forum rules in RB Chapter 10. The court shall, of its own motion, check its authority.

181. The court may not, due to the provisions in Chapter 10, entertain controversies assigned to authorities other than the courts or to the special courts, or required by law or decree to be determined by arbitrators.[179] The Code does not give any guidelines on how to answer the question under which circumstances the decision-making authority of an administrative authority excludes ordinary court competence. However, development of the case law so far shows that ordinary court competence has been deemed to be excluded as soon as statutory authorization has been given to an administrative authority to examine certain issues comprehensively and definitively.[180]

182. It was established by the Supreme Court that land courts are to be regarded as special courts.[181] Therefore, it is not possible to join claims that must be entertained by ordinary courts with cases that must be entertained by environmental courts.[182] In addition, it is, in principle, not possible for the defendant in an environmental court to assert a debt by way of set-off, if the debt is based on circumstances, which the environmental court is not competent to examine. The reverse is also true.[183]

---

178. This central rule is RB 10:17.
179. RB 10:17 para. 1, 1.
180. B. Wennergen, *Förvaltningsprocesslagen M.M. En Kommentar* 14, 19 (2001). *See, e.g.*, NJA 1987, p. 780.
181. *See* the plenary judgment NJA 1979, p. 107.
182. The land courts was abolished 2009 and replaced by the environmental courts.
183. *See* KRB 10:39.

183. Ordinary courts are not competent to entertain controversies which are to be brought in a certain court if, by law or decree, that court is exclusively competent to entertain such controversies.[184]

184. Certain controversies are by law assigned exclusively; certain special district courts or the division of marital or co-habitants property, if the controversy is brought to a court other than the proper one.[185] This mainly concerns maritime cases and other issues concerning maritime law.[186] Other examples are freedom of the press cases, where damages are not claimed, and cases where damages are claimed because of violation of the freedom of expression. In these cases, the district court of Stockholm is normally exclusively competent.

185. Disputes concerning the right of succession or the validity of testamentary dispositions, as well as controversies concerning certain land cases, are exclusively assigned to special courts.[187] Ordinary courts are furthermore not authorized to hear matrimonial cases according to the rules in Chapter 10 of the Code.[188] There are also special provisions stipulating which courts are competent with regard to attached property or stipulating the validity of a contract concerning personal property remaining in the possession of the seller subsequent to sale.[189]

186. According to the rules in Chapter 10 of the Code, the court cannot become competent for controversies that can be entertained by the courts without the need for summons.[190] This exception has its greatest importance in relation to court matters. It is of no relevance if the individual case has been initiated by summons or not. The crucial point is whether a summons is necessary to initiate an action.[191]

187. Pursuant to the rules in Chapter 10 of the Code, the parties may not institute an action in any other way than that prescribed by the law.[192] According to the Expert Drafting Committee, the reason for this is that the parties' right to agree on the forum should not imply the power to agree to bring an action in another court than that prescribed by law.[193]

---

184. RB 10:17 para. 1, 2.
185. RB 10:17 para. 1, 3.
186. *See* Prop. 1969:44, 244. The Code applies to the internal competence of the maritime courts.
187. RB 10:17 para. 1, p. 4. Cf. RB 10:9–10.
188. RB 10:17 para. 1, p. 5. In matrimonial cases the authorization for the ordinary courts is laid down in ÄktB.
189. RB 10:17 para. 1, p. 6. A special rule about the competent court can be found in UB 2:24.
190. RB 10:17 para. 1, p. 7.
191. *See* NJA 1943, p. 113.
192. RB 10:17 para. 2.
193. NJA II 1943, p. 114.

II. Main Claims and Ancillary Claims

188. Main claims and ancillary claims cannot be entertained by the same court unless it is competent to try both. Similarly, a claim for set-off may not be entertained by a court that is not competent to entertain a dispute concerning the debt asserted as a set-off claim.[194]

III. Overview of the Case Load of the Different Courts

189. Administrative cases and cases exclusively designated to special courts or tribunals are not to be examined by the ordinary courts. The following statistics offer an overview of the total number of civil cases filed at the Swedish judiciary in 2019.

190. The number of civil cases filed at the district courts was 201,741, at the appellate courts 30,040 and at the Supreme Court 6,787. The number of cases filed at the county courts was 176,760 while at the administrative appellate courts there was 44,541 and at the Supreme Administrative Court 7,100.

§2. Venue

I. Factors to Be Taken into Account

191. Generally, the competent court for civil cases is the court of the place where the defendant resides (*forum domicile*).[195] This includes both actual and legal 'persons'. The place where the defendant is registered is deemed his residence.[196] This is not a presumption that must be rebutted by counter-evidence concerning the defendant's real residence. Hence, if the actual residence does not correspond with the registration, the defendant is not obliged to appear at his real residence.[197] If a person does not have a real residence outside the jurisdiction, but is still registered in Sweden, no forum is designated.[198] The provisions in the Code do not apply automatically if a person has a residence both in the jurisdiction and outside it.[199]

192. A corporation, partnership, cooperative or association, or a society, foundation or similar institution, is considered to reside at the place in which the governing board has its permanent seat or, if the board has no permanent seat (or when there is no board), at the place from which the administration is carried out. The

194. RB 10:17 paras 3 and 14:6. *See also* para. 184 *supra* and para. 304 *infra*.
195. RB 10:1 para. 1.
196. RB 10:1 para. 2.
197. NJA II 1943, p. 96.
198. *See* NJA II 1943, p. 97 and NJA 1965, p. 172. Cf. NJA 1965, p. 351.
199. S. Dennemark, *Om svensk domstols behörighet i internationellt förmögenhetsrättsliga mål* 208 (1961).

same applies to municipalities or similar communities.[200] The residence of a joint-stock company or an economic association registered in Sweden is the place within the country where the board is located according to the articles of the association or the association charter, respectively.[201]

193. If a legal entity is registered abroad, and according to the articles of association has its residence abroad, a Swedish court has jurisdiction over it only if the information in the articles regarding the residence is fictitious or fraudulent.[202] When a legal entity does not have its activities registered in any country, but has a Board for which a permanent seat has been decided, the actual seat should be decisive with regard to the competence issue, if this is other than the permanent seat decided in the articles of the association.[203] A branch office of a foreign company, with independent administration in Sweden, is probably obliged to appear at a Swedish forum.[204]

194. The estate of a deceased person is subject to suit at the place where the deceased would have been required to respond.[205] Generally, this is the place where he has been registered for census purposes. A defendant without a known residence, either in or outside the territory, is subject to suit at the place where he is sojourning. If he is a Swedish citizen and sojourning outside the territory, or at an unknown place, he may be sued at the place within the territory where he last resided or sojourned.[206] As mentioned above, this rule does not imply that a person residing abroad, but who temporally sojourns in Sweden, can be sued in a Swedish court. The competence of the court shall be determined with respect to the facts existing at the time the defendant is served with the summons.[207]

195. In civil cases in general, the Crown is subject to suit at the place where the authority charged with representation of the Crown's interest in the subject-matters has its seat.[208]

196. The forum for a person without a known residence within the territory for controversies concerning debt obligations is the place in which his property is located (*forum arresti*).[209] Any property with an economic value can provide the basis for exercising jurisdiction.[210] The rationale behind this rule is that, from the

200. RB 10:1 para. 3.
201. *See* 2:4 the Act on Joint-Stock Companies (SFS 1975:1385) and 2:2 the Act on Economic Associations (SFS 1987:667).
202. Dennemark, *supra*, 87.
203. NJA II 1943, 98.
204. KRB 10:9.
205. RB 10:1 para. 4.
206. RB 10:1 para. 5.
207. RB 10:15.
208. RB 10:2.
209. RB 10:3 para. 1.
210. NJA II 1943, p. 99.

point of view of execution, it is important to organize a fast and effective enforcement.[211] The majority view in the commentaries is, therefore, that only such property that can be attached can provide the basis for exercising jurisdiction.[212] This forum rule is subsidiary to the general forum rule and, to some extent, in competition with it.[213] According to the wording of the provision at issue, it only applies to claims asking for performance. Whether it can be used for claims for declaratory relief is debatable.[214]

197. *Forum arresti* has not been deemed to apply when the defendant is a foreigner who possesses property for personal use during a temporary stay in the country.[215] Moreover, the provision probably does not apply to worthless property.[216] A claim concerning a purchase which was set down for security has been regarded as belonging to the defendant and thus providing the basis for jurisdiction in Sweden.[217] In addition, a claim belonging to a foreign defendant has, per se, been deemed to grant competence to a Swedish court, but if the plaintiff tries to create jurisdiction in Sweden through an omission to pay a debt, and the defendant proves that the plaintiff had this intention, the determination will be the reverse.[218] The *forum arresti* rule is dispositive which, *inter alia*, means that an action instituted against a foreigner who is not obliged to answer before a Swedish court can be entertained and brought to trial if the defendant does not raise any objection against the forum.[219]

198. In controversies involving personal property, the defendant may be sued in the place where the property is located.[220] This provision not only applies to disputes concerning the title to personal property, but also to disputes concerning limited rights to personal property and contractual claims regarding the right to possess personal property located in Sweden.[221]

---

211. *Ibid.*
212. Dennemark, *supra*, 153 et seq., P.O. Ekelöf, *Rättegång II* 27 (8th ed., 1996). *But see* Hj. Karlgren, *Kortfattad lärobok i internationell privatoch processrätt* 159 (1974) and Hjerner, *Anmälan av* Dennemark, *supra*, in SvJT (1963), 197.
213. If the plaintiff can choose between certain courts these are called 'competing courts', *see* Ekelöf, *Rättegång II*, 22.
214. Dennemark, *supra*, 151. Concerning performance and declaratory claims, *see* para. 232 *infra*.
215. NJA 1981, p. 386.
216. NJA 1988, p. 440.
217. NJA 1970, p. 487.
218. *See* NJA 1962, p. 354. This judgment has been criticized in the doctrine, *see* Dennemark, *supra*, 129; L. Welamson, *Svensk Rättspraxis. Civiloch straffprocessrätt 1958–1962*, SvJT 403 (1964); Hj. Karlgren, *Svensk Rättspraxis. Internationell privat-, straffoch processrätt 1961–1965*, SvJT 520 (1967) and L. Pålsson, *Svensk rättspraxis i internationell processrätt*, hereafter '*Svensk rättspraxis*', 64 (1989).
219. P.O. Ekelöf, *Rättegång II*, 26, note 26. *See also* NJA 1928, p. 149.
220. RB 10:3 para. 1, p. 2.
221. Dennemark, *supra*, 183.

199. A debt evidenced by a promissory note, or by any other document for which presentation is a condition of payment, is deemed located where the instrument is. Other debt claims are considered located in the district in which the debtor resides. If the debt is secured, the place in which the security is kept may also be considered the location of the debt.[222]

200. If a person without a known residence within the jurisdiction has entered into a contract or has otherwise incurred a debt in the jurisdiction, he may be sued in a controversy concerning the contract or debt in the place where the contract was formed or in the place where the debt was incurred (*forum contractus*).[223] A debt is deemed to have been incurred in Sweden even if only certain preparatory negotiations have taken place in the country.[224] Furthermore, it is required that the defendant or his attorney sojourned in the territory when the contract was finally entered into.[225] Consequently, a contract agreed to over the telephone between representatives for a Swedish company and a foreign company is not regarded as being entered into in Sweden.[226]

201. A person engaged in farming, mining, manufacturing, handicraft, commerce or some similar business with a permanent establishment in Sweden may be sued in the court where the establishment is located (*forum negotii*)[227] regarding a controversy stemming directly from these business activities. This forum rule contradicts the general forum rule and is, to some extent, a replacement rule, namely with respect to physical or legal persons who are not subject to jurisdiction within the territory.[228] In addition to the businesses listed above, this forum rule also applies to banks, insurance companies, shipowners and other transport or communication activities, hotels, theatres, cinemas and similar businesses.[229]

202. Anyone who has entered into a contract, or otherwise has incurred a debt at a place where he has been residing for a considerable period of time may be sued with respect to such an obligation at the place of his temporary residence while present at that place. The same rule applies for disputes regarding food, lodging and the like.[230] This forum rule contradicts the general forum rule and provides a default forum for actual or legal persons who are not otherwise subject to jurisdiction within the territory. In addition, it only applies to disputes concerning an obligation to pay debts.[231]

---

222. RB 10:3 para. 2. *See, e.g.*, NJA 1998, pp. 361 and 1999, p. 16.
223. RB 10:4.
224. *See* NJA 1925, p. 330.
225. Dennemark, *supra*, 189.
226. This opinion has been confirmed in NJA 1940, p. 354. Considering the technical developments in communications since 1940, it is possible that the outcome would be different today.
227. RB 10:5.
228. N. Gärde et al., *Nya Rättegångsbalken* 86 (1949).
229. NJA II 1943, p. 100. With regard to the requirement that the claim must arise directly out of the activity carried on at the establishment, *see* Dennemark, *supra*, 197, Ekelöf, *Rättegång II*, 32; Pålsson, *Svensk Rättspraxis*, 80. Concerning 'permanent establishment', *see* NJA 1992, p. 3.
230. RB 10:6.
231. SOU 1938:44, p. 145. Gärde et al., *supra*, 87. But *see* Ekelöf, *Rättegång II*, 31, note 62.

203. Controversies relating to administration by guardians, custodians or trustees may be instituted in the court in which the guardianship, custodianship or trusteeship is or was last registered, or in the court in the place where the administration has been performed. If any other person has administered property belonging to another, controversies relating to that administration may be instituted in the court in the place where the administration has been performed (*forum administrationis*).[232] This forum rule contradicts the general forum rule and provides a default forum with respect to persons who are otherwise not subject to jurisdiction in Sweden.

204. An action for tort damages may be instituted in the court in the place where the tortuous act occurred or had its impact (*forum delicti*). If the act or its impact occurred at places located in different court districts, the action may be brought in any of these districts.[233] According to this rule, the forum contradicts the general forum rule in civil procedure and provides a default forum when the defendant has no residence in Sweden. *Forum delicti* does not apply to claims based on a failure to perform contractual obligations.[234] Furthermore, it does not only apply to actions instituted against the person who has caused the tort damage, but also to anyone else who, pursuant to law or a contract (e.g., an insurance company), is responsible for the damage.[235] The plaintiff is free to choose between the court in the place where the act occurred and the court where an impact of the act happened.[236]

205. In controversies between a consumer and a merchant relating to a service, a product or some other kind of utility that has been provided mainly for personal use, an action against the merchant may be instituted in the place where the consumer resides.[237] However, this rule only applies if it can be presumed that a single legally qualified judge will handle the action.[238] The background to this rule is that a consumer in such cases is not entitled to compensation for legal costs for an attorney in the place where the merchant is located, while the merchant, who in any case generally has to engage an attorney, might as well engage an attorney in the place where the consumer resides.[239]

206. Disputes concerning the right of succession or the validity of testamentary dispositions should be brought to the court in which the deceased would have been required to respond in civil cases in general (*forum hereditatis*). Controversies about the division of joint property between spouses or co-habitants should be brought to the court where either is required to respond in civil cases in general. If any of them is deceased, controversies relating to property division should be brought to the

232. RB 10:7.
233. RB 10:8.
234. NJA II 1943, p. 102, Gärde et al., *supra*, 88.
235. *See* the statement of the Council of Legislation in NJA II 1943, p. 103 and Ekelöf, *Rättegång II*, 31. *See also* NJA 2001, p. 335.
236. NJA II 1943, p. 103 (stated by the Council of Legislation).
237. RB 10:8 a.
238. *See* RB 1:3 d.
239. Prop. 1973:187, p. 158.

court where the deceased would have been required to respond. If there is no competent court in these cases, the action should be instituted in the Stockholm District Court.[240]

207. Controversies involving title to land, the use and enjoyment of land, an easement or other special right in land, or possession of land shall be brought to the court in the place where the land is situated. The same applies to controversies concerning the obligation of an owner or possessor of land to perform any obligation required of him in this capacity or, when a right to use land or other special rights to land has been granted, to controversies concerning consideration for the grant in question, the maintenance of buildings or other similar matters.[241] Disputes arising out of a temporary grant of the right to use and enjoy land or a house, or a part of a house for the storage of vehicles, shall not be considered as a leasehold dispute. When the premises of an estate are located in different court districts, or when a controversy involves more than one estate located in different court districts, the controversy shall be brought to the court of the district in which the main part is located.[242]

208. The rationale behind this rule concerning *forum rei sitae* is that the investigation and presentation of evidence relating to the real property can best be carried out at the court where the real property is located.

209. Disputes regarding title to land include disputes about ownership of the land and disputes about the validity or cancellation of a real estate purchase.[243] The defendant's claim must centre on the issue of ownership, which, *inter alia*, means that the *forum rei sitae* rule does not apply if the ownership issue has a substantive effect on the case.[244] Controversies regarding the right to use real property include those relating to site-leasehold rights and rights to electrical power. Controversies concerning an easement shall always be brought to the court where the encumbered property is located. Issues concerning amendments and termination of an easement are regulated in the Act on Real Estate Construction. Thus, these are not handled by the ordinary courts, but by a special authority. 'Other special rights in land' refers, *inter alia*, to disputes concerning security. A Swedish court is, in principle, not authorized to handle disputes concerning title to land, the right to use land or other rights to real estate outside the country.[245]

210. In addition, the following actions can be instituted in *forum rei sitae*:

(1) controversies concerning the purchase price in a real property sale or other similar claims arising out of the transfer of the ownership of the property;

240. RB 10:9.
241. This rule does not apply on tenancy disputes.
242. RB 10:10.
243. NJA II 1943, p. 105.
244. Ekelöf, *Rättegång II*, 29. Concerning the meaning of 'substantive effect' *see* para. 412 *infra*.
245. *See, e.g.*, NJA 1929, p. 466, 1968, p. 78.

(2) claims against the owner of real estate for personal satisfaction of a debt secured by a mortgage, provided that the personal claim is joined with a claim for satisfaction out of the estate;
(3) controversies concerning damage to or other intrusions upon land;
(4) claims for compensation for work done on real property; or
(5) claims for compensation for breach of a covenant of title.[246]

211. According to this provision (RB 10:11), *forum rei sitae* contradicts the general forum rule in civil cases or another competent forum.

212. The forum rules elucidate on what is regarded as real property according to Chapter 10 of the Code: buildings situated on the land of another. Hence, mine buildings and installations are considered real property.[247] This diverges from the general provisions concerning what belongs to the category of real property.

213. Controversies concerning attorneys' fees and expenses, the division of litigation costs among jointly liable parties or other persons, and other similar claims arising out of litigation may be instituted in the court that originally adjudicated the case.[248] The rationale for the rule is that this court is in the best position to decide if the attorney's fee is reasonable.[249] This forum rule contradicts the general forum rule. The term 'controversies concerning attorneys' fees' refers to disputes between the principal plaintiff and the attorney, but expenses for the attorney relating to the principal plaintiff are also considered to be such claims.[250] The provision also applies to a defendant with a residence abroad.[251]

214. The parties can agree about the competent forum to hear their disputes.[252] Such an agreement must be written. It can refer to a controversy already existing or to one that may arise in the future, if the contract in which the agreement is embodied refers to a legal relationship from which the dispute is emanating. There are certain limitations on the right of the parties to stipulate a forum. They may not, for example, agree that the case shall be brought to the Court of Appeal, if according to the law an ordinary lower court is competent. In addition, they may not go against the rules for exclusive competence.

215. When a court has heard a case, the general rule is that a higher court may not review the competence of the lower court.[253] However, there are certain exceptions to this rule which allow a higher court to review the issue of competence:[254]

---

246. RB 10:11.
247. RB 10:12.
248. RB 10:13.
249. NJA II 1943, p. 107.
250. *Ibid.*
251. Dennemark, *supra*, 195.
252. RB 10:16.
253. *See* para. 223 *infra*.
254. RB 10:19.

(1) where a challenge has been raised and rejected in the lower court and the party appeals this decision;
(2) if a challenge is raised for the first time in appellate proceedings by a party entitled to do so;
(3) if the controversy is of such a nature that it falls within the competence of special courts or authorities other than the courts;
(4) if the controversy should have been brought before a higher court;
(5) if by law or decree the dispute must be settled by arbitration.

216. If a higher court declares that a lower court lacked competence to try an action instituted in that court, the higher court may refer the case to a competent lower court on request of a party.[255] Nevertheless, a case cannot be referred to an independent special court. A 'lower court' also refers to an ordinary court that functions as a land court.[256]

II. Main Claims and Ancillary Claims

217. In the Code, there is a forum rule that makes it possible to join several claims related to one another in a single action at the same court.[257] According to the rules in Chapter 10 of the Code, claims based on essentially the same grounds against several defendants may be brought before the court in which any of the defendants is required to respond, when the claims are brought simultaneously.[258] However, if the plaintiff and one of the defendants have stipulated a competent forum in a written contract, this contract does not create an obligation for the other defendants to answer at the same court.[259] In addition, the court will be competent with respect to all defendants, simply because one of them fails to raise an objection with respect to the competence of the court and the court thus becomes competent with regard to him.[260] If the controversy is such that all interested persons must be bound by the same judgment, the action may be instituted in the court at which any of the defendants is required to respond.[261]

218. Counter-claims shall be instituted in the court before which the main action is pending. In this court, certain other claims must be instituted, if they are related to the main claim. These cases will be discussed later.[262]

255. RB 10:20. It is provided in RB 10:20 that a district court which lacks competence can refer the case to a competent court, *see* Prop. 1995/96:115, p. 125.
256. *See, e.g.*, NJA 1973, p. 703; 1976, p. 711; 1983, p. 331.
257. RB 10:14.
258. Cf. RB 14:2–5 described in paras 296–307 *infra*.
259. NJA II 1943, p. 108.
260. The terms 'simultaneously' and 'essentially the same grounds' are explained in paras 297–298 *infra*.
261. This situation is described more in detail in para. 253 *infra*.
262. *See* para. 301 *infra*.

III. Overview of the Different Rules

219. Figures 1–4 show diagrams of the different applicable rules:

Figure 1 Civil Cases in General

Kind of Dispute	Rule of Competence
Defendant resides in Sweden	The district court in the place where the defendant resides, RB 10:1 paragraph 1
Defendant without a known residence either within or outside Sweden	The district court in the place where the defendant is sojourning, RB 10:1 paragraph 5
National defendant without known residence either within or outside Sweden, sojourning outside Sweden or at an unknown place	The district court in the place where the defendant last resided or sojourned, RB 10:1 paragraph 5

Figure 2 Provisions Competing with, or Exclusive of, the Provisions Applicable in Civil Cases in General

Kind of Dispute	Rule of Competence
Non-resident defendant concerning a payment obligation	The district court in the place where property belonging to him is located, RB 10:3 paragraph 1
Non-resident defendant concerning personal property located in Sweden	The district court in the place where the property is located, RB 10:3 paragraph 1 p. 2
Non-resident defendant concerning a contract entered into or a debt incurred in Sweden	The district court in the place where the contract was entered or a debt incurred, RB 10:4

Figure 3 Regardless of Defendant's Residence

Concerning disputes arising out of a permanent establishment →	The district court in the place where the establishment is located, RB 10:5
Concerning an obliation for a debt incurred at a place of temporary residence →	The district court at the place of the defendant's temporary residence while present at the place, RB 10:6: the same rule applies for food, lodging and the like at a temporary residence
Concerning the administration of property by guardians, custodians or trustees →	The district court at the place where the guardianship etc. was registered or has been performed, RB 10:7
Concerning tort damages →	The district court in the place where the tortuous act occurred or had its impact, RB 10:8
Concerning consumer disputes →	The district court in the place where the consumer resides, RB 10:9
Concerning the right of succession, testamentary dispositions or division of joint property →	*See* RB 10:9 and 10:1
Concerning real property →	The district court in the place where the property is situated (competing in other), RB 10:10 and 10:11
Concerning certain litigation expenses →	The district court in the place where the expenses were incurred, RB 10:13

Figure 4 Multi-Party and Multi-Claim Litigation

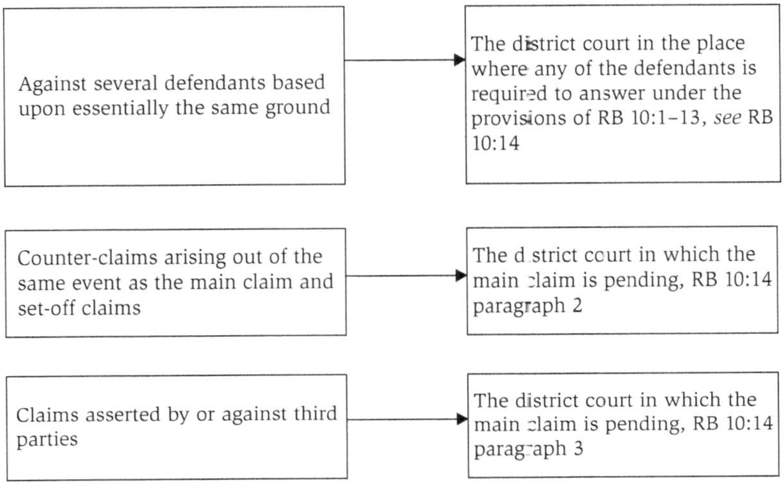

§3. Resolution of Jurisdictional Conflicts

220. The legislature has not delegated any decision-making power to the courts as far as the forum rules in Chapter 10 of the Code are concerned. Instead, it is prescribed that an action *may* or *shall* be entertained at a certain court.

221. The concept 'dispositive' is usually reserved for those forum rules that give the defendant the final right to decide upon the court's competence. Thus, that a forum rule is dispositive means that it is the defendant who decides if an action shall be dismissed if the plaintiff has brought the case in the wrong forum. For example, suppose there is a written contract in which the parties can decide which court will adjudicate the dispute. If the defendant does not have any decision-making right with regard to the forum issue, the forum rule is mandatory.

222. Most of the forum rules in Chapter 10 of the Code are dispositive. A conclusion can be reached regarding which forum rules are mandatory by studying the list set out in 10:17 of the Code. The court must observe this list on its own motion. 10:18 of the Code refers to 10:17, which makes it obvious that a forum rule is dispositive if it not is mentioned in 10:18. If it is so mentioned, it is also exclusive, which means that the defendant can have the dispute adjudicated only at the court designated in that rule. Furthermore, 10:18 states that the controversy shall be deemed to have been brought in a competent court, unless the defendant has interposed a timely objection to the competence of the court.

223. Objections to the court's competence are specifically regulated in the Code.[263] The rule in question implies that any party who wishes to assert an objection that the court lacks competence shall do so when he first addresses the court on the case. According to the preparatory legislative works, this means that the defendant, when the case is orally prepared, shall assert the objection at the first preparatory session and when the preparation is written, in the answer to the summons.[264] If the objection is not asserted within the prescribed time, but the party has a legal excuse for his failure, the objection shall be presented as soon as possible after the reason for failing to object has ceased to exist. A legal excuse exists if a person was impeded from doing what was required of him by reason of a breakdown in the general modes of communication, sickness or another circumstance which he could not have anticipated, or if the court otherwise regards the excuse as valid.[265]

224. If a party has made a timely objection to the court's competence, the court shall issue a separate order thereon as soon as possible.[266] If the court overrules the objection and the order is pronounced at a hearing, the party must give a formal notice of exception immediately or otherwise within a week of service of the order upon him. If he fails to do this, he forfeits his right to appeal the order. If a timely exception is taken, the court shall decide, with reference to the particular circumstances involved, whether an appeal shall be taken separately or only in conjunction with an appeal from the judgment or final order on the case.[267]

225. If an action has been instituted in violation of a mandatory forum rule, any objection from a party will have no legal relevance, since the court on its own motion must observe this rule. However, if the party asserts an objection and the court approves it, the action shall be dismissed by a special order. If the objection is overruled, the party must observe the above-mentioned rule about formal notice of exception. Nonetheless, failure to observe this rule does not mean that the party cannot later allege circumstances relevant to the competence issue, if the case is such that the court on its own motion should have taken notice of them. The court in this situation must entertain the competence question, but in such a case the party cannot demand a special order relating to the issue.[268]

263. RB 34:2.
264. SOU 1938:44, p. 377.
265. RB 32:8.
266. *See* RB 34:3 and 49:3.
267. RB 49:4.
268. SOU 1938:44, p. 377.

Chapter 2. International Jurisdiction

§1. Rules Applicable in the Absence of a Treaty

226. The Code contains no general provisions defining the competence of Swedish courts in cases with international aspects.[269] Competence to adjudicate has been deemed to exist if the Swedish law has designated a forum for review of the dispute in question. Although the lack of a forum in Sweden has not been deemed to constitute an absolute hindrance for the competence of a Swedish court, the relevant case law implies that there is a presumption against competence for Swedish courts when a forum has not been designated. One can, therefore, conclude that special reasons must be present in order for a Swedish court to be competent in such cases.[270]

227. If, however, a forum is provided for in the Code or some other Swedish legislation, it follows that a Swedish court is competent to adjudicate the controversy.[271] With respect to disputes with international aspects, it should moreover be observed that certain rules in the Code presuppose competence for a Swedish court to adjudicate the dispute. This is true concerning, for example, *forum deprehensionis* (10:1 paragraph 5), *forum arresti* (10:3) and *forum contractus* (10:4). These provisions can also be used as rules, which give the court competence to adjudicate, something that is also true with reference to most of the rules in Chapter 10 of the Code.[272] With regard to the application of the rules in Chapter 10 on individual cases with international aspects, I refer to what has been stated in the above paragraphs.[273]

§2. International Treaties

228. The Lugano Convention on International Competence of the Courts and Enforcement of Judgments Concerning Private Law was accepted by Sweden in 1988 and is given the force of a law in Sweden. The Lugano Convention, which is an important Convention in Sweden in this area, is thus incorporated in the Swedish legal system. This is true also with respect to the Brussels Convention on International Competence of the Courts and Enforcement of Judgments Concerning Private Law, which came into force on 1 January 1999 (SFS 1998:358). However, the Brussels-I Decree, which came into force in March 2002, has in principle overtaken these Conventions. The new Lugano Convention, adapted to the Brussels-I

269. It is obvious that Swedish courts lack competence to adjudicate if a legal subject has immunity, *see* the Act on Immunity and Privileges for Certain Cases (SFS 1976:661).
270. *See* NJA 1944, p. 75; 1917, p. 417 and 1980, p. 188 and Pålsson, *Svensk Rättspraxis*, 49 et seq.
271. Although local competence exists according to Swedish rules on jurisdiction, the court, after a discretionary review, can decide not to use the power to adjudicate, *see, e.g.*, NJA 1966, p. 450 and 1981, p. 386 and, in addition, Pålsson, *Svensk Rättspraxis*, 54.
272. Pålsson, *Svensk Rättspraxis*, 51.
273. *See* paras 191–216 *supra*.

Decree, was approved in 2007 by the Swedish Parliament.[274] A new Brussels-II Decree was adopted in 2003 and came into force in 2005. Also important to mention are the European Enforcement Order for Uncontested Claims (2004), the European Order for Payment Procedure (2006) and the European Small Claim Procedure (2007).[275] A revised Brussels-I Regulation was adopted on 12 December 2012, aimed at further improving cross-border enforcement of judgments in the EU by making it easier and faster. This regulation began to apply on 10 January 2015. Due to the new regulation, some changes have been made in Swedish law. The old Brussels-I Regulation of 2000 became binding and directly applicable in all Member States, except Denmark, and has thus not required any implementation. The Amsterdam Treaty subsequently moved Member State's civil-law cooperation from the third pillar of the Union to the first. This treaty could issue provisions corresponding to the Brussels Regulation issued in the form of directives or regulations. Consequently, in relation to Denmark, a parallel convention concluded between the EU and Denmark applies, which entered into force on 1 July 2007 (Denmark Convention). Supported by this agreement it has been declared that the 2012 Brussels-I Regulation will be applied in relation to Denmark. A new Lugano Convention was adopted in October 2007 (The Lugano II Convention). The new Lugano Convention applies, like the old one, between the European Free Trade Association countries and was signed by Denmark, Iceland and Switzerland. The Convention is binding and is directly applicable in Sweden, but in the same way as the Brussels-I Regulation, it required some constitutional amendments.

229. The competence rules in the above-mentioned Conventions and decree correspond for a large part with the Swedish forum rules, but there are also important divergences. In this respect, it should be observed that the Lugano Convention lacks a general *forum arresti* and rules on *forum contractus*, in the sense that the latter is referred to in 10:4 and 10:6 of the Code.[276] The implication of these divergences is that a Swedish court can no longer support its competence on these provisions with regard to a defendant who has his residence in a state that has accepted the convention. However, they apply to a defendant who does not have his residence in a state party to the Convention, if the rules of the Convention do not apply independently of the defendant's residence.

230. In addition, it should be mentioned that the Conventions and Decree at issue also contain some rules of competence that are new for the Swedish legal system. An important example is *forum solutions*, as a special forum for contractual disputes.

231. Among other international Conventions ratified by Sweden which contain competence rules, the following can be mentioned:[277]

---

274. Prop. 2008/09:205.
275. *See* M. Berglund, *Cross Border Enforcement of Claims in the EU* (2009).
276. *See* L. Pålsson, *Luganokonventionen* 65 (1992).
277. In this context it should be mentioned that there are a number of Conventions in force between the Nordic countries, mainly in the area of family law.

- The Hague Convention on Recognition of Divorces and Judicial Separations (1 June 1970). Compare the Act on Recognition of Certain Foreign Divorces and Judicial Separations (SFS 1973:943) and, in addition, the decree on application of that law (SFS 1975:634).
- The Convention on Freight Contracts Concerning the International Delivery of Goods by Road (CMR) (Geneva 19 May 1956). Compare the enabling Act (SFS 1969:12). *See also* the Act on Obligation for Foreign Plaintiffs to Deposit Security for Legal Costs (SFS 1980:307) and, in addition, the Government's announcement on Exemption in Certain Cases for Foreign Plaintiffs to Deposit Security for Legal Costs (SFS 1996:625).
- The Convention on International Railway Traffic (COTIF) (Bern 9 May 1980). Compare the Act on International Railway Traffic (1985:193).
- The International Convention on Sequestration and Similar Interim Enforcement Measures Regarding Shipping (Brussels 10 May 1952).
- The Convention on Responsibility for Damage Caused by Oil Pollution (Brussels 1969).
- The Warsaw Convention on International Air Transport (Warsaw 12 October 1929). Compare Chapter 9 of the Aviation Act (SFS 1986:166).
- The Convention on Liability for Damages on the Area of Atomic Energy with additional Conventions (Paris 29 July 1960). Compare the Act on Atomic Energy (SFS 1968:45).

Part III. Actions and Claims

Chapter 1. Actions

§1. Definition

232. Two principal forms of action are recognized in the Code, namely actions concerning performance and declaratory claims (*fullgörelseoch fastställelsetalan*).[278] Significant for a performance claim is that the plaintiff claims that the court shall oblige the defendant to perform something, most often to pay an amount of money. However, a performance claim can also refer to the omission of something. In addition, a performance claim sometimes refers to a 'negative performance', for example, the plaintiff requests that the defendant be obliged to cease doing something disturbing, or to stop infringing the right to a patent or the name of a firm. In such cases, the judgment is called 'a prohibition judgment'.[279]

233. The principal rule is that the court may entertain a performance claim for review, only if the time for performance has taken place. However, there are five exceptions to this principal rule:

(1) the claim is for periodic payments and either does not depend upon the performance of a past or future reciprocal obligation or is in the form of a pension or an annuity owed by reason of a reciprocal obligation already performed, and that at least one of the payments is due;
(2) the claim will fall due immediately upon default of a primary obligation which constitutes the principal claim in the case;
(3) the claim is for interest which will follow as a result of the principal claim in the case;
(4) it is important for the plaintiff that the performance be discharged within the agreed time and there is reason to believe that the defendant will disregard his obligation; or
(5) the institution of such a claim is otherwise authorized by law.

278. RB 13:1 and 13:2.
279. *See* K. Olivecrona, *Rätt och dom* 170 (1966); NJA II 1943, p. 158 and S. Larsson, *Fullgörelsetalan, Festskrift till P.O. Ekelöf*, 466.

234. The first exception refers to periodic performances. The reason why a claim concerning a future obligation is not permitted, with the exception of claims referring to pensions or life annuities, is that the debtor would then be put in a disadvantageous position. Thus, a creditor cannot, based on an instalment plan, institute an action concerning future performance.[280] Institution of an action with regard to future rental payments is similarly disallowed.

235. The second exception refers to the situation where several different performance claims have been put forward, and one of these refers to a claim not due for performance until another has been completed, for example, if the plaintiff claims possession of some property and, in addition, claims damages if this is not possible. The third exception deals with a situation, which is rather obvious and, therefore, needs no further comment. An example of a situation where the fourth exception applies is where the performance concerns delivery of bricks to be used for a building, and the bricks shall be used according to the progress of the construction. Another example is the delivery of goods that the buyer has, in his turn, already sold. A third example is where a tenant is removed from an apartment, which is immediately occupied by a new tenant.[281] It is not enough that the plaintiff says that the conditions in the fourth exception exist; he must also prove them.[282] With respect to the fifth exception, it can be concluded, for example from the rules about maintenance to children, that an action may be instituted whenever the performance shall occur.

236. A condition for all situations mentioned above is that one of the debts is mature for payment and the debtor has not paid. It is also obvious in all cases that the plaintiff cannot enforce the judgment until the expiry date has passed.[283]

237. If a plaintiff institutes a declaratory claim, he does not request enforcement of a judgment. Instead, such an action seeks to determine whether a legal relationship exists. Two more conditions must be fulfilled to enable the court to entertain a declaratory claim: an uncertainty must exist as to the legal relationship, and this uncertainty must be to the plaintiff's detriment.[284]

238. The requirement that the issue concerns a legal relationship means that it is not possible to institute a declaratory claim concerning the interpretation of a rule *in abstracto*, that is to say an interpretation that is not linked to a concrete dispute. Hence, if the plaintiff asks the court to declare that a legal rule has a certain meaning, the court shall dismiss the action. In addition, it is not permitted to institute a

280. NJA II 1943, p. 159.
281. Ekelöf, *Rättegång II*, p. 108.
282. Larsson, *supra*, 466.
283. KRB 13:15.
284. RB 13:2. The rule is optional for the court, *see* NJA 2005, p. 517 and NJA 2007, p. 108.

declaratory claim concerning the question if a certain event has occurred. The reason for this is that it would become too difficult to predict the consequences of such a declaratory judgment.[285]

239. In general, the prerequisite that an uncertainty must exist does not cause any problems. The prerequisite is fulfilled if the defendant has contested the claim. If, however, the defendant has consented to the claim, it might seem as if the prerequisite at issue cannot be fulfilled. However, in case law, there are examples showing that it has been deemed to be fulfilled even in certain such cases.[286] The meaning of the word 'detriment' is that the uncertainty must make it difficult for the plaintiff to plan his economic activities or in some other way create a disturbing uncertainty for him.[287]

240. A declaratory claim is also possible when the adjudication of the instituted claim depends on whether a certain disputed legal relationship between the parties exists. This dispute shall thereby concern a legal relationship with substantive significance in a subsequent action. An example of this res judicata effect would be a landlord's claim for rent from a tenant where there is a controversy with regard to the validity of the rental contract. In such a case, the landlord can request that the court remove the tenant from the apartment, and also that the court declare the rental contract valid. The prerequisite that the plaintiff be detrimentally affected need not be fulfilled as far as substantive legal relations are concerned. In addition, an issue with substantive significance must be reviewed even if it is not the subject of a declaratory claim, but if a declaratory claim has been instituted, the substantive issue will be binding for the future.[288]

241. Moreover, a declaratory judgment may be entertained for review when this is permitted in some law other than the Code. Such provisions are common, particularly in the area of intellectual property law.

242. Some scholars as a third group of claims regard constitutive claims. These are common in the area of family law. They principally concern a change in status, for example divorce or adoption. Hence, a status judgment establishes a social classification, which is a reason why it has been urged that a constitutive claim is something other than a performance or declaratory claim. The classification issue is debatable, but overall has no practical significance.[289]

285. Ekelöf, *Rättegång II*, *see, e.g.*, NJA 1994, p. 66; 1996, p. 94; 1985, p. 72 and 1998, p. 438.
286. KRB 13:25.
287. Ekelöf, *Rättegång II*, 113.
288. Concerning res judicata, *see* paras 410 et seq. *infra*.
289. *See* KRB 13:6, Olivecrona, *Rätt och dom*, 167; Agge, 47, Gärde et al., *supra*, 130 and NJA II 1943, p. 158. *See also* para. 396 *infra*.

§2. ADMISSIBILITY

243. The definition of the subject matter in Swedish litigation presupposes that the right to commence an action with regard to the disputed subject matter exists and, in addition, that it is possible to institute such an action. Whether a party has the capacity to institute an action is another issue that must be decided, preferably before the court enters upon a review of the disputed subject matter. The answer to the question of capacity as a party is easy to determine: if an individual or entity, according to substantive law, can acquire rights and incur obligations, the individual or entity has capacity as a party in his or its own name. Thus, even a newborn baby can have capacity as a party.[290]

244. If a party does not exercise control of the disputed property, or the dispute involves a legal transaction that the party is not competent to effect, the legal representative of the party shall sue or be sued on his behalf.[291] With respect to minors, there are rules in the Parental Code, which limit their ability to undertake legal actions.[292] The ability to undertake legal acts is, in several cases, also limited with respect to those who have a guardian.[293] In addition, any corporation, partnership, cooperative, association or similar society, foundation or similar institution, which can acquire substantive rights and assume legal liabilities, can also sue or be sued. This is also true with respect to the Crown, the municipalities and similar communities. The representatives of such parties have the authority to present the claims and defences.[294]

245. As indicated above capacity must be distinguished from capacity to present or defend against a claim, i.e., procedural capacity. One who has party capacity can lack procedural capacity, thus the representative of a legal person must present the claims and defences. However, it is unclear whether an association has procedural capacity. Some have argued that an association has procedural capacity, but that it must act through its representative, while others have argued that an association does not have procedural capacity and, thus, has to act through a representative.[295] Nevertheless, it seems clear that this terminological dispute has no significance in practice.

246. Normally, the representative's procedural capacity coincides with that of the party, in which case he, himself, can present the claim or defence. Thus, the representative can undertake all necessary measures in the proceedings, with binding effect on the party. In addition, the representative is subject to the same procedural obligations as the party. If there is more than one authorized representative for the party, the above applies to all of them. If a party has more than one legal representative the court may, however, direct one or more of them to appear in person.

290. RB 11:1 para. 1.
291. RB 11:1 para. 2, p. 1.
292. *See* FB Ch. 9.
293. *See* FB 11:7.
294. RB 11:2.
295. Ekelöf, *Rättegång II*, 50, E. Söderlund, *Kommentar till RB kap.* 1–12, 295 (1979).

247. A special issue, which has been addressed several times, is whether a stock company, which has ceased to exist, can appear as a party. Obviously, the answer should be negative, since a non-existing entity cannot acquire rights or incur obligations. This is also the main rule. However, there are precedent cases where such an entity has been allowed to appear as a party, *inter alia* when the stock company has ceased to exist and has been removed from the stock company register during a pending action.[296]

248. A procedural act undertaken by anyone who lacks procedural capacity is, in principle, invalid. The court shall, on its own motion, observe if a party lacks the capacity in question and, in that case, dismiss the action.

249. A third concept of importance in the context of capacity is standing to sue, which means that a party has sufficient stake in an otherwise justiciable controversy to obtain judicial resolution of that controversy. In modern Swedish legal language, this term has at least two meanings. According to one of them, the concept refers to the subjective side of the legal relationship. For example, if it is stated that the creditor has standing to sue, the concept in question refers to the subjective side of that legal relationship.[297]

250. However, the question of whether standing to sue exists also arises when dealing with the issue of whether or not a procedural hindrance exists. This is the second and more interesting meaning of the concept. If standing to sue is lacking, the claim shall be dismissed. Thus, it is obvious that a defect in standing to sue constitutes a fundamental procedural hindrance. Standing to sue in this sense must not be confused with capacity as a party and procedural capacity. Anyone who has capacity as a party can lack standing to sue in cases of a certain kind, thus the former is not linked with the ability to acquire rights and incur obligations. In addition, standing to sue differs from procedural capacity in the way that a defect in standing to sue cannot be remedied by a representative for the party. Thus, a legal subject who lacks standing to sue cannot be a party in a dispute concerning the subject matter in question, but must be replaced by another legal subject that possesses standing to sue.

251. The principal rule is that the court in dispositive cases does not examine whether standing to sue exists. The reason for this is that a creditor must be able to institute an action against the person he considers the debtor. Hereafter the issue to be litigated is whether the creditor has the rights that he claims. That the creditor makes claims on his own behalf thus leads to standing to sue for both him and the debtor-defendant.[298] One could also say that if the principal rule is that the parties outside the proceedings can settle the dispute, they also ought to have the possibility to avoid intervention from the court regarding questions concerning standing to sue. Hence, only in those cases where the trial can lead to effects which the parties

296. *See, e.g.*, NJA 1993, p. 723 and 1998, p. 608.
297. Ekelöf, *Rättegång II*, 54.
298. *Ibid.*, 74.

outside the proceedings could not have agreed upon are there reasons for the court to observe other interests than those of the parties, by means of, for example, an examination of standing to sue.[299]

252. The most important exception concerns bankruptcy. A person declared bankrupt may not exercise control over the property belonging to the bankrupt estate. Rather, it is the bankrupt estate that administers and has recourse to this property. Under this provision, it is the bankrupt estate and not the debtor who will prevail in a controversy between the debtor and a third person concerning the title to certain property.[300]

253. If two people own land together and a dispute arises about, for example, an easement to the land, the owners are said to possess 'necessary procedural unity'. If the plaintiff has sued one of the owners and planned to sue the other one later in another trial, the claim shall be dismissed.[301] However, this situation is not an example of standing to sue in the sense mentioned above, since a lack of standing in this case cannot be eliminated by another legal subject-bringing suit, but only by bringing the other owner into the proceedings.[302] The reason for dismissal in this case is that if both cases could be adjudicated, a possible outcome is that both cases would be decided differently. In such a situation, it would be impossible to enforce contradicting judgments.[303]

254. If anyone sues for the benefit of another person, i.e., if the plaintiff claims that someone other than himself is entitled to performance from the defendant, the claim shall be dismissed.[304]

255. With regard to cases, which are not dispositive, case law shows that the courts in all kinds of cases belonging to this category – thus not only in cases concerning the status of a person – perform an examination of standing to litigate.[305]

§3. Vexatious Litigation

256. As a rule, there are no prohibitions in the Swedish legal system against instituting an action concerning an alleged legal relationship, however preposterous it might seem. However, in certain obvious cases, the court can refrain from serving the summons.[306] This omission presupposes that the plaintiff's claim for relief does not contain legal reasons for the claim, or that it is otherwise obvious that the claim

299. KRB 13:10 a.
300. Ekelöf, *Rättegång II*, 72. *See also* NJA 1978, p. 347 I and II and KRB 13:10 p.
301. L. Welamson, *Domvillobesvär av tredje man* 125 (1956).
302. KRB 13:10.
303. Ekelöf, *Rättegång II*, 73.
304. NJA 1984, p. 215. *See* P.H. Lindblom, *Processhinder* 196 (1974) and Ekelöf, *Rättegång II*, 72, both critical of the judgment.
305. KRB 11:14.
306. RB 42:5.

is unfounded. In such cases, the claim is not dismissed but disapproved. Apart from this situation, a claim can be dismissed only if it can be deemed to concern something that conflicts with common moral views (*pactum turpe*).[307]

257. The Code provides three types of sanctions for vexatious or negligent proceedings: fines, requirement to pay the other party's legal costs and preclusion from introducing new legal facts and new evidence.

I. Fines

258. A fine shall punish a party who, against better knowledge, commences or causes the commencement of a civil action.[308] Liability according to this rule requires that the claim is unfounded and that the party knows it.[309] According to the wording of the rule, it also applies to the defendant. In case law, fines have been imposed on a debtor who in bad faith contested an obligation to pay.[310] It has, however, been maintained that it is incorrect to apply the rule in question when a debtor, who has not paid his debt on request and been summoned, admits the claim. An application of the rule on the debtor in such cases would imply that unwillingness to pay is criminal, which is not the case.[311]

259. If a party appeals a judgment or an order against his better knowledge that the appeal is clearly unfounded, the party shall be punished with a fine.[312] The case law shows that this rule is seldom used, due to difficulties in proving an intentional abuse of trial.[313] In RH 1985:121, intentional abuse of litigation was not deemed to be proved in a case where a party applied for re-opening of a case ten years after a default judgment. In NJA 1985 p. 622, an attorney's appeal against the decision of a police authority to issue a parking fine was deemed to constitute intentional abuse of litigation, since the appeal only contained the general statement that he was in the process of loading and unloading.

260. A fine shall punish a party who endeavours to prolong the course of litigation by raising clearly unfounded allegations or defences, by withholding evidence or by any other improper measure.[314] While the above-mentioned rules refer to the commencement of an action, this rule applies to certain kinds of vexatious proceedings when an action is pending. It is not required that the litigation has actually been prolonged, but rather that the party directly intended to delay the proceedings.

307. Lindell, *Civilprocessen*, 223 et seq.
308. RB 9:1.
309. NJA II 1943, p. 89.
310. NJA 1950, p. 526; 1967, p. 348.
311. Ekelöf & Edelstam, *Rättegång I*, 206.
312. RB 9:2.
313. Söderlund, *supra*, 190.
314. RB 9:3.

II. Legal Cost Sanctions

261. A party who by carelessness or oversight causes the opposing party to incur expenses shall reimburse that party, regardless of how costs in general are to be distributed.[315] The carelessness can consist of the party's failure to appear in the proceedings, to observe an order issued by the court, or by making statements that he ought to have realized were irrelevant. From these examples, it can be concluded that the types of procedural activities to which the rule refers can be related to either substantive or formal assertions, or both.[316]

262. The rule in question, which applies both in dispositive and non-dispositive cases, also includes objections concerning procedural hindrances. According to an investigation carried out by the Trial Committee, the rule is very seldom used in practice.[317] A disadvantage of the rule is that, in principle, it can only be used against the party who wins the case.[318] However, for the parties it can often be difficult to foresee the outcome. The preventive effects of the rule should therefore not be underestimated. Nonetheless, maintaining its compensatory and deterrent functions presupposes that it applies not too infrequently.[319] Application of the rule is mandatory.

263. If the winning party is found to have initiated the action without provocation from his adversary, or otherwise deliberately or negligently has caused unnecessary litigation, he shall reimburse his adversary for litigation expenses. However, if the circumstances so justify, each party shall bear his own expenses.[320] This provision not only refers to proceedings brought about by carelessness, but also to situations where the whole trial was unnecessary.[321] In practice, the issue whether this rule should apply has often been raised in connection with abandoning settlement offers. Thus, if a debtor has offered to pay a part of the creditor's claim and the court approves the claim to that part, the rule applies.[322] Application of the rule is obligatory with optional clauses.

264. If the losing party neither knew nor should have known of the circumstance determining the outcome prior to the commencement of the action, the court may direct that each party shall bear its own expenses.[323] This rule does not directly aim at proceedings brought about by carelessness, yet the losing party's lack of knowledge about a relevant circumstance can sometimes depend on an oversight.

---

315. RB 18:6.
316. U. Jacobsson, *Parts kostnad i civilprocess* 206 (1964).
317. SOU 1982:26, p. 214. *See, e.g.*, NJA 1961, p. 157 and 1983, p. 167.
318. Prop. 1986/87:89, p. 221.
319. Lindell, *Processuell preklusion* 132 (1993).
320. RB 18:3 para. 1.
321. Jacobsson, *Parts kostnad i civilprocess*, 164 and KRB 18:11.
322. *See* Ekelöf, *Rättegång II*, 167. For case law *see, e.g.*, NJA 1937, p. 167 (II); 1955, p. 329, 1966, p. 445; 1967, p. 202; 1972, p. 551; 1977, p. 704; 1980, p. 366 (I); 1982, p. 366; 1983, p. 635 and 1984, p. 469.
323. RB 18:3 para. 2.

The word 'circumstance' in this rule refers only to legal facts.[324] According to the preparatory legislative works, the court ought to use the possibility to set-off the legal cost with great caution.[325] Application of the rule is discretionary.

265. In the Code, there is also a rule concerning an obligation for the party's representative, attorney or assistant to reimburse the adversary for legal expenses in completely or in part. Such compensation presupposes an act or conduct as described in Chapter 18, section 3, paragraph 1; or such carelessness or oversight as referred to in Chapter 18, section 6. The court may impose joint liability for costs upon the party and his representative, attorney or assistant, even if not requested to do so. Application of the rule is discretionary.

III. Preclusion of New Legal Facts and New Evidence

266. Legislation within the last decade has increased the possibilities for the court to preclude new circumstances and evidence. The rules in question only apply in dispositive cases, since it is deemed incompatible with the principle of the court's inquiry on its own motion that dismissal could occur in non-dispositive cases.

267. During the preparation in a dispositive case, the court may direct the party to definitively state the legal facts and the evidence to be presented if the court deems it necessary due to the manner in which they were presented at earlier proceedings.[326] This rule is meant to be used in cases where there are reasons to believe that the party is attempting to delay a judgment without acceptable reasons, or where a party does not properly participate in the proceedings.[327] An order for preclusion becomes part of the final judgment in the case and is thus subject to appellate review.[328] The order shall be formulated in a manner appropriate to the circumstances in the individual case and can include counter-claims and claims for redress.[329]

268. If, after expiration of the order for preclusion or the preparatory stage has been closed, the party wants to present new evidence or legal facts which are relevant to adjudication of the case, he must show that he has a valid excuse. The rule is mandatory, which means that the court must dismiss new legal facts or new evidence alleged by the party if he cannot offer such an excuse, even if the material in question is crucial to the outcome of the case.

---

324. SOU 1938:44, p. 232.
325. SOU 1938:44, p. 233. *See also* NJA 1972, p. 77 and 1986, p. 263. Note that set-off in this context does not mean that the costs are divided into two equal amounts but that each party shall bear his own expenses.
326. RB 42:15.
327. Prop. 1983/84:78, p. 77.
328. *Ibid.*, 36.
329. *Ibid.*, 76.

269. Examples of situations in which a legal excuse is deemed to be present include the following typical cases, which are mentioned in the preparatory legislative works:[330]

(1) The party has become aware of the new evidence after the expiration of the time limit for an answer in the order for preclusion. It is thereby presupposed that the party has conducted reasonable investigations into the facts relevant to the case.
(2) The new evidence is motivated by the adversary's activities in the proceedings.
(3) The party had not realized the significance of a circumstance in the case before expiration of the time limit.
(4) The party had not alleged certain material related to the proceedings for economic reasons, believing that what he already had presented would be sufficient to win the case.[331]

According to RB 42:15 a, the court may, in a dispositive case, announce that the preparation of the case shall be deemed to be accomplished at a certain date. In such a case, a party may not, after that date, present new evidence or legal facts, if he cannot show legal excuse (cf. RB 42:15) or if the examination of the case will not be unreasonably delayed. This rule was adopted because RB 42:15 was not regarded as enough effective in making the parties to present all their evidence and legal facts before the main hearing.[332] As stated above, RB 42:15 requires an attempt to delay or gross negligence.

270. If a party amends a statement previously made by him in the action during the main hearing in the district court, adds something thereto, or claims a circumstance or evidence which was not mentioned prior to the commencement of the hearing, the matter thus presented may be disregarded, if it can be assumed that the party's conduct was designed to delay the proceedings or to accomplish some other improper purpose, or if it was the result of gross negligence.[333] The prerequisite 'gross negligence' was added to the rule in 1987, since the rule was regarded as insufficient with only the 'improper purpose' requirement, which is difficult to prove.[334] This rule is optional according to its wording, but in practice, it is regarded as almost obligatory.

271. In applying the prerequisite of 'gross negligence', it is important that the court produces a written compilation of the parties' point of view in the dispute, as

330. *See also* Lindell, *Processuell preklusion*, 306 et seq.
331. *Ibid.*, 77.
332. *See* Prop. 1999/2000:26, p. 69.
333. RB 43:10.
334. *See* Prop. 1986/87:89, p. 221.

understood by the court.[335] A written compilation shall be based on the court's opinion about what has occurred during the preparation. It thereby represents an important instrument of control for the parties.[336] The purpose of the compilation is to reduce the risk of surprises later on, which improves the possibilities of having a consolidated trial immediately.[337] A compilation may also make it easier for the judge to write the judgment.[338] If a compilation has been made and a party alleges new legal facts or evidence during the main hearing, strong reasons are required in order to deem that gross negligence is not present.[339] If a party, who has already had an order imposed on him according to 42:15 of the Code, alleges new legal facts or evidence during the preparation of the case, this rule, rather than 43:10, applies during the main hearing.

272. It is obvious that there must also be rules of preclusion in the higher courts. Thus, a party who alleges new legal facts or evidence in an appellate court or in the Supreme Court must show that he has a legal excuse.[340] With regard to the application of the preclusion rules in the higher courts, guidelines can be sought in the above-mentioned typical cases, since the required legal excuse and the standard of proof are the same in those rules as in 42:15. However, since the purpose is that it should be more difficult to present new relevant evidence or legal facts in an appellate court, the possibilities to complete the procedural material are rather small as far as the appellate courts are concerned and very limited in the Supreme Court (if the case goes so far).

273. As has already been mentioned, the rules of preclusion can be used not only in cases where a party intentionally tries to prolong the litigation or to accomplish some other improper purpose, but also in situations where a party has not understood the relevance of a legal fact or of evidence and has, therefore, not alleged it earlier.

274. If the court orders that a new legal fact or new evidence be disregarded, the order can be appealed only in conjunction with an appeal against the judgment. This is also true for an order according to 42:15, which thus cannot be appealed separately.

---

335. Such a compilation is set down in RB 42:16. *See* further para 364 *infra*.
336. Prop. 1986/87:89, p. 221.
337. *Ibid.*
338. *Ibid.*, 86.
339. *Ibid.*, 22.
340. In the appellate court RB 50:25 para. 3 (which was made more stringent in 1989) applies and in the Supreme Court RB 55:13. However, if a party in an appellate court alleges old legal facts, that is to say such legal facts which were alleged already in the district court, RB 43:10 applies. *See also* para. 465 *infra*.

Chapter 2. Claims and Defences

§1. Definition

275. In the summons application, the plaintiff must present a fixed claim for relief and must state in detail the circumstances upon which the action is founded.[341] To claim something is the same as to request something. However, the plaintiff's claim, for example on payment, is not directed to the other party, but to the court. The claim must be understood as a request that the court renders a judgment with a certain content.[342]

276. It has been stated that the defendant does not set forth any claims, with the exception of set-offs and counter-claims. The reason given for this opinion is that contesting and admitting the plaintiff's claims cannot be regarded as claims. However, the better view, and one that is more in accordance with reality, is that these procedural acts should be regarded as claims.[343]

§2. Distinctions

277. To support a claim, facts, laws of general experience and legal rules can be alleged. However, the notion 'allege' is mainly used in respect to legal facts.

278. In the preparatory legislative works to the Code, the legislature made a distinction between circumstances of direct relevance and circumstances of indirect relevance.[344] If a circumstance is of direct relevance, a legal consequence is linked to it, while a circumstance of indirect relevance is of importance because of its evidentiary value with respect to a legal fact. Commonly, circumstances of indirect relevance are called evidentiary facts, and circumstances of direct relevance are called legal facts.

279. The substantive legal facts, which the plaintiff must from the outset allege in the summons application, are usually called the foundation of the claim for relief.[345] Other substantive legal facts are called counterfacts. If, for example, the purchaser claims payment and the vendor alleges that the purchased product is defective, the purchase is the foundation of the claim and the alleged defectiveness a legal counter-fact. A counter-fact, if proven, means that another alleged legal fact (in this case the purchase) does not have the legal consequence it otherwise would have had.

---

341. RB 42:2.
342. Ekelöf & Edelstam, *Rättegång I*, 39.
343. *Ibid.*
344. SOU 1938:44, p. 208. *See also* paras 595–596 *infra*.
345. Ekelöf & Edelstam, *Rättegång I*, 41, R. Boman, *Om åberopande och åberopsbörda i dispositiva tvistemål*, hereafter '*Åberopsbördan*' 10 (1964).

280. The adversary can make one or more substantive objections with respect to a legal fact. These objections must be separated from objections concerning procedural hindrance, which means that the claim shall be dismissed. However, a substantive objection is put forward with the purpose that the claim shall be disapproved, totally or in part. There are three types of substantive objections:

(1) The defendant can make an objection in point of law. that the facts alleged by the plaintiff lack relevance.
(2) The defendant can allege that the legal facts alleged by the plaintiff do not exist (denial).
(3) The defendant can allege the existence of a counter-fact.

281. As mentioned above, the defendant also can make objections with regard to procedural hindrances. Some procedural hindrances are mandatory (e.g., res judicata or lack of capacity as a party or procedural capacity) and thus shall be raised by the court on its own motion and be cause for dismissal, even if the case has reached an appellate court. However, as was mentioned before, a procedural hindrance can also be dispositive.[346] If the defendant does not make an objection at his first appearance in the action, his right to do so will disappear, unless he can prove that he had a legal excuse for not doing so.

I. Amendment of Claims

282. The summons application sets out the framework of the controversy. The possibilities for the plaintiff to change or make amendments to the summons are limited.

283. The principal rule is that the presentation in the summons application may not be amended.[347] The rationale behind this prohibition, despite many exceptions which are elaborated below, is that respect for the other party and the court requires it.[348] If the plaintiff were free to make amendments to his claim, it is obvious that the object of the litigation would become uncertain, because of which both the court's supervision of the proceedings and the adversary's possibilities to defend himself would be obstructed. In addition, the principle of consolidated proceedings would collapse.[349]

284. However, as has already been mentioned, there are several important exceptions to the general prohibition against amending the claim. The plaintiff may thus:

346. *See* para. 221 *supra*.
347. RB 13:3 para. 1.
348. SOU 1938:44, p. 184.
349. K. Olivecrona, *Grunden och saken*, TJFF 312 (1954) (Concerning the abbreviation 'TJFF', *see* para. 62 *supra*).

(1) by reason of a circumstance that occurred or became known to him during the proceedings, demand a performance other than that initially requested;[350]
(2) request a declaratory judgment pursuant to 13:2 of the Code;[351] or
(3) claim interest or other auxiliary obligations, arising from the principal obligation, and may also assert an additional claim based upon essentially the same ground as the original claim.[352]

285. With respect to the plaintiff's possibilities to demand another performance than that initially requested, the most usual situation is that the original claim concerned transfer of personal property that the defendant claims he no longer possesses. In that case, the plaintiff is entitled to an appropriate replacement.[353] The new circumstance alleged by the plaintiff must then be a legal fact, but it is not required that it occurred after the proceedings at first instance; the essential point in time is when the plaintiff acquired knowledge about the legal fact in question. However, if the plaintiff ought to have had knowledge about the legal fact earlier, the court can disregard it.[354]

286. According to the tenor of the discussed provision, the new claim must refer to 'another performance'. From the preparatory legislative works, it can furthermore be concluded that the basis of the claim must not be changed.[355] However, case law demonstrates that quantitative changes of claim can also be subsumed under the rule in question and, in addition, that it has been applied in cases where the foundation of the claim has changed.[356] The way in which the application of the rule has developed in case law means that there is no practical difference between this rule and the one referred to in the third exception listed above.[357] This will be further elaborated below.

287. The second exception refers to 13:2 of the Code, a rule that regulates declaratory claims. If, for example, a landlord has claimed that the tenant must pay the rent, he may, according to this rule, also request that the court establish the validity of the rental contract.

288. It is maintained in the preparatory legislative works that strong practical reasons support the possibilities for the plaintiff to assert auxiliary obligations.[358]

350. RB 13:3 para. 1, p. 1.
351. RB 13:3 para. 1, p. 2.
352. RB 13:3 para. 1, p. 3.
353. SOU 1938:44, p. 184.
354. Lindell, *Processuell preklusion*, 352. It ought to be mentioned that RB 13:3 para. 1, p. 1 can also be used at the first instance.
355. SOU 1938:44, p. 184.
356. *See* Lindell, *Processuell preklusion*, 349 and NJA 1971, p. 317; 1971, p. 620; 1974, p. 604; 1981, p. 1201; 1984, p. 807 and 1989, p. 47.
357. Lindell, *Processuell preklusion*, 351.
358. SOU 1938:44, p. 183.

The same reasoning is present with regard to the general permission to assert additional claims supported upon essentially the same grounds, for example, if the plaintiff asserts several claims against a contractor founded on carelessness in the performance of the construction work.[359]

289. The meaning of the vague phrase 'essentially the same grounds' is hard to grasp. In the commentaries, it has been said that there is a connection between this prerequisite and the prerequisite 'original subject-matter' in paragraph 3 of the Code, a rule that will be elaborated below.[360] However, the opinion is that two or more claims are supported on essentially the same grounds only if the grounds are substantially the same as the ones alleged in the application.[361] The court decides within its discretion what kind of ... can be accepted.[362]

290. In practice, claims asserted in cases concerning discrepan ing following a purchase or administration assignment have been de ported on essentially the same grounds.[363] This solution is practica lead to any inconveniences, since the assignment limits the possibiliti ing the material relevant for the litigation. This is also true in cases co appeal from tenancy inspection. A tenancy inspection is where a tenant periodically inspect the leased premises to determine its value and adju accordingly. In this case, there are similar considerations regarding the ap of the prerequisite in question.[364]

291. The plaintiff is free to assert new claims supported on essentially the same grounds during the preparation of the case and during the main hearing, if, in the latter case they can be examined without inconvenience. Additional claims may not be presented in appellate proceedings apart from claims pursuant to exception number (1) stated above.[365]

292. The rule on amendments of claims also entails a legal definition, which states that the plaintiff's reduction of the claim does not constitute an amendment. In addition, an allegation of new circumstances in support of the claim does not constitute an amendment if the original subject-matter does not change.[366]

---

359. NJA II 1943, p. 171.
360. Olivecrona, *Grunden och saken*, 332.
361. Hassler, *supra*, 121 and 134. Cf. Ekelöf, *Rättegång II*, 159 and Lindell, *Procesuell Preklusion*, 340 f.
362. Gärde et al., *supra*, 136. *See, e.g.*, NJA 1995, p. 664 and 1996, p. 553.
363. NJA 1964, p. 38 and 1966, p. 193.
364. NJA 1990, p. 660. It ought to be mentioned that in this case the plaintiff was allowed to amend his claim after the expiration of the prescribed time limit for such an action. However, the action was instituted in due time. *See also* the similar judgment in NJA 1990, p. 336.
365. RB 13:3, para. 2.
366. RB 13:3 para. 3. *See, e.g.*, NJA 1988, p. 161. NJA 2005, p. 295 and NJA 2011, p. 718.

293–298

293. A reduction of the claim occurs, e.g., when the plaintiff lowers the amount of his claim.[367] Reduction of a claim must be distinguishable from withdrawal of a claim,[368] where, if the [illegible] has already responded to the claim, he has the right to demand that the [illegible] nonetheless be adjudicated. The difference is that the reduction conce[illegible] the claim and the defendant is thereby protected by res judicata from [illegible] new claims referring to the same subject matter, while the plaintiff, [illegible]awal, is entitled to institute a new claim on the same issue.

29[illegible] [illegible] decide which new circumstances the plaintiff can allege without [illegible]ginal subject matter, it is obviously necessary to identify the original [illegible]ter. This issue will be elaborated upon below in the discussion of res [illegible]

[illegible]e rules concerning the amendment of a claim are, in general, mandatory [illegible]gatory, which means, *inter alia*, that it is of no relevance if the adversary [illegible]es of the amendment.

Joinder of Claims

296. When several claims are joined in a single action, it is possible to achieve lower litigation costs, since procedural material, which is relevant for the adjudication of several actions, only has to be presented once. Another advantage is that issues, which are related to one another, can be adjudicated together.

297. If the plaintiff asserts an additional claim at the same time against the same defendant, they will be joined in a single action if they are supported on essentially the same grounds.[370] The joinder is original if the time difference between the different summons is short and, therefore, of no practical importance; it is thereby obligatory. It has been maintained that the prerequisite 'essentially the same grounds' does not mean that the majority of the circumstances which constitute the foundation of the claim must coincide. The most important aspect from the perspective of minimizing the costs of litigation is that the circumstances in question are usually disputed in cases of this type.[371]

298. It has been noted above in paragraph 289 that the prerequisite 'essentially the same grounds' is also an element of the rule concerning amendments to a claim when it is relevant to the plaintiff's ability to assert additional claims. In that situation, it cannot be required that the combined circumstances are disputed. If the plaintiff asserts an additional claim pursuant to 13:3 paragraph 1 p. 1 of the Code, which constitutes an independent subject matter, the court must join the claims in a

367. *See, e.g.*, NJA 1987, p. 707 and NJA 1994, p. 23.
368. Concerning withdrawal of a claim, *see* RB 13:5 and paras 502–505 *infra*.
369. *See also* paras 410 et seq. *infra*.
370. RB 14:1.
371. Ekelöf, *Rättegång II*, 167.

single action. Since the joinder in that case is obligatory, it cannot be required that the mutual circumstances must be the subject of dispute.[372] In addition, it should be mentioned that joinder of claims reduces the litigation costs, even if the common circumstances are not disputed, by reduction of appearances and a more concentrated argumentation on the legal topics.[373]

299. A plaintiff against more than one defendant can institute claims at the same time or by more than one plaintiff against one or more defendants. In such cases, the claims shall be joined in a single action if they are supported on essentially the same grounds.[374] This rule on original subjective joinder applies, for example, if the plaintiff institutes actions against several persons who have caused the same damage. To ease such joinder, there is a corresponding rule on *forum connexitatis*, which makes it possible for the plaintiff to bring all the claims to the court in which any of the defendants is required to respond.[375]

300. In the following sections, subsequent joinder will be described. These rules are obligatory. This kind of joinder presupposes that the cases are joined in a single action before the main hearing in the district court.

301. The parties can be alternately plaintiff and defendant, in which case the original claim is called the main claim and the claim instituted later is called the counter-claim. The defendant can institute an action against the plaintiff concerning the same or a related matter or concerning a debt that may be set-off against the plaintiff's claim.[376] However, it is unusual that the claims concern the same subject matter. In those rare cases, the controversy probably concerns cases in which the parties' claims have the same or a similar purpose, or cases where the counter-claim is founded on a circumstance, which also is alleged to support the main claim.[377] The most common situation where the rule in question is applicable concerns cases in which a performance claim instituted by one of the parties is joined with a declaratory claim from the other party.[378] Another frequent situation is one in which the defendant alleges a debt that may be set-off. Since the rule on joinder in this case is obligatory, the right to institute a set-off can be used by a party as security if the other party should be bankrupt. There is a forum rule linked to this rule that makes it possible to institute a counter-claim in the court where the main action is pending.[379]

302. Instead of instituting a counter-claim, the defendant can assert his claim in the form of a defence. Thus, if the defendant has a claim against the plaintiff, he may assert it as a set-off defence. A set-off defence does not require a summons

372. Lindell, *Processuell preklusion*, 341.
373. *Ibid.*
374. RB 14:2.
375. RB 10:14 para. 1, 1.
376. RB 14:3.
377. Ekelöf, *Rättegång II*, 169.
378. KRB 14:10.
379. RB 10:14 para. 2.

application, but can be asserted orally, even in the appellate court, although it can be dismissed in an appellate court if it cannot be examined without inconvenience.[380]

However, the defendant should bear in mind that the examination of a set-off defence with regard to the rules on res judicata does not have the same meaning as it does with regard to a counter-claim.[381]

303. If an intermediate party (*mellankommande part*), who is not a party to the original action, requests a joint procedure when instituting a claim against both of the original parties or against one of them concerning the disputed matter, the claims shall be joined in a single action.[382] The intervening party can, for example, institute an action against the plaintiff in a case concerning payment, while alleging that he is the rightful possessor of the claim. The rule on *forum connexitatis* is also applicable in this case, meaning that the intervening party's action shall be instituted in the court in which the main action is pending.[383]

304. If a party, in the event that judgment is entered against him, wishes to present a claim for recovery of damages, indemnification or the like against a third party, he may institute his claim against the third party in a joint procedure in the pending action. This rule also applies if a third party, because of the outcome of a pending action, wishes to institute such a claim against one or both of the parties.[384] Thus, if *A* and *B* together have entered a surety bond, and *C* sues *A* on payment according to the surety bond, *A* can, in turn, sue *B* and assert a claim to recover all or part of the bond in the pending action. Another example of the application of the rule is the following: if *A* and *B* damage a car, which together they have leased from *C*, and *C* sues *A* for damages, *B* can institute a declaratory claim against *C* that he bears no responsibility for the damage. He can thus avoid a claim from *A*; in which *A* tries to recover part of the damages from *B*. The above-mentioned rule on *forum connexitatis* is also applicable in this case, stating that a claim for partial or complete recovery of damages shall be instituted in the court where the main action is pending.[385]

305. The Code also offers a general possibility of optional joinder concerning claims between the same or different parties in cases other than those described above, if it benefits the investigation of the case. Such claims may later be served and processed separately.[386] Joinder pursuant to this rule might be adequate if some of the conditions, which are necessary for obligatory joinder, are lacking. For example, when the creditors' claim against the debtor and the surety has been handled by different district courts but the appeals reach an appellate court at the

380. RB 50:25 para. 3 and 55:13.
381. *See also* para. 424 *infra*.
382. RB 14:4.
383. RB 10:14 para. 3.
384. RB 14:5.
385. RB 10:14 para. 3.
386. RB 14:6.

same time.[387] Another case is that in which the grounds of the claims are not essentially the same, but they coincide with respect to the evidence required.[388] An application of the rule can also be motivated only by the fact that one or more of the parties does not have to appear so many times in court.[389] Finally, the situation should be mentioned in which the grounds have certain similar features but they differ from each other with respect to time and place, for example, several terrace houses sold by the same building constructor have the same faults.[390]

306. In order to join claims according to the rules described above, the claims must have been instituted in the same court, the court must be competent to try the claims, and the same rules of procedure must apply to each.[391] The criteria to decide whether one or more claims are present are partly the same as those used in deciding the identity of the disputed subject matter. Thus, one determining factor is normally whether the additional claim changes the original legal consequences in a qualitative way. For example, a claim concerning transfer of personal property and indemnification because of damage to the property constitute two separate claims, since the legal consequences at issue are qualitatively different. If, however, the plaintiff alleges alternative grounds for a claim, this does not lead to an additional claim, since the legal consequence has not been changed.[392]

307. If an action pursuant to 14:3–5 of the Code has been instituted after the commencement of the main hearing, or if the main claim has been brought to final adjudication in some other way, the court may handle the actions separately if they cannot be joined in a single action without inconvenience. This rule shall also apply if one of the parties institutes a claim pursuant to 14:3–5 after expiration of the time limit for answering an order for preclusion according to 42:15 or after the expiration of the time laid down in 42:15a.[393] Thus, 42:15 prescribes an examination of whether the party has a legal excuse, while pursuant to 14:7, the court will examine whether joinder leads to inconveniences even though the party has not answered the order for preclusion in due time.[394]

387. Ekelöf, *Rättegång II*, 178. *See also* SOU 1938:44, p. 195 and KRB 14:16. Thus, this rule concerning joinder of claims can be used in an appellate court.
388. Ekelöf, *Rättegång II*, 178; KRB 14:16.
389. Ekelöf, *Rättegång II*, 178; KRB 14:16.
390. Ekelöf, *Rättegång II*, 178; SOU 1938:44, p. 195 and KRB 14:16.
391. RB 14:7.
392. Cf. Ekelöf, *Rättegång II*, 157 and para. 399, 419 *infra*. But *see also* NJA 1994, p. 23; 1995, p. 610 and 1999, p. 520.
393. Concerning RB 42:15, *see* paras 267–268 *supra*.
394. Lindell, *Processuell preklusion*, 361. Concerning special and necessary joinder, *see* para. 495 *infra*.

Chapter 3. Sanctions Applicable to Procedural Irregularities

§1. Formal Requirements

308. Sanctions applicable to vexatious litigation and procedural irregularities coincide to some extent. With respect to the former provisions, *see* the discussion above. In addition, a party may fail to proceed correctly through various acts or omissions.[395]

309. It is, of course, very important that the parties do their very best to achieve a fast and effective procedure throughout the proceedings. However, not all relevant rules in this context impose obligations on the parties, for example, the preclusion rule which is of great importance for speedy litigation, does not impose a duty to allege legal facts and evidence as soon as possible. Thus, the parties can wait. However, they do take a risk; the court may disregard new circumstances if in the court's opinion, they are alleged too late.

310. With regard to the content of the summons application, there are certain mandatory rules in the Code, which are touched upon above. If the summons application fails to comply with these regulations or is otherwise incomplete, the court shall direct the plaintiff to cure the defect.[396] If the plaintiff fails to obey such a directive, the application shall be dismissed if it is so incomplete that it cannot, without essential inconvenience, be used as basis for legal proceedings. It shall also be dismissed if it is manifested that the case cannot be heard owing to a procedural hindrance.[397]

311. An order for the plaintiff to complete the summons application shall contain a warning that it can be dismissed if it is not completed.

§2. Time Limits

312. Normally the court fixes the time limits. When a party or any other person, pursuant to a court order, is required to appear before the court or to perform any other act in the proceedings, he shall be given reasonable time to comply with the court's order.

---

395. *See also infra* on default judgments.
396. RB 42:3.
397. RB 42:4.

Part IV. Proceedings

Chapter 1. Proceedings in First Instance

§1. Adversary Proceedings

I. Ordinary Proceedings

A. Introduction of the Claim

313. An action shall be initiated by summons, unless otherwise prescribed.[398] Particular rules in this regard are mainly to be found in the area of family law. Thus, spouses can apply for divorce and, in cases concerning custody; a party may request maintenance without applying for a summons.[399] In addition, a summons is not required for necessary joinder of claims when another party enters the action on an existing party's side.[400]

314. An action is deemed to be initiated when the summons application is filed with the court or, if a summons is not necessary, when the claim is presented to the court.[401]

315. In Chapter 42 of the Code, there are provisions concerning the summons and the preparation of the case as well as judgment without trial. These rules will be outlined in the following paragraphs. To begin, the requirements on the summons application will be elaborated. It shall consist of:

(1) a fixed claim;
(2) a detailed statement concerning the circumstances alleged as foundation for the claim;
(3) a statement about the evidence that will be presented and what the plaintiff aims to prove with each piece of evidence; and
(4) the circumstances rendering the court competent, unless this appears from the allegation.

398. RB 13:4 para. 1.
399. ÄktB 14:4 and 5, FB 6:17 paras 2 and 4.
400. NJA 1988, p. 78.
401. RB 13:4 para. 3.

316. If the plaintiff has any preferences regarding the proceedings, he should inform the court of these in the application, which shall be signed by the plaintiff or his attorney. Originals or certified copies of documentary evidence in the plaintiff's possession should be annexed to the application.[402]

317. The rules stating the requirements of the summons application were changed in 1987 with respect to language and disposition. In addition, some substantial changes were made. One of these was an amendment providing that the plaintiff shall give a 'detailed statement' of the circumstances alleged in support of the claim. The word 'detailed' was added in order to stress that it is not enough that the summons application has such a content that a default judgment can be based on it, but also that it must be so itemized that the defendant can give a complete answer to it.[403]

318. According to the preparatory legislative works to the amendments in question, it is an advantage to offer a detailed description of the background to the dispute and other circumstances of relevance. The risk of unnecessary work if it appears later on that there is no real dispute between the parties is regarded as small, since the summons application is supposed to be used only in such cases where a real dispute exists.[404]

319. In addition, a detailed description can make the defendant understand that he has no reason to contest the case. It will be easier for him to determine which circumstances he should not dispute. Moreover, the plaintiff might have reasons to give more details than the rule in question requires. Thus, if he suspects or knows that the defendant will allege a counter-fact he can anticipate it and elaborate upon it in advance in the summons application.[405]

320. The plaintiff's personal identity number, e-post address and postal address shall be specified in the summons application. Occupation, telephone number and any other circumstance of importance for service shall also be stated. If the plaintiff has a legal representative or has retained an attorney, that person's name and postal address shall be stated. The same particulars shall be stated with respect to the defendant and to witnesses whom the party wishes to present during the main hearing, if the information is easily accessible for the plaintiff. The plaintiff shall notify the court of any changes in the facts or circumstances in question immediately.[406]

---

402. RB 42:2.
403. Prop. 1986/87:89, p. 189 and Prop. 1983/84:78, p. 37.
404. Prop. 1986/87:89, p. 190.
405. *Ibid.*
406. *See* RB 33:1 which applies in applications, notices and other writings with reference to the action.

1. Service

321. A new Act on Service took effect on 1 April 2011. The old Act (1970:428) had then served for just over forty years.

322. The new Act improves the conditions for service, safeguards better possibilities for electronic communication and imposes a bigger responsibility on the parties than the old law. Furthermore, the rules on service have become clearer and simpler.[407]

323. From an academic point of view, service of documents is considered to be a rather boring and peripheral subject. However, in order for the administration of justice to work quickly and effectively, it is fundamental that there is a *safe system for service of documents* to the parties, and for witnesses and others who are entitled to the documents in the case. It is furthermore notorious that it is difficult to service certain legal subjects as, for example, companies which often change the address.

324. The way in which a document shall be served should be chosen with respect to what is appropriate with respect to the content and scope of the document. Furthermore, it should cause as little inconvenience as possible and must not be inappropriate with regard to the circumstances of the matter.

325. When simplified service is used, the document is sent to the recipient in an ordinary letter. The next working day, a *verification message* is sent to the recipient that the document has been sent.

326. Simplified service is based on the assumption that the recipient knows that the matter is pending in court and, therefore, monitors his or her mail.

327. Only authorities may use simplified service since it must be possible afterwards to prove that the document has been served.

328. Special service in relation to a legal person is carried out in the same way as simplified service. This service can be used for legal persons that are registered in certain registers, e.g., the bank register or the insurance register. In addition, it can be used only if ordinary or simplified service of a legal representative for the legal person has failed.

329. If the assumption is that service cannot be performed according to the methods mentioned above, a service officer, or someone else who is certified to deliver the document to the recipient may perform service. This method also means, e.g., that the document under certain circumstances can be handed over to a family member or to someone at the receiver's workplace.

---

407. Prop. 2009/10:237, p. 91. *See* C. Andersson & S. Synnergren, *Delgivningslagstiftningen. En kommentar* (2011).

330. Service through announcement may be used, e.g., if the receiver has no known residence and it cannot be found out where he or she is located.

331. Service through announcement is carried out in the following way: the document to be served is kept available for ten days at the authority or at a certain place decided by the authority. Information about this and about the main content of the document shall normally be announced in the Official Gazette and, if there are reasons for it, in regional newspapers.

2. Service Abroad

332. With regard to Norway, Denmark, Finland, Iceland and Norway, there is a treaty concerning mutual legal aid in service and obtaining of evidence that was concluded in Copenhagen on 26 April 1974. Service in any of these countries can be accomplished pursuant to this treaty. The Swedish court directly addresses the assigned authority in the other state, and consequently obtains its confirmation of service when executed. An alternative is postal service through an internationally recommended post, with a receipt of confirmation annexed to it. This method is simple, fast and effective. Moreover, it can be used in most countries around the world and is thus available with regard to countries, which have not ratified the Treaty on Service of Documents in Cases and Matters of Civil or Commercial Nature (The Hague, 15 November 1965). If service is performed according to the treaty in question, which has been ratified by Sweden, a request for service will be sent to a central organ in the state where the person wanted for service has his residence, or temporary residence. The request is made on special forms. With regard to other states, service can be carried out – in addition to the postal service mentioned above – with the help of the Ministry for Foreign Affairs.

The European Council Decree No. 1345/2000 on Service of Articles within the Member States in Cases and Matters of Civil or Commercial Nature came into force on 31 May 2001. The Decree applies when an article is sent from one Member State to another and it contains twenty-five sections. The Decree takes over rules in bilateral or multilateral agreements entered by the Member States, in particular Article IV in the Protocol to the Brussels Convention from 1968 and the Hague Convention from 1965.

3. Registration by the Court

333. Chapter 6 of the Code contains provisions about the registration of information in a case. The aim of the register function is to document the entertainment of a case and to give the general public insight into the courts' activity. The cases are numbered in consecutive order with reference 'T' for civil cases generally and 'FT' for civil cases which presumably will be tried by a single judge pursuant to 1:3 d paragraph 1 of the Code. According to 6:1 of the Code, the register shall show measures taken with respect to the case, when the case is decided and, if it is appealed, the day when the appeal was submitted.

334. It is provided in 6:4 of the Code that the circumstances and the evidence that the parties refer to during a meeting that is held during the preparation shall be recorded briefly. Through the reform A Modernized Procedure, it is provided that other circumstances necessary for a judgment without a main hearing shall be recorded.

335. In addition, the provision in 6:6 of the Code was changed through the reform in question. According to the first paragraph, oral evidence shall be video-recorded, if there are not special reasons against it. The provision is mandatory in the district court and optional in the Court of Appeal.

336. In order for the court to entertain a summons application, the plaintiff must pay the prescribed application fee.[408] An application for re-opening a case after default judgment is free of charge. The same applies to cases of injunction to pay and cases concerning assistance, referred to ordinary trial.[409] A summons is required for a counter-claim and, thus, is subject to a charge.[410] A set-off defence in a pending action is, however, free of charge.

337. If an application for provisional attachment has been made before the summons of application has been instituted, the fee for civil cases must be paid before the court tries the provisional attachment. A new fee will not then be claimed if an action is instituted within the prescribed time. A person who is entitled to legal aid does not pay a fee for application or costs registration, since these fees are costs covered by legal aid. Such an applicant still pays a variable sum towards his legal costs.

338. The fee must be paid when the summons application is handed over to the court. If this is not done, the court will not hear the case, but will direct the applicant to pay the fee to avoid dismissal of the summons application.[411] Thus, if the applicant does not pay, the summons will be dismissed.[412]

B. Progress of the Proceedings

1. Preparatory Measures

339. When the summons is issued, the preparation of the action shall commence.[413] The defendant's answer shall contain:[414]

(1) the procedural objections he wishes to make;

---

408. *See* the decree on fees at the ordinary courts (SFS 1987:452). The fee amounts at present to SEK 450.
409. Prop. 1989/90:85, p. 73. Concerning summary proceedings, *see* paras 696 et seq. *infra*.
410. JO 1968, p. 165.
411. RB 42:3.
412. RB 42:4.
413. Preparation of the case is thus obligatory.
414. RB 42:7.

(2) a statement with regard to what extent the plaintiff's demand for relief is accepted or opposed;
(3) if the plaintiff's demand for relief is opposed, the ground therefore, including the defendant's position as to the basis of the plaintiff's claim and a statement of the circumstances urged in defence and;
(4) information about the documentary evidence to be offered by the defendant.

340. The defendant should immediately present the originals or certified copies of the documentary evidence in his possession. The information required in the answer is similar to that relevant for the summons. However, while the plaintiff in his summons application must describe the alleged circumstances in detail, the defendant only has to express his opinion with regard to these circumstances and, in addition, state the circumstances he himself wants to allege.[415] The fact that the defendant need not give a detailed statement is linked to the fact that it is the plaintiff who outlines the framework of the litigation through his summons application.

341. In cases where out-of-court settlement is permitted, the court can direct the defendant to answer; otherwise, a default judgment might be entered against him.[416] In addition, in such cases the court may direct the plaintiff, within a certain time, to state whether he or she withholds the action. If the plaintiff does not reply before the expiration of the time stated in the order, a default judgment may be rendered against that party. The purpose of this rule is to make it possible for the court to finalize the case without a main hearing where the plaintiff obviously has no interest in continuing the action.[417]

342. The purpose of the preparation of the case is to elucidate the parties' claims, objections and the meaning of the circumstances they want to allege, as well as to ascertain the extent to which the parties disagree about facts relevant to the case, to find out the evidence the parties want to present and the evidentiary theme for each evidence and, finally, to determine what further investigations or other measures the parties deem necessary before the court renders a judgment. The court shall also examine whether there are grounds for a settlement of the dispute.

343. Before a change in the legislation in 1987, the principal rule was that the preparation should be oral. The principal rule today is that the answer shall be written, followed by one oral session at which the preparation ought to be concluded.[418] According to the preparatory legislative works, more than two oral sessions should be an exception.[419] Nonetheless, in practice, it is not unusual to have more than two oral sessions in complicated cases.[420]

415. *See* RB 42:2, p. 2 and 42:7 para. 3.
416. RB 42:11.
417. Prop. 1999/2000:26, p. 88.
418. RB 42:9.
419. SOU 1982:26, p. 86, Prop. 1986/ 87:89, pp. 81 and 199.
420. T. Brolin & M. Widebeck, *Effektivare handläggning av tvistemål*, SvJT 587 (1990).

344. Considering the nature of the case, it may be appropriate in certain cases for the answer to be stated at an oral session for preparation. An example of this mode of procedure is where the defendant, in a simple case, litigates without an attorney. In such a case, it might sometimes be better if the defendant states the answer at an oral session, in order to allow the court to elucidate circumstances that are incomplete or unclear. This proceeding might also be suitable if the plaintiff knows or can foresee the defendant's objections.[421]

345. In considering 'the nature of the case', notice may be taken of material that is not relevant to the subject matter in dispute. If a party litigates without an attorney, there is usually an oral session. However, the court should thereby determine whether the possible advantages of an oral session outweigh the costs and inconveniences, an oral session might cause. The reasons favouring a written preparation grow stronger as the economic value of the dispute decreases.[422]

346. The Code does not prevent the entire preparation, even in a huge and complicated case, from being purely written, but such a procedure is, of course, not to be recommended, considering the risk of misunderstandings between the parties. Obviously, if oral sessions are held it is easier for the court to carry out its duty in attempting to elucidate the subject matter of the dispute.[423] In addition, the possibilities of reconciling the parties will be reduced to a minimum of at least one oral session is not held.

347. In dispositive cases, each party shall be directed to appear at a session for preparation; otherwise, a default judgment may be entered against the absent party. If the parties are to appear in person, the court shall direct them to do so under penalty of fine.

348. In non-dispositive cases, the plaintiff shall be directed to appear; otherwise, the claim will be dismissed without prejudice to the commencement of new proceedings. If the plaintiff is to appear in person, the court shall direct the plaintiff to do so under penalty of a fine. The same applies to the defendant. The rules about attending sessions and the consequences for not appearing at a session were changed through the reform A Modernized Procedure, Prop. 2004/05:131. It is now possible to entertain both substantive and procedural issues during a session. This means that even if the session concerns, e.g., provisional attachment of the defendant's property the plaintiff must appear, or otherwise face a default judgment. The same is true if the parties shall be heard for evidentiary purposes and one of them does not appear. However, an exception is made for sessions about a procedural hinder, e.g., there is a dispute about whether or not there is a valid arbitration agreement. Such issues must always be decided before the court examines the substantial

---

421. Prop. 1986/87:89, 197 f.
422. *Ibid.*, 199.
423. *Ibid.*

issues. Because of the above-mentioned reform, the special provision about telephone conferences was omitted. However, telephone conferences are still used under the general provision on audio- and picture recording.

349. In January 2000, experiments were initiated with audio- and picture conferencing (video conference) in a number of selected courts.[424] The pilot studies gave good results and were extended until 1 January 2007. Through the reform A Modernized Procedure, which took effect on 1 November 2008, a new general provision was introduced in the Code, enabling those who would like to participate in proceedings through audio- and picture recording to do so. The provision is laid down in Chapter 5 section 10 of the Code. The main rule to be present in the courtroom remains. However, if there are reasons for it, the court can decide that a party and others may instead participate through video conference. Participation through video conference is not allowed if it would be inappropriate with regard to the purpose of the meeting and other circumstances. The court shall consider the costs and inconveniences involved with participating in a meeting in the courtroom. Certain general interests will then be weighed against individual interests. In the Government Bill, it is emphasized that the quality of the proceedings and legal security must not be jeopardized.[425] The provision is indispositive, i.e., the parties do not dispose over the way they can participate. If, for example, a witness would insist upon coming personally to the courtroom, it is not admittedly prohibited; however, the witness would not then be compensated for the additional costs that this would cause. Factors of significance for the overall assessment are, e.g., the parties' attitude and the nature and objectives of the meeting.[426]

350. As mentioned above, telephone conferences are still used but they fall under the same general rule as video conferencing. However, if there are evidentiary questions involved, video should be used instead of a telephone conference.

351. During the preparation, each party states the additional circumstances it wishes to allege and responds to his adversary's allegations. In addition, each party specifies the evidence upon which the party desires to rely and what it intends to prove by each specified item, to the extent not previously stated. Documentary evidence not already presented shall be immediately submitted. Upon request by the adversary, a party is obliged to indicate what other items of evidence it has in its possession.[427]

352. It is essential that preparatory sessions be devoted to an immediate oral exchange of opinions. The general rule is, therefore, that the parties may not submit or read any written statement on one's position or other written presentation. However, there is one important exception to this prohibition. The parties may submit or read written statements if the court finds that it would make it easier to understand

---

424. About the terminology, *see* para. 55, *supra*.
425. Prop. 2004/05:131, p. 95.
426. *Ibid.*
427. RB 42:8 para. 1.

a statement, or in some other way would facilitate the proceedings.[428] This might be the case, for example, when a case is very complicated. It is thereby possible for a party to make its opinion clearer than would be possible through an oral presentation.[429] There is a corresponding provision for the main hearing.[430]

353. During the preparation, as well as during the main hearing, a party is obliged to give truthful statements regarding the circumstances it alleges and regarding the information given by its adversary. A party must truthfully answer all questions put to him.[431] In general, a distinction is made between a negative and a positive obligation to tell the truth. The former means that a party is obliged to refrain from knowingly stating something that is not true, or to refrain from knowingly denying something that it knows is true. The latter means an obligation to give true information.[432] If a party makes statements, which are inconsistent with an assertion previously made by the party, or if an inconsistency otherwise appears in the party's statements, it shall be asked to give an explanation for the discrepancy.

354. As appears from the above, the preparation normally proceeds gradually in accordance with a scheduled pattern: the plaintiff shall state its claim for relief and the grounds and evidence it thereby alleges in a summons; the defendant, if opposing the claim, presents the grounds, therefore, and the evidence it wants to present. In more complicated cases, this pattern will continue by means of allegations of further legal facts from each party, according to the principle of successive relevance and successive verification.[433] The meaning of this principle, which is not codified, is mainly that in dispositive cases, it can be concluded from the burden of proof which of the parties must allege and prove a legal fact in order for the court to base its judgment on it.

355. It is evident from the provisions elaborated above that the legislature has tried to induce the parties to state their claims, grounds and evidence as soon as possible. This aim is furthered by the rule that before the session for preparation, the parties shall elaborate the case in such a way that, if possible, no further session will be necessary.[434]

356. As has been previously mentioned, the court has an obligation to ensure that facts relevant to the dispute are observed. This intervention by the judge in

---

428. RB 42:13. *See also* para. 74 *supra*.
429. Prop. 1986/87:89, p. 204.
430. RB 43:5.
431. RB 43:6.
432. *See* H. Wiklund, *God advokatsed* 524 (1973). This rule has no sanction, but if a party who, during the main hearing, after declaring that he will tell the truth, gives untrue information or withholds the truth, he shall be sentenced to imprisonment for at most two years or, if the crime is petty, to pay a fine or to imprisonment for at most six months. If the act is committed due to gross negligence he shall be sentenced for giving a 'careless statement' to pay a fine or to imprisonment for at most six months. BRB 15:2 and 3.
433. Olivecrona, *Rätt och dom*, 208.
434. RB 42:14 para. 2.

order to clarify the disputed issue and the way to entertain it is mandatory. However, it is debated how much intervention is appropriate.

357. Intervention of the judge is practised during the preparation as well as during the main hearing.[435] During the preparation, the court shall attempt to ensure that disputed issues are clarified and that the parties specify everything they wish to present in the case. In addition, the court shall attempt, by means of questions and reminders, to remedy unclear or incomplete statements.

358. It is obvious that intervention should be practised mainly during the preparation of the case, since new circumstances alleged during the main hearing might cause delays and other inconvenience. For this reason, the provision regulating intervention during the main hearing is more restricted than the provision that applies to the preparation. Pursuant to the former rule, the court must make certain that the action is fully developed and that irrelevant matters are not presented. It shall furthermore attempt, through questions and reminders, to remedy any unclear or incomplete statements made in the course of the proceedings. It should be emphasized that the court, according to the wording of the rule applicable during the main hearing, is not obliged to ensure that the parties state everything they wish to allege in the case.

359. Intervention by the judge can embrace claims, legal facts, evidentiary facts, issues concerning the burden of proof and the application of the law. However, if a party has overlooked a legal fact, which the party initially would have alleged had it observed it, the court might preclude it if it is alleged later.[436] At the same time, the rules on intervention impose an obligation on the court to ensure that the action is fully developed. Thus, while the rule on preclusion makes the parties responsible for presenting all relevant material in due time, the rules on intervention impose an obligation on the court to clarify the disputed issues. This division of conflicting responsibilities between the parties and the court has no definite boundaries.[437]

360. Failure of the court to fulfil its obligations according to the rules on intervention has, in practice, been considered to be a procedural error which – if it cannot be remedied in an appellate court without inconvenience – results in a reference back to the lower court for correction.[438] It also appears from practice that the requirements on intervention should be higher when a party is litigating without a legally qualified attorney, than if the party is represented by an attorney.[439]

361. In order to have all relevant evidence available in an uninterrupted sequence at the main hearing, orders shall be issued during the preparation for

435. RB 42:8 para. 2; 43:4 respectively.
436. *See* paras 266–274 *supra*.
437. Lindell, *Processuell preklusion*, 210.
438. *See, e.g.*, NJA 1976, pp. 489 and 504.
439. *See, e.g.*, NJA 1982, p. 27 and NJA 1985, p. 738.

obtaining expert opinions, documentary production or objects for view, or inspection, or for taking any other preparatory measure. If evidence is to be taken outside the main hearing, orders thereon should also be issued during the preparation. It is not possible to take oral evidence during the preparation of the case because of the principles of immediacy, oral presentation and concentration.[440]

362. If it is not regarded as unnecessary, the court shall make a time plan for the entertainment of the case and – in addition – give the parties a list of questions, which should be addressed during the preparation, if such a measure would benefit the handling of the case. In 2005, an amendment was made that the parties must check the time plan and inform the court if they think that it cannot be upheld. Before the preparation is concluded, the court shall make a compilation of the parties' opinions as they have been understood by the court.[441] The word 'summary' was changed to 'compilation' through the reform 2004/05:131 at the same time the rule became mandatory.

363. A party who wants to rely upon an item of evidence at the main hearing, which the party did not present during the preparation, shall immediately notify the court and the opposing party, and shall indicate what it intends to prove with such item.[442] The obvious purpose of this rule is to prevent surprises during the main hearing. The wording of this rule gives the impression that it is applicable only to evidence; however, it is also deemed to apply to legal facts.[443] If a party does not observe the rule, it risks preclusion of the evidence or the legal fact.

364. It is prescribed by 42:6 of the Code that the court shall examine whether an out-of-court settlement or a solution based on mutual understanding is possible to reach. This general rule, which from 2006 is also applicable in non-dispositive cases, is supplemented by another obligatory rule in 42:17 paragraph 1 of the Code, which prescribes that the court in dispositive cases shall try to conciliate the parties during the preparation if it does not appear inappropriate with regard to the nature of the case and other circumstances. This rule was changed in 2011. Before the amendment, it was stated that settlement activities should appear appropriate. Thus, the amendment means that there is a presumption for conciliation.

365. Since the RB was enacted in 1942 and came into force in 1948, the view on the court's contribution to settlement has changed. Initially, the legislature had a rather restrictive view of settlement activities, mainly because of the fear that the

---

440. In doctrine this is regarded as a defect in our procedural system. Ekelöf has raised the question whether it ought not to be permitted to hear an important witness during the preparation. *See* Ekelöf, Edelstam & Boman, *Rättegång V*, 40, note 87 and also L. Heuman, *Bevisupptagning under förberedelsen i syfte att främja förlikningsverksamheten*, 137 et seq., in *Process och Exekution* (1990).
441. *See* 42:6, 42:14 and 42:16. This rule was sharpened 2016, see prop. 2015/16:39, 69.
442. RB 42:22.
443. Pauli, Åberopsbördan, 43, Ekelöf, Edelstam & Boman, *Rättegång V*, 37, note 73.

court might undermine its objectivity in the eyes of the parties. However, as mentioned above it is now regarded as quite acceptable and even appropriate for the court to give concrete proposals on settlement.[444]

366. In general, the parties' willingness to settlement increases the longer the preparation of the case proceeds. This depends mainly on the fact that the disputed issues become clearer, which makes it easier for the parties to estimate their chances to win the case.[445] Approximately 60% of all dispositive cases at the district courts are settled.[446] It is also possible for the parties to settle in appellate courts.

367. It is not possible to specify particular groups of cases where an attempt to settle should not be made.[447] However, certain circumstances can make a case more or less suitable for settlement. In this respect, the so-called black and white cases should be taken first, that is to say, such cases where the preparation has shown that it is obvious that one of the parties would win the case. In such cases, the general opinion has been that the court should not contribute to a settlement not corresponding to such an outcome.[448] Correspondingly, the view has been that the court should be cautious with settlement attempts in cases where the outcome is obvious, but it depends on circumstances, which a party says he can prove.[449]

368. Furthermore, settlement has not been regarded as appropriate in cases where the crucial issue solely concerns a question of law. The reason is that the judge might be suspected of having decided the outcome in advance if he declares how a settlement could be constructed.[450] Another factor is that the case may be beneficial in setting a precedent in the area in question. However, it can be maintained that creating precedents is not a task for the parties.[451] Today the legislator's view is that now cases should be excluded from settlement beforehand.[452]

369. If the parties are represented by advocates or legally qualified attorneys, one can count on the fact that attempts to settle the case have been made and thus that the chances of settlement are smaller than when the parties are litigating without legal representation.[453]

370. The rule on court-annexed mediation was also changed in 2011. Furthermore, the Swedish Act on Mediation in Certain Private Disputes came into force at the same time. Through the Act, the Directive of the European Parliament and the

---

444. *See* B. Lindell, *Civilprocessen – rättegång samt skiljeförfarande och medling* 367 et seq. (2017).
445. SOU 1982:26, p. 137.
446. *Ibid.*
447. Prop. 1986/87:89, p. 113.
448. SOU 1982:26, p. 148.
449. *Ibid.*
450. SOU 1938:44, p. 437.
451. Ekelöf, Edelstam & Pauli, *Rättegång V*, 68.
452. Prop. 1986/87:89 p. 113.
453. SOU 1982:26, 151.

Council – Directive 2008/52/EU of 21 May 2008 about certain aspects on mediation – was implemented. The objective of the directive is cross-border disputes, but the Act applies also to purely domestic extrajudicial mediation procedures. According to 42:17 paragraph 2 of the Code, if it is not inappropriate to act for a settlement the court may, with the consent of the parties, make a decision about special mediation. Furthermore, it is stated in the Government Bill that judges should consider special mediation more often and that it should be placed on an equal footing with settlement activities in court.[454] To date, special mediation has been seldom used. The main reason for this can be found in the obligation of the judge to try to resolve the dispute between the parties through settlement. In addition, a network of trained mediators has not yet developed in Sweden. Therefore, there is no infrastructure in the area.[455]

2. Purely Written Procedure

371. The Code distinguishes between judgments and orders. Normally, a judgment concerns a substantive issue, while an order concerns a procedural issue. A person may appeal separately – and not in conjunction with the judgment – from a final court order.[456] This appeal procedure is normally written. However, if examination of a party or a third person is found necessary for the investigation, the courts of appeal shall direct that such an examination be held. Court matters are normally handled in writing, but an oral hearing is also possible in these cases. As far as the possibilities for the court to deal with substantive issues in writing are concerned, *see* paragraphs 455–458 below.

3. Determination of the Trial Date

372. The court shall fix a date for the main hearing when a time plan for the case is made.[457] If possible, this date should be decided after hearing the parties. Consultation with the parties might be necessary in order to give them enough time to prepare their cases. A main hearing may be scheduled for the disposition of a procedural issue or of a portion of the disputed matter that may be decided separately, although in other respects the action is not yet ready for trial.

454. Prop. 2010/11:128, p. 39.
455. *See* B. Lindell, *Alternativ tvistlösning – särskilt medling och skiljeförfarande* 117 (2000). *See also* Part XI *infra*.
456. *See also* para. 474 *infra*.
457. RB 42:6. Prop. 1999/2000:26, p. 68.

4. Trial

373. When the main hearing starts, the court shall ascertain whether there is any impediment to an immediate full hearing and final disposition of the action.[458]

374. The concept 'main hearing' is not defined in the Code. Instead it is defined by the principles of orality, immediacy and concentration. In short, these principles mean that parties, witnesses and others come to the courtroom to tell their stories in front of the judge. However, the meaning of the concept 'main hearing' is no longer evident because of the new technique, video conferencing. The technique allows parties to be present through a video screen, even though they can be far away from the courthouse. Furthermore, the technique does not affect the quality of the proceedings as far as the evaluation of evidence is concerned. In effect, orality, immediacy and concentration have got a new meaning compared with the situation when the Code came into force in 1948. This also means that it can be difficult to draw the line between the preparation of the case and the main hearing. If evidence would be presented during the preparation, it would be possible to entertain the case without ever having a main hearing. It is likely that a development of that kind is in the pipeline. However, today the main rule is still that the parties shall come to the courtroom, which they are also entitled to do if the case is disputed. The main rule is that all relevant material must be presented orally. In 2005 it became possible for the parties to refer to documents. By doing so, the material referred to is brought into the procedure and may be considered by the court. Thus, the plaintiff can refer to the summons application; the defendant to the answer. Furthermore, the parties can refer to maps, i.e., other documents earlier presented, instead of presenting them orally. The parties are not only allowed to refer to documents; but they may also refer to a summary made by the court or to a tape from video conferencing. Reference to video however, is, intended to be made in a restrictive manner. [459] The rule in question has few limitations. However, the summation must be oral since it is based on circumstances brought up during the proceedings.[460]

5. Main Hearing in Simplified Form

375. The main hearing may be held in simplified form if no impediment to an immediate full hearing exists and the parties consent thereto. Such a main hearing may take place in immediate conjunction with the preparation or, provided that the same judge sits in the court, within fifteen days of completion of the preparatory hearing. Regardless of the consent of the parties, a main hearing in simplified form

---

458. RB 43:1. Postponement of the action is elaborated upon in paras 505 et seq. *infra*.
459. *Ibid.*, p. 131.
460. Prop. 2004/05:131, p. 147.

may be held in immediate conjunction with the preparation if the appropriate resolution of the controversy appears obvious to the court.[461] The controversy is obvious when it is clear that the circumstances alleged by the plaintiff will not be accepted by the court, as well as when the defendant's opposition is clearly unfounded.[462]

376. If the oral preparation of the case has been held by telephone, a hearing in simplified form may also be held by telephone in immediate conjunction with the preparation. Videoconference is another option, *see supra* paragraph 350. If some evidence has been sound and video-recorded earlier, it may be presented in this way during the simplified main hearing.

377. At a main hearing in simplified form, all the attendant circumstances at the session when the preparatory hearing was concluded shall be considered to have occurred at the main hearing, without the need to be repeated at the latter.

378. A main hearing in simplified form is meant to be used in cases that do not require comprehensive investigations. The court decides at its discretion if this mode of proceeding is adequate.

6. Ordinary Main Hearing

379. The court shall direct the parties to appear at the main hearing in person if their presence can be assumed to be of importance to the investigation.[463] In general, their personal presence is more important during the main hearing than during the preparation, since it might be necessary to hear them when evidence is taken.

380. Three stages are included in the main hearing: the opening presentation of the facts in dispute, proof taking and summation.[464] The opening presentation is commenced by the plaintiff, who states the circumstances, which support his claim. After that, the defendant shall indicate whether he consents to or opposes the plaintiff's explanation of these circumstances. Furthermore, the parties, each in turn, present their allegations and respond to the allegations of the opposing party, so that it becomes clear which issues are disputed. If, for example, the defendant wants to make an objection to a point of law or allege a counter-fact, he may do so. The plaintiff can in turn, deny the exception, make an objection to a point of law, or maintain his version of the events. Subsequent statements according to this scheme might be necessary in complicated cases.

381. The opening presentation of the facts in dispute should be based on a legal analysis of the facts presented and should, therefore, be handled by the attorneys.

461. RB 42:20 para. 2.
462. NJA II 1943, p. 534.
463. RB 11:5 para. 1.
464. RB 43:7–9.

However, if the parties are present in person, there might be reasons for letting them state their opinions at this stage.[465] It is important that the parties perform the opening presentation with care in order not to miss any legal fact of relevance.

382. It is also important that the division of the main hearing in these three stages is upheld. During the opening presentation, it might, however, be appropriate to read written documents aloud. However, the parties should never state the content of oral evidence which will be presented later, since the court thereby might adopt a preconceived view on the evidentiary issues.[466] It is sometimes an advantage to touch upon the questions of law even in the opening presentation, since reference to a legal rule is sometimes the best way to clarify the meaning of a legal fact.[467]

383. Since the hearing shall be oral, the parties are not permitted to read aloud their opening presentation. However, they may use short notes as memoranda and may also read from papers if it would assist the understanding of a statement or in some other way help the proceedings.[468] However, reading from notes has become more and more unusual. Today, the plaintiff usually uses PowerPoint to present his or her case, at least if the case is more complicated. This technique makes it easier for the court and the public to follow the opening presentation. Insert after the last sentence: As mentioned in paragraph 376 *supra*, a new rule was introduced in 2005 which allows the parties to refer to documents in the case.

384. The taking of evidence will be explained in Part VII. Some short remarks concerning the order in which the evidence should be presented will, however, be put forward here. If a party is to be heard for evidential purposes regarding a particular circumstance in the case, such an examination should be held prior to the taking of witness testimony concerning the circumstance in question.[469] The reason for this is that the party shall not be able to adjust his statements to the testimonies in the case. Documentary evidence shall have been submitted during the preparation. Such evidence should be read aloud in those parts where it has evidentiary value.

385. If both parties want to present witnesses in favour and against the same evidentiary theme, the party alleging the circumstance to be proved shall present his witnesses first, and thereafter the adversary shall present his witnesses. It might be necessary to hear the witnesses against each other. In such cases the court ought to be cautious in permitting one of them to leave after testifying.[470]

386. After the evidence has been presented, the parties may state what they regard as necessary for the summation of their positions.[471] The summation shall be

465. Ekelöf, Edelstam & Pauli, *Rättegång V*, 83.
466. *Ibid.*
467. *Ibid.*, 83.
468. *See* paras 76 and 352 *supra*.
469. RB 43:8 para. 2.
470. Ekelöf, Edelstam & Pauli, *Rättegång V*, 89.
471. RB 43:9 para. 1.

performed in a free oral speech and can embrace evidentiary issues as well as issues concerning the application of law. The summation presupposes that the parties analyse the problems in the case with care. In respect to questions of law, the parties can allege legal rules, precedent cases and comments on the doctrine. Although the court examines evidentiary and legal issues on its own motion, a skilful summation might focus the court's attention on the hard issues and, therefore, be of importance. The summation is commenced by the plaintiff and is usually concluded by the defendant. In complicated cases, the parties might want to speak several times. Procedural guidance might occur during the summation.

C. Judgment

1. Deliberation

387. Before rendering a judgment, the court shall meet to deliberate.[472] The court is free to decide about the arrangement of the deliberation. When a main hearing has been held, deliberation shall take place either on the same day or on the next working weekday. The reason for this is that the impressions from the main hearing should be as fresh as possible.[473] The main rule is that the judgment shall be read out in open court prior to adjournment. It is thereby sufficient if the reasoning in support of the judgment and the ultimate order is read. If a dissenting opinion has been expressed, it shall also be notified to the parties. However, even if this is the main rule the court, in simple cases only, will deliver a judgment immediately after the main hearing.

388. When the nature of the case is such that a considerable period is required for the determination and composition of the judgment, the court may defer its pronouncement. However, unless there is an extraordinary obstacle, the judgment shall be set out in writing and pronounced within two weeks of conclusion of the main hearing. Such obstacles can be present if the case is very large and complicated.[474] The Code does not contain any maximum permitted length for an adjournment when extraordinary obstacles exist, but it has been said that the time limit of two weeks should not be extended for more than one or two weeks.[475] The court shall always notify the parties when and how the judgment will be pronounced.

389. The rules stated above concerning deliberation and pronouncement of the judgment shall apply to actions finally adjudicated at a preparatory hearing.[476] If a case is decided on the merits without a main hearing, there are no time limits regarding deliberation and pronouncement in national law.

---

472. RB 17:9 para. 1.
473. NJA II 1943, 214.
474. RB 17:9 para. 2, Gärde et al., *supra*, 189.
475. JO 1966, p. 218 and 1971, p. 21.
476. *See* RB 42:18.

390. If there are dissenting opinions at the court's deliberation, voting shall take place if the members of the court cannot agree.[477] The members of the court shall at that time state their opinions, starting with the judge who has presided at the preparation of the case, followed by the judges in order of seniority. Each member of the court shall state the grounds upon which he bases his opinion. The content of the voting rules will be explained in the following sections.

391. The court shall vote separately upon procedural issues.

392. The general rule concerning the disputed subject matter is that the court shall vote once about all matters related to it. However, this rule has many important exceptions.[478] If there are several claims in an action, the court shall vote separately upon each claim. It shall also vote separately on a debt asserted as a set-off defence. However, sometimes the court must also vote separately in a single action. This presupposes that there are divergent opinions within the court on separate issues of fact, each of which may bear directly upon the outcome of a claim. Such issues shall be allocated for separate voting to the extent required by the nature of the matter in dispute. An example of the application of this rule is where the defendant in a case involving a loan agreement alleges, in the first place, that the period of limitation has run out and second, that the loan agreement is not valid because of fraud. In such a case, each issue can be voted on separately. Thus, the rule does not mean that the court votes separately about the conclusions, but about the reasons for the conclusions. It, therefore, becomes possible to use the capacity and competence of the court in the optimal way.[479] In this respect, it must be observed that a member of the court who has been outvoted on a particular issue is obliged to participate in subsequent voting, accepting as a premise thereof the position of the majority on the issue on which he dissented.

393. The vote of the majority shall prevail. In the event of a tie, the chairman's vote is decisive. However, when voting separately about permission to grant review in a higher court, approval of one member will be decisive on the matter.[480]

394. If there are more than two opinions, none of which prevails pursuant to the rule stated above, and the issue concerns a monetary demand or any other quantitative demand for relief, the votes for the highest amount shall be counted with the votes for the next highest amount and, if necessary, the counting shall continue on the same basis until a determination with the required support is reached; otherwise, the opinion obtaining the most votes or, when two or more opinions have an equal number of votes, the opinion supported by the most senior member among those voting for one of the opinions shall prevail.[481]

477. RB 16:1.
478. *See* RB 16:2.
479. NJA II 1943, p. 194.
480. RB 16:3.
481. RB 16:4.

395. When the rules concerning counting of votes are applied, the votes are counted with respect to similarity in conclusions without reference to the reasons supporting those conclusions. If different conclusions are asserted regarding the legal issue, 16:3 of the Code applies analogously, in which case the court will base its judgment on the votes deciding the outcome.

2. Different Sorts of Judgment

396. The different types of judgment that exist correspond to some extent to the different types of claims that can be instituted in an action. A performance or a declaratory claim results – if approved – in a judgment on respective performance or declaration. Besides these two types of judgments, a third has been recognized, constitutive judgments, which obviously correspond to constitutive claims.[482] Sometimes constitutive judgments are divided into sub-groups, referring to the actual change of the legal relationship the plaintiff seeks to accomplish. However, it seems impractical and of doubtful value to divide judgments into different divisions with respect to the content of the final order. A more simple, and for most purposes sufficient division, is to differentiate only between performatory and declaratory judgments, distinguished from one another by the element of executability.[483]

397. According to the Code, two kinds of separate judgments are possible in an action. These are part judgment (*deldom*) and intermediate judgment (*mellandom*).

398. Part judgment may be entered when several claims amenable to severance are joined in a single action.[484] The court may enter a judgment upon any of the claims separately, although the processing of the remaining claims has not been terminated. The advantage of part judgment is that the parties and the court can obtain a better overview over the procedural material, which benefits the evaluation of evidence and, in addition, makes it possible for the entitled party to get an execution title immediately.[485] A part judgment can be entered not only in a complete case but also in a part of a case, if this part has been conceded. This is true even if the defendant has asserted a set-off defence on a smaller amount than the main claim.[486] However, a main debt claim and a debt asserted by the defendant by way of set-off must be adjudicated simultaneously. The reason for this is that the defendant would otherwise risk losing his counter-claim if the plaintiff subsequently becomes bankrupt.

399. According to the prevailing opinion, the order in which one or several claims are presented should be solved in accordance with the criteria defining the

---

482. *See* para. 242 *supra*.
483. Ekelöf, *Rättegång II*, 122. Cf. KRB 13:4.
484. RB 17:4.
485. Ekelöf, Edelstam & Pauli, *Rättegång V*, 230.
486. NJA II 1943, p. 306.

identity of the subject matter.[487] The meaning of the prerequisite 'claims amenable to severance' is either that the different claims are quite independent of each other or – if there are any mutual circumstances – those are not disputed.[488] If a mutual circumstance is disputed, nothing will be gained by a part judgment as far as procedural costs, since the same evidence is relevant and thus must be presented again.

400. It is possible for the court to schedule a special preparation session and a special main hearing for issues that can be decided through a part judgment.[489] Default judgment is possible, as well as judgment without trial in certain cases.[490] Appeal from a part judgment (which has the same legal consequences as an ordinary judgment) follows the normal rules.

401. While an independent section of the case is decided through a part judgment, an intermediate judgment refers to an issue of relevance for the rest of the case.[491] Intermediate judgment is possible in three situations:

(1) the adjudication of a particular claim depends upon the outcome of another claim, joined in the same action;
(2) there are several circumstances in respect of the same claim, each of which is of direct significance for the outcome, and separate adjudication is found to be appropriate in view of the nature of the inquiry; and
(3) an issue primarily of relevance for the application of the law is of direct significance for the outcome.

402. A mutual condition for all these situations is that an intermediate judgment is found to be appropriate with respect to the inquiry, which means that the judgment in question will benefit the procedural costs. This purpose will be reached if the whole case can finally be solved through adjudication of a separate issue in it. The court decides ex officio if an intermediate judgment should be rendered. However, this does not mean that the parties are not heard.

403. The first situation in which an intermediate judgment is possible is when a declaratory claim is joined with a performance claim. For example, a landlord asks the court to declare that a tenancy agreement is valid and, in addition, claims that the tenant shall be obliged to pay the due rent.[492] In the second situation mentioned above, it is possible to render an intermediate judgment upon a legal fact. The legal fact can concern cumulative or alternative grounds alleged by the plaintiff, or cumulative or alternative objections alleged by the defendant.[493] For example, the plaintiff alleges in the first place that no binding contract has been entered between him and the opposing party, and, second, that the contract, if deemed to be entered, is

487. Cf. paras 306 *supra* and 421 *infra*.
488. NJA II 1943, p. 205.
489. RB 42:12 and 42:20.
490. RB 42:18.
491. RB 17:5. R. Boman, *Deldom* 10 (1975).
492. NJA II 1943, p. 207.
493. Concerning these notions, *see* paras 414–415 *infra*.

not valid because of fraud. In such a situation, the court can render an intermediate judgment on either of these legal facts, if it believes that the case thereby will finally be settled. The possibility to enter an intermediate judgment on an issue mainly concerning the application of law was introduced in 1990.[494] Examples of such questions are whether a contract should be regarded as a purchase contract, which national law should be applied to a certain legal relation, and whether a particular declaration of intent constitutes a binding offer pursuant to the law on contract.[495]

404. It is also possible to schedule a special preparation session and a special main hearing for intermediate judgments. Default judgment is also possible. However, if the intermediate judgment mainly concerns a question of application of the law, the difference between ordinary judgments will be small.[496] An intermediate judgment pursuant to points (2) and (3) above only has intraprocedural binding force; thus, the res judicata effect will be limited to the case in which it has been rendered.

405. Finally, it should be mentioned that if the parties agree upon a settlement of the disputed matter and they both request it, the court shall confirm their settlement agreement by giving a judgment.[497] Such a judgment has the same legal consequences as an ordinary judgment.

3. Formal Aspects of the Judgment

406. A judgment shall be in writing. In separate sections, the court shall specify the court, time and place of pronouncement of the judgment, the parties and their attorneys or assistants, the ultimate order of the court, the parties' demands in support of the judgment, the circumstances upon which they are founded and the reasoning in support of the judgment, including a statement of what has been proved in the action. Moreover, a judgment rendered by an appellate court shall, to the extent necessary, describe the judgment of the lower court. If a party appeals against a judgment or apply for re-opening of a default judgment, the judgment shall, in addition, state the steps he must take to do so.[498]

407. In order to decide the extension of res judicata and to make performance possible, it is important that the final order clearly states if the judgment relates to a performance claim, to a declaratory claim, or to both.[499] How comprehensive the recital should be is, to some extent, unclear. However, it is beyond any doubt that claims and legal facts must be stated. With respect to objections on points of law

494. As far as the distinction between questions of fact and questions of law are concerned, *see* B. Lindell, *Sakfrågor och rättsfrågor* Chs. 1 and 10 (1987).
495. Prop. 1989/90:71, p. 43.
496. KRB 17:21.
497. RB 17:6.
498. RB 17:7.
499. Gärde et al., *supra*, 186.

and denials, it has, however, been maintained that these need not be mentioned.[500] The rationale behind the rule regarding the content of a judgment is to make the reasoning supporting the judgment easier to understand by setting out the framework of the dispute. Therefore, it may be justified to present a description of denials and demurrers if the case essentially concerns such issues.

408. The reasons supporting the judgment should be detailed, describing issues concerning the evidence in the case, as well as issues relating to the application of law. Such a particularization is of importance for legal security, for assisting the judge in structuring his own thoughts, and for a party who wishes to appeal. In addition, it is of importance for the appellate court in order to examine if the judgment is correct.[501] It is obvious that these arguments are of particular relevance if the case is complicated.

409. The court must state that not only the legal and evidentiary facts deemed to be proved, but it must also account for the evaluation of evidence. With respect to the application of the law, it is not enough that the court states the relevant legal rules; if the court has interpreted the law extensively or restrictively, or has applied a rule analogously, the reasons for this should be stated if they are not obvious.[502]

4. Res Judicata

410. Judgments are given binding force to secure a level of security in society with regard to economic and other consequential decisions people make, without fear of economic or other losses. Hence, the rule on res judicata obtains its ultimate legitimacy from the benefits which it bestows upon society. The principle of irrevocability does not imply whether there are any criteria for determining when a judgment has binding force, but legitimates a decision based on other criteria.[503]

411. The binding force of a judgment comes into being when the judgment is no longer open to attack by appeal or other ordinary means. It attaches only to the judgment order and not to the grounds of decision.

412. There are two situations in which the effects of res judicata appear. First, a prior judgment can be used as the basis for a subsequent action. For example, suppose that *A* has won a case against *B* concerning title to land. After this judgment is no longer open to attack, *B* institutes an action against *A*, claiming indemnity,

500. *See* KRB 17:23 and Ekelöf, Bylund & Edelstam, *Rättegång III*, 176. *See also* NJA 1985, p. 410 and Lindell, *Civilprocessen*, 405.
501. NJA II 1943, p. 211.
502. Pursuant to RB 17:8 RB, it is possible to render a judgment in simplified form if the case is uncomplicated. It is thereby presupposed that it is a default judgment or a judgment where the defendant has consented to the claim, or a judgment where an appellate court simply confirms a judgment rendered by a lower court. However, according to KRB, this rule is obsolete, since it is possible to render a simplified judgment pursuant to RB 17:7.
503. Lindell, *Processuell preklusion*, 50.

alleging that he is the owner of the land. In cases like this, the first judgment is said to have a substantive effect on the second action. Since the claim in the second action is not the same as that in the first, the court shall judge the latter on its merit, but not approve the claim.[504] Secondly, the same controversy already resolved by the judgment is renewed between the same parties. The former judgment then constitutes a procedural hindrance, and the court shall dismiss the second action. This is sometimes called the negative effect of res judicata.[505] The court shall, ex officio, observe the negative as well as the substantive effect of res judicata.[506]

413. It should be emphasized that there is a relationship between the possibilities for the plaintiff to allege new circumstances in support for his claim and the extension of the res judicata effect. The plaintiff may allege new circumstances in support of his claim as long he does not change the subject matter in dispute.[507] This means that the following question ought to be posed when deciding whether a new circumstance, alleged by the plaintiff, should be allowed or not: supposing the court renders a judgment against the plaintiff, would it then be possible for him to institute a new action on the same claim and get this new action tried? If the answer is no, the new action in question ought to be tried with the original action; otherwise it will be excluded from all adjudication.[508] This point will be elaborated upon in the following sections, since it is of great importance in order to understand the Swedish concept of res judicata.

414. The plaintiff can change his claim in different ways. He can, for example, allege competing grounds in support of his claim. Significant for those is that the defendant cannot be obliged to perform according to both.[509] Competing grounds are either cumulative or alternative.[510] In the former case, they can exist beside each other, while in the latter case the existence of one of them excludes the other. An example of cumulative grounds is the allegations of formal defects and mental illness, as grounds for the invalidity of a will.[511] Allegations of compulsion and fraud are examples of alternative grounds for a claim; a contract cannot at the same time have been induced by fraud as well as by compulsion.[512]

415. Claims can also be cumulative or alternative. Two claims can be of such a nature that they cannot be fulfilled alongside each other, in which case they can be

---

504. Ekelöf, Edelstam & Pauli, *Rättegång III*, 230, 421.
505. *Ibid.*, 194.
506. *Ibid.*, 113.
507. However, such circumstances can be precluded pursuant to RB 42:15, RB 42:15a, 43:10, 50:25 para. 3 or 55:13. Concerning these rules, *see* paras 266 et seq. *supra* and Lindell, *Processuell preklusion*, 46 et seq.
508. *See* Olivecrona, *Rätt och dom*, 317, I. Agge, *Bidrag till läran om civildomens rättskraft* 138 (1932) and U. Jacobsson, *Argumentation i civilprocessen*, 349 et seq. in *Festskrift till L. Welamson* (1988). The principle that there is an immediate relation between RB 13:3 para. 3, p. 2 and 17:11 para. 1 is laid down in NJA 1984, p. 733.
509. P.O. Ekelöf, *Processuella grundbegrepp* 106 (1956).
510. *Ibid.*, 107.
511. *Ibid.*
512. *Ibid.*

said to be alternative. For example, a purchaser requests that the court cancel a purchase or alternatively reduce the claimed purchase amount. Two claims can instead refer to two legal consequences both of which are possible to perform; for example, a landlord brings a claim for indemnity and, in addition, requests that the tenant be obliged to move out of the apartment.[513]

416. There are three possible relationships between the provisions on amendments of a claim and the provisions on res judicata:[514]

(1) the possibilities of amending the claim are equal to the extension of res judicata, which means that the binding force of a judgment includes all amendments permitted pursuant to 13:3 of the Code, no more and no less, and irrespective of whether the amendments have actually taken place or not;
(2) the possibilities of amending the claim are smaller than the extension of res judicata, which means that the binding force of a judgment includes more than those amendments permitted pursuant to 13:3; and
(3) the possibilities of amending the claim are greater than the extension of res judicata, which means that during a pending action it is possible to make such amendments which are not included in the binding force of a judgment.

417. As mentioned above, alternative number (1) above is deemed relevant for the grounds supporting the claim. However, what are the criteria used to identify the subject matter? This issue has been touched upon and is elaborated upon below.[515]

418. According to Olivecrona, the expression 'subject-matter' in 13:3 paragraph 3 and 17:11 paragraph 1 of the Code refers to both the claim and the alleged circumstances. In doing so, he distinguishes between the historical content of the former rule and the meaning it should be given for practical use.[516] With regard to changes in the grounds of a claim, Olivecrona maintains that the court shall compare the actual circumstances alleged in the first action with those alleged in the second action. If the latter, compared to those alleged in the first action, represent an independent event, the court should not dismiss the action.[517]

419. Ekelöf, however, relates the identity of the subject matter to the legal consequences of the alleged circumstances, that is to say, he stresses the content of the norm rather than the actual circumstances. Thus, if new grounds to support the claim are alleged, but the claim is unchanged or changes only in respect to quantity, the subject matter always remains the same. If, for example, the plaintiff has claimed in the summons that the court should declare a will invalid, he may, according to these

513. *Ibid.*, 109 f.
514. Lindell, *Processuell preklusion*, 51.
515. *See* paras 306 and 399 *supra*.
516. Olivecrona, *Rätt och dom*, 260 et seq.
517. *Ibid.*, 320 et seq. This means that the time and place for the event must have changed. In TJFF 1954, *supra*, 332 Olivecrona speaks about essential changes of the alleged circumstances. Since this work is older it is likely that he has modified his view.

criteria, subsequently alternatively allege that the will is invalid because of the testator's mental illness.[518] However, it should be observed that a comparison between two events can hardly take place without influence from the content of the rule(s) in question, since the rules determine which events are to be compared. In addition, legal terms are often used when describing an event.[519] This implies that it cannot be maintained that Olivecrona only compares facts, but to some extent, also the legal rules in question.

420. Ekelöfs proposal on how to solve issues of res judicata is easier to apply than Olivecrona's, since, in general, it is easier to determine whether the legal consequence has changed in a qualitative way than to determine whether a new event, alleged by the plaintiff, is independent from the one examined and adjudicated upon in the first action.[520] However, in most cases Olivecrona's and Ekelöf's criteria lead to the same result.[521] It is stated in NJA 1994 p. 24 and NJA 1995 p. 610 that a purchaser of real estate must claim cancel of the purchase or reduction of the purchase amount in the same action. Thus, although these legal consequences are qualitatively different they must be brought in the same proceedings. In addition, it is stated in NJA 1999 p. 520 that res judicata as a hinder for litigation should be limited to claims with the same legal consequence or to a legal consequence which is alternative and equal from an economic point of view.

421. As far as claims are concerned, a distinction must be made with respect to the instance at which an additional claim is asserted. In the district court, alternative number (3) above is relevant, that is to say that the possibilities for the plaintiff to amend his claim are larger than the extension of res judicata. It is thus possible for him either to assert an additional claim or to institute a new action. This means, *inter alia*, that a person who has been injured in a traffic accident in the first action can institute claims regarding, for example, loss of income and expenses for medical care (which claims then will be joined in a single action), but if he wishes, he can separate these claims into two single actions.

---

518. Ekelöf, Bylund & Edelstam, *Rättegång III*, 198. Both Ekelöf and Olivecrona argue that statements in the preparatory legislative works to the Code support their opinions. These statements (*see* SOU 1938:44, s. 186, cf. SOU 1926:33) seem to support rather Olivecrona than Ekelöf, but *see* Ekelöf, *Yrkandet talan och saken*, SvJT 521–546 (1959) where he elaborates his view in detail.
519. Lindell, *Sakfrågor och rättsfrågor*, 35 et seq. and 364 et seq.
520. There is not a single precedent case after 1948 where HD has applied RB 13:3 para. 3, p. 2 in a dispositive case and thereby resolved the issue whether a new legal fact can change the subject-matter. Amongst the precedent cases NJA 1959, p. 658 appears to deal with an independent event, which thus was not deemed to change the subject-matter in dispute. In this case, objections were raised against the validity of a will. The plaintiff alleged that the testator had written the will under the influence of mental sickness. After a judgment rendered against him at the district court, he appealed and then also alleged that the will – which the testator had torn to pieces and thereafter repaired – had been withdrawn. *See* Lindell, *Processuell preklusion*, 47. However, there are some cases in which the binding force of a judgment has not been regarded to preclude all grounds, but these cases are rather old. *See also* NJA 1977, p. 618.
521. KRB 13:40.

422. Additional claims are, in principle, not permitted in an appellate court. The only exception from this prohibition is the one stated in 13:3 paragraph 1 p. 1.[522] If the plaintiff wishes to extend his claim regarding the same subject matter, and thereby does not allege a new circumstance that occurred or became known to him during the proceedings the claim has been dismissed in practice.[523] This is an example of alternative (2) above, where the possibilities of amending the claim are smaller than the extension of res judicata. Fortunately, it also seems to be the one and only example of such a situation.[524]

423. If the plaintiff has instituted a declaratory claim concerning payment of a debt, and the court renders a judgment against him and, in a second action, he institutes a performance claim regarding the same debt, the court shall dismiss the action because of res judicata. If, however, the sequence between the actions is reversed, so that the plaintiff in the first action institutes a performance claim on payment of a debt – which the court does not approve – and thereafter institutes a declaratory claim on the issue, the court shall adjudicate upon the merits and render a judgment against him because of the substantive effect of the first judgment. It is also possible that the plaintiff institutes an action on payment which the court approves and that the defendant later institutes a declaratory claim that he is not obliged to pay. In such a case, the court shall dismiss the action because of a procedural hindrance. Thus, in this case a judgment on performance has the same binding force as a declaratory judgment and consequently, the symmetry with the reverse situation is not complete.[525]

424. A judgment has binding force to the extent that the court has examined a debt obligation as a set-off.[526] A defendant who has a counter-claim, which is possible to use as a set-off defence, is not obliged to allege it as a defence, but if he does so the judgment has binding force to the extent that the examination includes the set-off. Hence, if the counter-claim amounts to a higher sum than the main claim and the set-off defence is approved, the binding force of the judgment only extends to that part of the counter-claim that covers the main claim.[527] If, however, still presupposing that the counter-claim amounts to a higher sum than the main claim, the

---

522. *See* para. 291 *supra.*

523. Ekelöf, *Rättegång II*, 140. If the plaintiff in the district court has claimed that a purchase of real estate shall be cancelled and the claim is not approved, he probably cannot in the appellate court make a claim of reduction of the purchase amount, unless he can allege a new legal circumstance (Lindell, *Civilprocessen*, 242).

524. Ekelöf argues that it ought to be possible for the plaintiff to extend his claim in an appellate court, if it refers to the same subject-matter, even in such cases where he does not allege a new legal circumstance relevant to RB 13:3 para. 1, p. 1. Suppose that the plaintiff by an oversight has claimed SEK 20,000 instead of the SEK 25,000, to which he is entitled. Making a mistake in counting is not a substantial legal fact and, consequently, RB 13:3 para. 1, p. 1 does not apply, according to its wording. The rule ought to apply analogously in these circumstances; *see* Lindell, *Processuell prekusion*, 52 note 105.

525. KRB 17:41 and S. Larsson, *Rättskraftslärans identitetsterminologi*, TfR 404–427 (1974).

526. RB 17:11 para. 2.

527. If the defendant brings a counter-claim the court will oblige the plaintiff to pay the excess amount.

set-off defence is not approved, in part or total, the court has examined the counter-claim in its entire amount, in which case the binding force of the judgment comprises the totality of it. This principle also applies if the set-off defence consists of several counter-claims. Thus, if the defendant asserts a set-off defence he risks losing everything. However, if the binding force of a judgment did not have this extensive scope, the defendant would be able to litigate the counter-claim several times, which would be unjust with respect to the plaintiff.[528]

425. Concerning the res judicata effect with regard to a third person standing outside of the litigation, the general rule is that he is not affected. This rule, which cannot be found in the Code, is linked to the parties' possibilities of controlling the disputed subject according to civil law at the time of the action; if the parties are not permitted to make agreements according to civil law affecting the legal position of a third party at the time for the action, then a judgment rendered by the court cannot have this effect.[529] Consequently, if *A* has transferred personal property to *B* before an action between *A* and *C* concerning the title to the property, a judgment in that action has no binding force in respect to *B* in a later action between him and *A* on the same subject-matter. If, however, the transfer in question has occurred during or after the pending action between *A* and *C*, the judgment also has binding force in respect to *B*, even though *B* might have been in good faith and thereby would have been entitled to keep the property. There are, however, certain exceptions to this general principle; for example, judgments regarding an individual's civil status in family law disputes have full binding force on anyone.[530] In addition, several judgments concerning environmental cases and cases related to real estate construction also have res judicata effect on everyone.

426. A judgment in which the court confirms a settlement between the parties has the same binding force as an ordinary judgment. However, such a judgment does not prevent a party from instituting an action claiming that the settlement is invalid.[531] As an alternative, a party can apply for re-opening of the case (*resning*); however, this is an extraordinary remedy.[532]

427. If the court dismisses an action because of a procedural hindrance, such a decision has, in principle, the same binding force as a judgment against the plaintiff, presupposing that the procedural hindrance and the disputed subject matter are the same in a new action.[533] Decisions by which the court strikes the case from the agenda have no binding force. Similarly, decisions during the trial have no res judicata effect, for example, a decision to joinder or separate actions, to preclude new circumstances or evidence or direct a party to appear in person.

528. SOU 1938:44, p. 224.
529. Ekelöf, Bylund & Edelstam, *Rättegång III*, 231.
530. *Ibid.*, 233.
531. NJA 1975, 507.
532. NJA 1974, 295.
533. Lindblom, *Processhinder*, 116 et seq. Cf. NJA 1982, p. 210.

428. The meaning of the concept 'subject-matter' is also crucial when deciding whether *lis pendens* is present. In order for *lis pendens* to exist, it is necessary that the first action is pending when the second action is instituted.[534] In addition, an earlier instituted and still-pending action constitutes *lis pendens* under the same conditions as a judgment rendered in this action would have led to dismissal of the action instituted later because of res judicata.[535]

429. Of great importance, apart from its binding force, are the evidentiary effects of a judgment. If the court earlier has adjudicated a dispute upon its merits and examined the facts in the case, the probability for this adjudication to be correct is great. Thus, if the plaintiff in action number (1) has claimed compensation because of a car accident caused by the defendant, and in action number (2) claims compensation for other damages caused by the accident in question, the presumption is that the investigation presented in the first action correctly describes how the accident occurred. The strength of this presumption depends on the circumstances in each individual case and is considered after a free evaluation of all relevant evidence.[536]

430. The existence of a *factum superveniens* and the rules on re-opening concerning relief for a substantive defect break through the binding force of a judgment.[537] A *factum superveniens*, that is to say a subsequent fact, is a circumstance which could not be tried in the first action.[538] If the circumstance occurred or became known after the conclusion of the proceedings, it is regarded as new.[539] The reason why a *factum superveniens* breaks through the binding force of a judgment is that it otherwise could constrain the possibilities for the parties to undertake dispositions according to civil law.[540] This tenet is obvious, if, for example, *A* has won over *B* in a dispute concerning the title to land, *A* might thereafter transfer the land property to *B*, in which case it must be possible to adjudicate upon a new dispute between *A* and *B* concerning the title to this land.

431. The relevance of a *factum superveniens* depends on which legal facts that have been alleged to support the final order of the judgment in the former action; a *factum superveniens* can support a new action only if it, together with the legal facts alleged in the first action, could have affected the outcome of the action.[541] In addition, it must be essential.[542] An evidentiary fact cannot be a *factum superveniens*.[543]

---

534. RB 13:6. *See, e.g.*, NJA 1997, p. 390 and 1999, p. 520.
535. Lindell, *Civilprocessen*, 365.
536. Gärde et al., *supra*, 196.
537. Relief for substantive defect is described in paras 485–488 *infra*.
538. Agge, *supra*, 283 and Lindell, *Civilprocessen*, 367 et seq.
539. Agge, *supra*, 285 and T. Eckhoff, *Rättskraft* 113 (1945). It is probably not an indispensable requirement that the circumstance is subsequent. Sometimes it might be sufficient that the knowledge is subsequent; *see* Lindell, *Processuell preklusion*, 76.
540. Lindell, *Civilprocessen*, 368.
541. *Ibid.*, 126.
542. Lindell, *Processuell preklusion*, 76.
543. Agge, *supra*, 285; Eckhoff, *supra*, 112.

5. Interpretation, Rectification and Supplementation of Judgments

432. The Swedish commentaries hardly devote any attention to the question of how to interpret judgments. However, it has been maintained that if it is doubtful how far the binding force of a judgment reaches, one should assume the smaller instead of the larger scope.[544] Furthermore, it has been argued that judgments, to a greater extent than contracts, should be interpreted in an objective way, and that the decisive factor should not be what the court meant, but the meaning of the judgment in respect to the relevant rules in force and their purpose.[545]

433. The court can rectify a judgment or an order if it, after complaint or otherwise, finds it evidently incorrect owing to an error in transcription, calculation or any similar oversight, made by the court or someone else.[546] In principle, everything that the court has adjudicated upon can be rectified, if it has been wrongly expressed in the judgment, irrespective of whether the judgment can be appealed or not. This means, *inter alia*, that the possibility of rectification is not open if the court has overseen a rule or a precedent case of importance to the outcome.

434. There is also a possibility for the court to supplement a judgment if it has accidentally failed to render a decision, which should have been pronounced simultaneously with the judgment or final order. Such a supplement, which must take place within six months after the expiration of the time to appeal the judgment, can for example, refer to a provisional measure or a matter concerning legal costs. If the court has forgotten to examine a question, supplementing is not permitted.

435. Before the court makes a decision about rectifying or supplementing, it must afford the parties an opportunity to be heard, if it is not obvious that this is unnecessary. A rectification or supplement shall, if possible, be entered directly upon the original judgment or order.

§2. Default Judgments

436. Chapter 44 of the Code deals with the consequences if one or both of the parties is or are absent. It draws a distinction between dispositive and non-dispositive cases.

437. A judgment in a dispositive case rendered because of the absence of either of the parties is called a default judgment. In Sweden, this procedural construction has been shown to be the most effective sanction against a party who refuses to appear at a session. The consequence of not appearing is that the procedural competence of a party will be precluded. The failure to appear is per se an essential legal

544. Kallenberg, *supra*, 1138.
545. Lindell, *Civilprocessen*, 369.
546. RB 17:15.

fact, causing the default judgment.[547] One disadvantage of other possible sanctions is that they will not advance the proceedings.[548] If a party appears before the trial is concluded, that is to say while the adversary and other procedural subjects are still present, he can avoid a default judgment provided that the case has not been handed over to the court for pronouncement of judgment.[549]

438. Failure to appear means that the party, neither in person nor represented by an attorney, attends a session. If a party has been directed to personally appear under penalty of a fine, but is represented by an attorney, the court shall impose the fine on him. An alternative is to conclude the preparation of the action or to adjudicate it upon its merits.[550]

439. In general, it is the defendant who does not appear.[551] There are several possible reasons for this, for example, he might have realized that the plaintiff has the law on his side, in which case a default judgment rapidly and cheaply ends a trial on a matter not in dispute. It is also possible that the defendant tries to delay the proceedings, in which case a default judgment ends this attempt. If the absent party should be the plaintiff, it is obvious that he has not proved the grounds for his action, which motivates a default judgment rendered against him.[552] In addition, a defendant who has appeared has a justified claim to obtain a judgment in the action, since otherwise the plaintiff, by not appearing, would be allowed to institute a new action on the same subject matter, which would violate the defendant's right to a judgment pursuant to 13:5 of the Code.[553]

440. In an action for payment instituted by summons, the normal procedure is that the defendant is directed to present a written answer, or a default judgment might be entered against him.[554] The party must have been served the directive in such time that he could comply with it.[555] A default judgment shall not be rendered against a party who can prove a legal excuse.[556]

441. The rule in question is optional, although the court normally directs the defendant to present an answer upon penalty of a default judgment being entered against him. An exception from this sanction should be made if the defendant probably lacks the ability to express his standpoint in writing or if the plaintiff expressly

---

547. Olivecrona, *Rätt och dom*, 180.
548. Lindell, *Civilprocessen*, 322 et seq.
549. NJA II 1943, p. 552.
550. RB 44:6.
551. If the defendant does not appear, the court on its own motion shall examine whether he has been sued in the right court, *see* RB 10:18.
552. Olivecrona, *Rätt och dom*, 181.
553. Concerning RB 13:5, *see* paras 500–503 *infra*. In addition, a passive plaintiff may be directed to state if he withholds his action, facing the risk of a default judgment if he does not reply before a certain date.
554. *See also* para. 341 *supra*.
555. RB 32:1.
556. RB 32:8. *See* para. 223 *supra*.

requests that this sanction shall not be a part of the order.[557] The defendant shall be deemed to have complied with an order to present a written answer if he has clarified his attitude to the plaintiff's claim and stated reasons that might be of importance for the disputed subject matter.[558] However, the defendant is not required to state his opinion in detail and nor should the court examine the truthfulness of the defendant's statement.[559] The court's examination of the legal relevance in the defendant's statement should, instead, focus on the task of separating the cases where it is obvious that the defendant's objections are irrelevant from the cases where they are of legal relevance.[560]

442. If the defendant has been ordered to present a written answer with the possibility that otherwise a default judgment might be entered against him but has not complied with the order, the court may enter a default judgment against him if the plaintiff does not oppose this. Before the court enters a default judgment, the plaintiff shall be given an opportunity to assert claims for legal costs, and he can request that the action shall continue instead of a default judgment being entered. Such a request might be put forward if the plaintiff suspects that the defendant would apply for re-opening of the default judgment. If the plaintiff requests that the action continue, the court may choose between oral preparation on a subsequent date or continued exchange of written statements. The court usually calls the parties to a session for preparation.[561]

443. A party shall be directed to appear at a hearing for oral preparation with the consequence that otherwise a default judgment might be entered against him. On request of the appearing party, such a judgment shall be entered.[562] This rule applies irrespective of whether the hearing is the first one or a continued hearing for oral preparation. If a default judgment is not requested, the case shall be written-off. However, if the absent party is the defendant, the action in this case – for the same reasons stated above – may be continued for oral preparation on a subsequent date on request of the plaintiff.

444. The sanctions for not appearing at the main hearing in dispositive as well as non-dispositive cases are the same as those that apply for absenteeism from oral preparation in each respective type of case.[563]

557. Prop. 1986/87:89, p. 201.
558. RB 44:7 a. *See* NJA 1989, p. 487.
559. Prop. 1986/87:89, p. 228.
560. *Ibid.*, p. 229.
561. *Ibid.*, 227.
562. RB 44:2. *See also* para. 341 *supra*. If there are several parties on one side, the principle rule is that each of them is responsible for his absence, which means that default judgments might be entered against some – but not all – of them. If only one judgment can be entered against all, (concerning necessary joinder, *see* para. 495 *infra*) all parties must be absent in order to make a default judgment possible. An intervenor who appears on the side of a party who does not appear can prevent a default judgment only if he has the capacity of a party in the trial; *see* RB 14:11 para. 2, commented in para. 495 *infra* and NJA 1976, p. 227.
563. RB 44:4.

445. A party shall be directed to appear at a continued main hearing or face the consequence that a default judgment might be entered against him.[564] If a party does not appear, the consequence will be a default judgment if the appearing party does not request that the court try the action on its merits. In such a case, the judgment entered will be an ordinary one, open to attack through ordinary means.

446. If one or both parties fail to appear at a special hearing for the disposition of a procedural issue, the issue may nonetheless be considered and determined if the preparation is to be continued. As mentioned in paragraph 350 *supra*, a default judgment will otherwise be rendered.

447. If the plaintiff supports his claim to payment with written evidence, or on a written promise concerning some performance other than payment, the court may enter a judgment against the defendant if he does not make well-founded objections.[565] This provision is optional, since it would sometimes be unfair to enter a default judgment against the defendant; for example, he might assert a set-off defence, which is connected to the main claim.[566] However, the rule in question does not apply if the plaintiff's claim is based on a contract calling for mutual obligations and the defendant objects with respect to his obligations, if a default judgment has been previously issued, or the plaintiff opposes this. If the plaintiff does not comply with an order pursuant to RB 42:11 paragraph 2 a default judgment may be rendered against him.[567]

448. A default judgment may not be entered in a case that is non-dispositive. If the plaintiff in such a case fails to appear at an oral hearing for preparation, and he was ordered to appear with the consequence that otherwise his claim would be dismissed without prejudice, the case shall be dismissed.[568] If it is the defendant who does not appear, the court, instead of directing him to appear on sanction of a new conditional fine, may order that he be brought before the court in custody, either immediately or on the date to which the session has been adjourned. In addition, it might be possible to conclude the preparation and adjudicate the action on the merits. If both parties fail to appear at an oral hearing for preparation, the case shall be dismissed, irrespective of whether it is dispositive or non-dispositive.[569]

449. The examination, which forgoes a default judgment, is summary.[570] The judgment shall be based upon the content of the documents in the action and other circumstances that have occurred in it. If the plaintiff has not appeared at a hearing, his claim shall be dismissed on the merits, unless the defendant has accepted the claim, or it is otherwise plain that the claim is well founded, in which case it shall be accepted. A judgment by default against the defendant shall be based upon the

564. RB 44:4 para. 2.
565. RB 44:7 b para. 1. In this case, a default judgment may be entered only once.
566. Prop. 1989/90:85, p. 149.
567. RB 44:7 b para. 2.
568. RB 44:3. *See also* para. 348 *supra*.
569. RB 44:1.
570. *See* RB 44:8.

plaintiff's allegations of the circumstances in the action; to the extent that the defendant has received notice of them and that, they are not contrary to generally known matters. To the extent that the allegations are insufficient to entitle the plaintiff to the relief requested, or if the claim is otherwise ill founded, the claim shall be dismissed.

450. A default judgment must not be served by the court. A month after a default judgment has been rendered it will be binding, *see* RB 42:11 paragraph 2 and 42:12 paragraph 2.

451. A party against whom a judgment by default has been entered may apply for re-opening of the case (*återvinning*) at the court in which the action was instituted, within one month of the date on which the judgment was rendered.[571] If re-opening is not applied for, the judgment becomes immune to attack to the extent that it is against the party in default.[572]

452. An application for re-opening shall be submitted in writing. When an application for re-opening is accepted, the action, to the extent re-opening has been applied for, shall be resumed at the stage it had reached prior to the hearing at which the party failed to appear. If the party again fails to appear and a default judgment is entered against him, his right to re-open the case is forfeited.[573]

453. In respect to the choice between oral or written preparation at re-opening, oral preparation should be used if the party in his application for re-opening has stated what he should have stated in a written answer. If, however, the party, neither in his application for re-opening, nor earlier during the proceedings, has given an account of his position and the reasons supporting it, it is more appropriate to order him once again to submit a written answer under threat of a default judgment being entered against him.[574]

454. If a default judgment totally or partially has been entered against the appearing party, he may appeal it by ordinary means. If a re-opening action is written-off because of the absence of both parties, the court should declare the default judgment vacated.[575]

§3. Proceedings Without Main Hearing

455. A district court may, without a main hearing:

---

571. RB 44:9.
572. A default judgment can immediately be executed pursuant to UB 3:5. However, a party applying for re-opening at the same time can also apply for inhibition.
573. RB 44:10.
574. Prop. 1986/87:89, p. 230, *see also* NJA 1989, p. 487.
575. NJA 1987, p. 560.

(1) decide upon a case in another way than through judgment, for example, write-off and dismiss cases;
(2) enter a default judgment;
(3) enter a judgment based upon a party's consent to or renunciation of a claim;
(4) confirm a settlement agreement; and
(5) enter a judgment if a main hearing is not necessary with regard to the investigation presented and is not requested by a party.[576]

456. Point (5) of the above-stated provisions opens a possibility for the district court to adjudicate upon disputed subject matters without a main hearing. It is thereby a condition that a main hearing is not requested with regard to the investigation in the case. Of crucial importance for the application of this provision is the rule that oral evidence may be presented only at the main hearing. An exception is permitted only if proof taking outside of the main hearing is permitted.[577] Thus, if oral evidence is to be presented, an examination based plainly on the merits of written documents submitted is permitted only in cases where proof can be taken outside of the main hearing. Similarly, the necessity of viewing the *locus in quo* excludes the possibility of adjudicating without a main hearing. Adjudication on the merits after *locus in quo* is thus permitted only in cases where it is permitted to arrange *locus in quo* outside the main hearing.[578]

457. Even where oral testimony or *locus in quo* does not occur, a main hearing might be necessary with respect to the investigation of the case. An oral hearing may benefit the investigation of the case by allowing the parties to develop their arguments and pleadings. In particular, such a disposition is often needed when the parties proceed without attorneys. In addition, the parties have a right to an oral hearing pursuant to Article 6 of the European Convention on Human Rights.

458. As indicated above, the possibility to adjudicate disputed cases without a main hearing is primarily meant to be used in cases where the parties do not dispute the facts relevant to the case, but rather the application of the law to these facts. Before a judgment is entered pursuant to point (5), the parties will be allowed to summarize their positions, if they cannot already be deemed to have done that.[579] This is also true when a default judgment is entered pursuant to 44:7 of the Code or – with respect to the plaintiff – pursuant to 44:7 b of the Code.

576. RB 42:18.
577. *See* RB 36:19 described in para. 631 *infra*.
578. Concerning *locus in quo*, *see* paras 662–666 *infra*.
579. RB 42:18 para. 2.

Chapter 2. Review Proceedings

§1. Appeal

459. An ordinary civil case can be appealed from a district court to a Court of Appeal.[580] However, according to a new rule, which became effective on 1 November 2008, review dispensation is required in all civil cases and court matters.[581] Dispensation is also required for adjudication in the Supreme Court. The following discussion will start with appeal in ordinary cases, thereafter so-called small cases will be dealt with and, finally, appeal to the Supreme Court will be described.

460. A party who desires to take a regular appeal from a lower court judgment in a civil action to the Court of Appeal, shall submit an appeal petition to the lower court within three weeks of the pronouncement of the judgment.[582] With respect to an intermediate judgment pursuant to 17:5 paragraph 2 of the Code, the district court decides whether it may be appealed separately or in conjunction with the final judgment.[583] In principle, the Court of Appeal will examine an appealed judgment only if a party in the district court has appealed it. The examination of the case in the Court of Appeal comprises both questions of law and questions of fact. Although these questions are re-examined, one cannot say that the case is 'totally' reviewed. A more correct description is that the Court of Appeal checks that the judgment is correct, since the appellant has limited possibilities to present new circumstances and evidence and, in principle, he may not assert additional claims.[584]

461. In the appeal petition, the appellant shall specify:[585]

(1) the judgment appealed from; and the reasons for dispensation;
(2) the particular part of the judgment attacked and the change in the judgment he demands;
(3) the grounds for the appeal, stating the ways in which he considers the fact finding and legal conclusions of the lower court to be erroneous;
(4) the evidence upon which he relies, indicating what he intends to prove by each specified item. If new evidence and circumstances are presented in a dispositive case, the reason why these have not been presented earlier in the lower court;
(5) if he wants the Court of Appeal to hear the testimony of a witness or an expert, or of a party under affirmation of truth (who has been heard in the lower court), or that the Court of Appeal view the *locus in quo*, he shall so state in the petition, indicating the reasons therefore; and

580. However, it should be observed that the parties, pursuant to RB 49:2, can agree not to appeal a judgment rendered by the district court.
581. Prop. 2004/05:130, pp. 180 et seq.
582. RB 50:1.
583. *See* RB 49:1. With respect to certain decisions a party must give notice of appeal within one week of the pronouncement of the decision, *see* RB 49:4–6.
584. *See* para. 291 *supra*.
585. RB 50:4.

(6) whether he desires the other party to appear in person at the main hearing.

462. Formerly, the petition had to be signed by the party or his attorney personally. This is no longer a requirement.

463. An appellant can base his appeal upon legal facts that he wishes to allege, upon faults in the evaluation of evidence, or upon faults in the application of the law in the judgment rendered by the lower court. If the appellant objects to the evaluation of evidence, a judgment in his favour can be rendered based on erroneous legal conclusions.[586] However, a court should not correct a lower court judgment based on issues of law without first advising the parties, thus avoiding surprise and allowing the parties to debate the legal issues.[587] Legal facts must be expressly alleged; in dispositive cases,[588] however, reference to the lower court judgment is sufficient.[589]

464. Concerning the preparation of the case in the Court of Appeal, there is currently a rule stating that the Court of Appeal, with respect to the intervention of the judge, shall apply the same rule as the district court during its preparation.[590] In the legislative preparatory works, it is stressed, *inter alia*, that there might be amendments to the claims which must be elucidated and, in addition, that it might be unclear which of the circumstances alleged at the lower court the parties also want to allege in the Court of Appeal. It is furthermore particularly emphasized in the legislative preparatory works that parties and attorneys often have problems in stating the evidence they want to present and what they intend to prove with their items of evidence. According to the preparatory legislative works, the role of the judge with respect to procedural guidance could be practised more efficiently in the Court of Appeal.[591] If it is of benefit for the disposal of the case, the Court of Appeal, prior to the termination of the preparation, should make a written summary of the parties' positions.[592]

465. In support of his position in the Court of Appeal, a party may assert a circumstance or offer a piece of evidence not previously presented only if he could not have presented it earlier, or if he demonstrates that it is probable that he had a valid excuse for his failure to rely upon it in the lower court. This rule, which is mandatory, received its present wording in 1989, when it was made more stringent. Today it is rather difficult for a party to present new circumstances and evidence in the Court of Appeal in cases that are not dispositive.[593]

---

586. P.O. Ekelöf & H. Edelstam, *Rättsmedlen* 53 (12th ed., 2008).
587. Lindell, *Processuell preklusion*, 271. *See also* Lindell, *Partsautonomins gränser* 38 et seq. (1988).
588. RB 17:3, p. 2.
589. Lindell, *Civilprocessen*, 386.
590. RB 50:12 with reference to 42:8 para. 2. The former rule was enacted in 1989. Concerning RB 42:8 para. 2, *see* para. 358 *supra*.
591. Prop. 1988/89:95, p. 49.
592. RB 50:12 a.
593. *See* para. 274 *supra* and Lindell, *Processuell preklusion*, 116.

466. With regard to re-presentation of oral evidence or another viewing of the *locus in quo* in the Court of Appeal, the rule is that representation is necessary only if the court finds that renewal of proof-taking is of real importance to the investigation.[594] The Court of Appeal decides on its own motion the matter of renewal; thus, it can be refused against the wishes of the parties.

467. Concerning evaluation of evidence, the Court of Appeals, in principle, may not change the evaluation without it being represented, if the evaluation is decisive to the outcome of the case.[595] Because of the new technique where oral evidence is video-recorded in the district court, statements of witnesses and others can be viewed on a screen in the Court of Appeal. Thus, witnesses and others do not have to appear in person again. However, the Court of Appeal may change the evaluation made by the district court only if there are particular reasons for doing so. Re-representation of evidence, e.g., a witness, is allowed only if further questions are deemed necessary. According to the Government Bill, further questions may be necessary if new evidence is presented or a witness statement is unclear.[596]

468. The requested change of the judgment must be to the advantage of the appellant, which usually presupposes a change in the final order of the judgment. Thus, reasons supporting a judgment cannot be appealed.

469. If the petition fails to comply with the regulations stated in points (1)–(6) above or is otherwise incomplete, the Court of Appeal shall direct the applicant to cure the defect. If the applicant fails to do so, the petition shall be dismissed if it is so incomplete that it cannot reasonably be used as the basis for the proceedings.[597] However, if the petition is manifestly unfounded, the court may immediately pass judgment.[598]

470. If the court entertains the appeal, the petition, with the papers annexed thereto, shall be served upon the respondent with a notice directing him to file a written answer. This answer shall contain a comment on the appellant's grounds for appeal and shall specify the circumstances upon which the respondent desires to rely. In addition, it shall contain the same information as mentioned above in (4), (5) and (6).[599] Further exchanges of documents should normally not take place.[600] During the preparation, sessions may be held – also by telephone – if required to process the case efficiently. The main hearing in the Court of Appeal essentially follows the same pattern as the main hearing in the district court.[601]

594. RB 35:13 para. 2.
595. RB 50:23. *See, e.g.*, NJA 1969, p. 45 I and II and 1998, p. 50.
596. L. Welamson & J. Munck, *Rättegång VI* 88 (2012)
597. RB 50:7.
598. RB 50:8.
599. RB 50:9.
600. RB 50:10.
601. RB 50:15.

471. In his petition, the appellant must specify the change requested in the judgment. If only one of the parties has appealed, the court may not change the judgment rendered by the lower court to his disadvantage (*nulla reformatio in pejus*). In order for such a change to be possible, the opposing party must also have appealed. Thus, the opposing party is not entitled to claim anything in his written answer other than that the judgment rendered by the lower court shall be confirmed. In that case it is assumed that the judgment, at least to some extent, has been entered against both parties. A party who has won in the lower court, therefore, should not appeal the judgment if his adversary appeals.[602]

472. The prohibition against *reformatio in pejus* can lead both parties to appeal, although in reality they would prefer the judgment rendered by the lower court to be the final one. This desire then depends on the fact that neither of them is willing to take the chance that the adversary alone has the opportunity of a more favourable judgment in the Court of Appeals. For this reason, there is a rule on, literally translated, 'connected appeal', stating that if a party has appealed a lower court judgment, the opposing party may also appeal the judgment within one week of the expiry of the ordinary time to appeal.[603] A party thereby can make his appeal dependent on what the opposing party does. It is obvious that the function of this rule is to reduce the number of appeals.

473. The Court of Appeal may always dispose of an appeal on the merits without a main hearing, if the counterpart accepts the appellant's claim or if it is plain that the claim is unfounded. In addition, a main hearing is not required if the case can be properly examined on the merits and the parties have not asked for a main hearing or not made any objections to an examination on the merits. Furthermore, an appeal may always be determined without a main hearing if it is manifest that such a hearing is unnecessary.[604]

474. With respect to appeals against orders, the Code distinguishes between orders that are final and those that are not. To final orders belong, for example, decisions to write-off or dismiss an action.[605] Through a final order, a lower court disassociates itself from a case. Decisions, which are not final, are pronounced either during the trial or in conjunction with the judgment, and can be appealed either separately or in conjunction with an appeal against the judgment. The latter is the main rule in these proceedings on the merits.

475. As mentioned, there is a requirement for dispensation in all civil cases and in court matters. Since the reform took place, the Supreme Court has rendered many judgments in order to clarify the meaning of the prerequisites for dispensation. It should be mentioned that the appellate courts are not obligated to state the reasons for not giving dispensation.

---

602. Ekelöf & Boman, *Rättsmedlen*, 37.
603. RB 50:2.
604. RB 50:13, Prop. 1998/1999:37, p. 24.
605. RB 49:3.

476. Review dispensation may be granted only if it is of importance for guidance in the application of the law that a Court of Appeal decides the case, if there are reasons to change the final order in the judgment rendered by the lower court, or if there are, in some other respects, extraordinary causes present that motivate a review.[606] A new ground for dispensation was introduced through the above-mentioned reform, which took effect on 1 November 2008. According to this ground, dispensation shall be granted if it is deemed necessary in order to understand if the judgment rendered by the lower court is correct. This ground is aimed, e.g., at situations where the reasons given in the district court judgment are vague or in some other way difficult to understand.[607]

477. The most common ground for review dispensation is that there are reasons to change the judgment. In order for the Court of Appeals to grant dispensation, it is sufficient that there are reasons to doubt the correctness of the judgment of the lower court.[608]

478. A party who wishes to make an ordinary appeal against the judgment rendered by a Court of Appeals shall submit a petition for review to the appellate court within four weeks of the pronouncement of the judgment.[609] Of course, review dispensation is – as mentioned above – also required in the Supreme Court in order to get a judgment or final order considered.[610] The conditions for such a dispensation to be granted are more limited than at the Court of Appeal, although the rules are rather similar.

479. Review dispensation may be granted only if:[611]

(1) it is of importance for guidance in the application of law that the Supreme Court decides the case; or
(2) an extraordinary reason exists for such review, such as existing grounds for relief against substantive defects, that there has been a grave procedural error, or that the outcome of the case in the Court of Appeal was plainly due to a gross oversight or a gross mistake.

480. In 1971, the rules on appeal to the Supreme Court were changed. Before this reform, dispensation for precedential purpose required 'extraordinary importance'. When enacting the present rule, this requirement was removed, since the legislator considered it important to increase the number of precedent cases emanating

606. RB 49:14. *See also* Lindell, *Processuell preklusion*, 124 et seq. and, e.g., NJA 1995, p. 367 and 1997, p. 41.
607. Prop. 2004/05:131, p. 188.
608. Ekelöf & Boman, *Rättsmedlen*, 29. If review dispensation is required, the appellate court decides upon this question after the exchange of documents has been concluded, RB 50:11.
609. RB 55:1.
610. RB 54:9.
611. RB 54:10.

from the Supreme Court.[612] According to the preparatory legislative works, precedent cases are mainly of importance when:

(1) there is a lack of precedent cases in respect to a certain legal matter;
(2) the legislation is not detailed enough or is silent in some legal area;
(3) a judgment rendered by an appellate court diverges from the interpretation or application adopted by the Supreme Court;
(4) a judgment rendered by an appellate court diverges from a general principle adopted by the Supreme Court; or
(5) the Supreme Court wants to change previous case law.[613]

481. Swedish courts are not obliged to follow precedent cases. When the JO criticized a judge in a lower court for not having followed a judgment rendered by the Supreme Court *en banc*, the Standing Committee on Civil Law Legislation criticized the JO, stating that, as a general principle, one should hold that only the weight of the arguments recited by the Supreme Court in support to the judgment should be decisive with respect to the judgment's impact on the lower court's adjudication. Although the lower courts are not formally obliged to follow judgments rendered by the Supreme Court it seems obvious that they should, unless the reasons supporting it are clearly erroneous.[614]

482. The possibilities for a party to be granted review dispensation with respect to extraordinary causes are strictly limited.

483. A review dispensation may be limited to a specified part of the judgment or order to which the appeal relates.[615] If such a limited review dispensation has been granted, the Supreme Court may – pending its review of the case in that respect – stay the proceedings in respect of review dispensation for the rest of the case or a portion of it. If review dispensation is granted without limitation to a portion of the case, it shall apply to the judgment or the final order in its entirety. Insofar as review dispensation is not granted, the judgment or final order of the Court of Appeal shall be immune from attack.

484. There is also a possibility for a district court to have a precedent issue arising in the district court referred directly to the Supreme Court.[616] However, this opportunity presupposes that the case is dispositive and the parties agree thereto.

612. Prop. 1971:45, p. 88.
613. *See* Prop. 1971:45, p. 88; *see also* B. Lindell, *Deklaratoriska och demonstrativa prejudikat, Festskrift till Per Olof Bolding* 289–307 (1992).
614. S. Strömholm, *En svensk prejudikatlära*, SvJT 934 (1984).
615. RB 54:11.
616. RB 56:13.

§2. EXTRAORDINARY APPEALS

I. Relief for Substantive Defects and Restoration of Expired Time

485. Under certain very limited conditions, there is a possibility to attack a judgment after the time for an ordinary appeal has expired. The remedy is a relief for substantive defects (*resning*). If such an application is granted, the Supreme Court normally will direct that the case be taken up anew by the court in which it was last pending.[617]

486. Relief for substantive defect may be granted in favour of any of the parties if:[618]

(1) a member of the court or an official employed at the court rendered himself liable for criminal conduct or for a misdemeanour in the discharge of his duties with respect to the case, or if an attorney or legal representative was guilty of an offence with regard to the case and the offence or misdemeanour can be assumed to have affected the outcome;
(2) a document presented as proof was forged or if a party examined under affirmation of truth, or a witness, an expert or an interpreter gave false testimony, and the document or testimony can be assumed to have affected the outcome;
(3) a circumstance or evidence that was not previously presented is asserted and presentation of the matter would probably have led to a different outcome; or
(4) the application of law forming the basis of the judgment is obviously inconsistent with the governing legislative provision.

487. Application for relief for a substantive defect, based upon a situation of the kind referred to in points (1), (2) or (3) must be submitted within one year of the time when the applicant knew the situation justifying the application. In respect to point (4), application must be sought within six months of the time when the judgment became conclusive.[619] In respect to point (3), relief for a substantive defect may not be granted unless the party convincingly demonstrates that he was unable to claim the circumstance or evidence in the court that pronounced the judgment or an appeal therefrom, or that on other grounds he had a valid excuse for failing to do so.[620]

488. Relief for a substantive defect will not be granted because of erroneous reasons supporting a judgment.[621]

617. RB 58:7 para. 1.
618. RB 58:1. Case law is extensive in particular with respect to p. 1.
619. RB 58:4.
620. Cf. RB 43:10, 50:25 st. 3 and 55:13, described in paras 266 et seq. *supra*. *See also* Lindell, *Processuell preklusion*, 69 et seq. and, e.g., NJA 1980, p. 19 and 1989, 843.
621. *See* NJA 1980, 179.

489. If a party has been prevented from using the ordinary means of appeal and has a legal excuse, he can apply for restoration of expired time *(återställande av försutten tid)*.[622] The application must be submitted to the Supreme Court within three weeks of the termination of the circumstances giving rise to the legal excuse and, at the latest, within one year of the expiration of the period.[623] The difficulties in applying this rule mainly relate to the meaning of the notion 'legal excuse'. There is a lot of case law on this issue. With respect to extraordinary remedies, time limits cannot be restored.[624]

II. Relief for Grave Procedural Errors (*Domvilla*)

490. There is a special remedy for procedural errors, which occurred in the trial if the judgment is no longer open for regular appeal. This remedy is available under strictly limited conditions. If the application is granted, the judgment will be partly or totally vacated. Errors are open to attack when:[625]

(1) the action was adjudicated on the merits, notwithstanding the fact that a procedural hindrance existed that a higher court is obliged to notice on appeal on its own motion;
(2) the judgment was directed against someone who was not properly summoned and did not appear in the proceedings, or if the substantive rights of a person who was not a party to the action were adversely affected by the judgment;
(3) the judgment is so vague or incomplete that the determination on the merits cannot be ascertained therefrom; or
(4) another grave procedural error has occurred in the course of the proceedings that can be assumed to have affected the outcome of the action.

491. The application shall be brought within six months after the judgment became conclusive or, with respect to point (2), within six months the judgment became known to the applicant. It shall be in writing and brought before the Court of Appeal if the attacked judgment was rendered by the district court, and in other cases before the Supreme Court.[626]

492. It should be observed that procedural errors can be corrected through appeal pursuant to Chapters 52 and 56 of the Code if an order is rendered on the issue. If the error has not been observed until the proceedings in the Court of Appeal, the appellant can then make the court aware of the fault if it has failed to observe it, as it should have done, on its own motion.[627]

622. RB 58:11. Concerning legal excuse, *see* para. 223 *supra*.
623. RB 58:12.
624. Lindell, *Civilprocessen*, 495.
625. RB 59:1.
626. RB 59:2.
627. RB 50:26–28.

Part V. Incidents

Chapter 1. Intervention

493. As far as the possibilities for a third person to participate in a pending action as an intervenor, the Code distinguishes between ordinary and independent intervention. First, the difference between these forms of intervention will be set out and thereafter their elements.

494. Regarding ordinary intervention, the Code states that an intervenor may take any procedural act open to the party whom he supports. However, he may not amend the party's claim or otherwise act in opposition to the party or appeal against a judgment or order, except by supporting the appeal of the party.[628] This means that he may not assert any claims. In addition, the predominant opinion is that he may not allege legal facts.[629] The reason is that the judgment does not have an evidentiary effect on him with respect to legal facts not alleged. Thus, the procedural competence of an ordinary intervenor is rather limited. He may contribute to the debate over the disputed subject matter, but above all he may present evidence in the action. Thus, it seems clear that the main purpose of the rule on ordinary intervention is to protect the third person from the evidentiary effect of the judgment.

495. The independent intervenor has the capacity of a party in the proceedings.[630] Concerning his legal position, the principles guiding special joinder are deemed to apply.[631] Special joinder applies when the nature of the disputed matter requires that all interested parties be bound by the same judgment or when necessary procedural unity exists. A judgment has res judicata effect against a third person, *inter alia* in an action concerning paternity.[632] Necessary joinder exists when a legal relation cannot be divided; only one judgment can be rendered upon the disputed issue.[633]

628. RB 14:11 para. 1. With respect to new evidence, *see* NJA 1994, p. 287.
629. Ekelöf, *Rättegång II*, 192, Boman, *Åberopsbördan*, 94.
630. RB 14:11 para. 2. However, this capacity is only formal; *see* NJA 1982, p. 10.
631. RB 14:8 para. 2. Ekelöf, *Rättegång II*, 205. *See also* KRB 14:42. It should be mentioned that ordinary joinder is regulated in RB 14:8 para. 1. Each of the parties is thereby regarded as an independent party. However, this does not prevent the parties from having a mutual attorney or having evidence presented in the action by one of the parties also being considered in favour of the other parties on the same side.
632. *See* para. 253 *supra*.
633. *See* para. 425 *supra*.

496. In order for intervention to be allowed, the disputed matter must be related to a legal right or obligation of a third person, who can show probable cause for his application in this respect.[634] The meaning of the requirement 'related to his legal right or obligation' has been debated in the commentaries. A number of typical cases, which should not be regarded as exhaustive, have been set out. These cases or groups are related to the execution of the judgment and the binding, respectively evidentiary, effects of it. On which of these groups the third person can rely on his application as an intervenor is of importance when deciding whether the intervention shall be classified as ordinary or independent.

497. The execution group includes cases where the enforcement of the judgment can prejudice the third person, although the binding force of the judgment does not affect him. An example of this situation is where enforcement is sought against a person who, with a limited right (e.g., a lease) possesses property belonging to a third person.[635] A similar case is where the third person will be directly influenced by the enforcement, although it is not aimed at him; for example, if a tenant who has sublet his apartment is evicted, the person subletting the apartment may not intervene in the action.[636]

498. In respect to the res judicata group, the general rule is that a third person will be bound by the binding force of a judgment in an action in which he does not participate, if the change in his legal position, which the binding force of the judgment would cause in the event of an incorrect outcome, could also have occurred by a disposition of the disputed subject-matter undertaken by one or both of the parties in that action.[637]

499. Ekelöf has argued that a third person, who in accordance with this rule will be bound by the binding force of the judgment, cannot participate in a pending action because of this res judicata effect.[638] The reason supporting this conclusion is that a right to participate as an intervenor would then lead to a groundless limitation of the parties' rights in civil law to dispose over the disputed subject matter.[639] The Supreme Court in NJA 1985 p. 466 has adopted this view.

---

634. RB 14:9. *See, e.g.*, NJA 1951, p. 6; 1973, p. 478; 1985, p. 466 and 1997, p. 190.
635. *See* P.O. Ekelöf, *Om interventionsgrunden* 219 f. (1937).
636. NJA 1962, p. 384. However, he will be protected by some rules in UB.
637. *See also* para. 425 *supra*. Concerning the evidentiary effect of a judgment, *see* para. 431 *supra*.
638. But of course other reasons supporting a right to intervene might be presented.
639. Ekelöf, Bylund & Edelstam, *Rättegång III*, 234.

Chapter 2. Withdrawal of an Action

500. If the plaintiff in a dispositive case withdraws his claim after the defendant has responded, the action shall be adjudicated if the defendant so requests.[640] It does not constitute withdrawal if the plaintiff reduces his claim or abstains from alleging a circumstance previously alleged. This distinction is of great importance, since the original, but later reduced, claim or circumstance will be encompassed by the binding force of the judgment, a rule that does not apply if the action is written-off after withdrawal.[641]

501. However, as was previously mentioned, the plaintiff cannot withdraw his claim after the defendant has responded and requested the adjudication of the withdrawn claim. According to the preparatory legislative works, the defendant shall not be deemed to have responded if he has only presented procedural objections with respect to the claim, which obviously assumes that the action has recently started.[642]

502. If the plaintiff rescinds his withdrawal, the case will be dealt with as if the withdrawal never occurred.[643] However, if the court has already written-off the case, the plaintiff may rescind his withdrawal only if extraordinary reasons are presented, for example if the withdrawal has been caused by a circumstance, which would allow re-opening of the case.[644]

503. In so-called mixed cases, that is to say cases which contain issues, which are both dispositive and non-dispositive, rules that are non-dispositive, are applied with respect to the rules guiding the proceedings, as it would be too complicated with a division, while the principle of disposition is used on the material on which the court forms its judgment.[645] However, from a precedent case one can conclude that 13:5 paragraph 1 of the Code applies when a dispositive issue is examined in a non-dispositive case. Thus, if a spouse in an action for divorce claims support, the opposing spouse is entitled to a judgment with respect to the dispositive issue of support, if the plaintiff withdraws his or her claim for support.[646] Nonetheless, the main rule in non-dispositive cases is that the case will be written-off if a judgment has not been entered. After the judgment, a withdrawal is without effect.[647]

640. RB 13:5 para. 1.
641. *See also* para. 293 *supra* and NJA 1994, p. 23.
642. NJA II 1943, p. 167. This opinion has been criticized by Ekelöf, *Rättegång II*, p. 145 and S. Larsson, *Svarandens rätt till dom*, p. 229, in *Festskrift till Agge* (1970).
643. *See, e.g.*, NJA 1977, p. 580.
644. *See* NJA 1986, p. 356.
645. *See also* para. 65 *supra*.
646. NJA 1985, p. 338.
647. RB 13:5 para. 2.

Chapter 3. Withdrawal of a Consent

504. A party's consent to a claim in a dispositive case can normally be withdrawn in the instance in which it has been given.[648] Such a consent is to be regarded as procedural in nature and not substantive unless special reasons exist.[649] With respect to the possibilities to withdraw a consent given in a lower court in a higher court, it has been deemed to be limited in accordance with the right to withdraw an appeal after the case has been written-off.[650] Thus, special circumstances are required. From case law, it appears that the Supreme Court has considered the circumstances under which the consent was given. If these circumstances have been essentially changed, the withdrawal of the consent has been accepted.[651]

648. A consent in a non-dispositive case does not constitute a binding disposition on behalf of the party, but must be examined by the court on its own motion.
649. *See, e.g.*, NJA 1972, p. 439; 1980, p. 56.
650. NJA 1981, p. 780. *See supra* 504.
651. Lindell, *Processuell preklusion*, 368. Concerning case law, *see, e.g.*, NJA 1972, p. 439; 1974, p. 36; 1977, p. 600; 1978, p. 55; 1980, p. 56; 1981, p. 780 and 1983, p. 148.

Chapter 4. Postponement of the Main Hearing

505. The rules on recess and post postponement have been brought together in one single provision. According to the previous rule on recess (RB 1:9), a session should continue during the required number of consecutive working days. However, if it could occur without inconvenience, a recess in the proceedings was allowed to take place as long as the session continued for a maximum of two or, if there was a special cause, three working days in one week. The purpose behind this rule was to uphold the principle of concentration and, at the same time, make it possible for the court to handle daily administrative routines. This rule, in conjunction with the provision on postponement, was regarded as too detailed and complicated. In addition, it put a straightjacket on the court since it could not adapt the procedure to the individual case. When RB 1:9 was removed the possibility of postponement was increased.[652]

506. The main hearing shall be cancelled and scheduled for a new date if:[653]

(1) a party who should be present in person makes his appearance through his attorney only;
(2) a witness or an expert who should be examined fails to appear;
(3) a party wishes to allege new important grounds or wishes to present new evidence and it is found that a postponement is required in order to provide the opposing party with a reasonable opportunity to consider the new grounds or evidence; or
(4) there is some other impediment to immediate trial and final disposition of the action.

507. If it can be assumed that the impediment will be removed prior to the con clusion of the session, the main hearing may be held.

508. If a party alleges new circumstances or evidence and these are not disregarded, the main hearing shall be postponed to another date. However, postponement on these grounds presupposes that the opposing party requires a 'reasonable opportunity to consider'. An important question is how to interpret this requirement. Suppose, for example, that the parties dispute the meaning of a contract and during the main hearing, the plaintiff presents a letter written by the defendant shortly before the proceedings concerning the meaning of the contract. In such a case, the defendant should not need any significant time to comment upon this letter, since he wrote it. In any case, a short pause ought to be sufficient for him to consider his answer. It can generally be maintained that cancellation of the main hearing should not be required regarding facts about which a party ought to have immediate knowledge. This principle primarily relates to information concerning

652. Prop. 1999/2000:26, p. 50.
653. RB 43:2.

the parties' own actions, but it might sometimes also be of relevance in respect to measures undertaken by a party's employee.[654]

509. The main hearing shall continue as far as possible without interruption until the action is ready for final disposal by the court, in order to realize the principle of concentration. If the main hearing does not require more than three days, it shall be performed within a week. In other situations, the main hearing shall continue at least three days each week, compare paragraph 507 *supra* and RB 43:11 paragraphs 1 and 2. A main hearing once commenced, may not be adjourned unless there is an impediment of the kind referred to in 43:2 (*see* above), but it can be assumed that the hearing would be subject to continuance at a later session without a new main hearing, and furthermore that segmentation of the hearing would not adversely affect inquiry into the merits. [655]

510. If the main hearing is suspended, the court may still take up oral evidence if the defendant has been serviced and the person to be heard is available and it is deemed appropriate.[656]

511. The Expert Drafting Committee stated that it was obvious that the rule in question should be interpreted in a restrictive way, and that postponement should be permitted only when it was necessary.[657] However, the rule was changed in 1987 in order to expand the possibilities of allowing postponement. As stated above, the provisions at issue have been softened further recently.

512. The rule on fifteen days has been removed in the new provision. The present rule states that a new main hearing shall be held if there have been so many adjournments that the purpose of a concentrated hearing cannot be fulfilled. Previously, it was provided that if an action had been resumed after one or more adjournments and the total adjournment time did not exceed fifteen days, the main hearing could be continued. Otherwise, the general rule was that a new main hearing must be held.

513. The main reason behind the removal of the previous rule, which in principle required a new main hearing after fifteen days, was that it made it difficult for the court to handle big and complicated cases. The previous rule sometimes made it impossible for the judge to take a holiday and for the advocates to be able to attend sessions two or three times a week for a very long time.[658]

654. Lindell, *Processuell preklusion*, 30.
655. It should be mentioned that the Code regulates adjournment during the main hearing in quite a different way than adjournment during the preparation of the case, where an adjournment always leads to continued preparation. The reason for the difference is that the principles of immediacy and the principle of the best evidence do not apply during the preparation.
656. *See* para. 121 *supra*.
657. SOU 1938:44, p. 450.
658. Prop. 1999/2000:26, p. 51.

514. At a continued main hearing, the action shall proceed from the stage it had reached at the conclusion of the previous hearing. At a new main hearing, the trial shall be commenced de novo. If an item of evidence was taken at an earlier hearing, the item shall be re-taken, provided that such re-taking is found to be of importance in the action and that no impediment thereto exists. When an item of evidence is not re-taken, it shall be presented from the court record or in another appropriate way.[659]

515. If a case is scheduled for a continued or new main hearing, the court may direct resumption of the preparation and issue the necessary instructions.[660] In particular, this step will often be necessary when a party wishes to present new circumstances or evidence.[661]

659. RB 43:13.
660. RB 43:12.
661. SOU 1938:44, p. 451.

Chapter 5. Substitution of Parties

516. If the plaintiff transfers the disputed matter, the transferee has the right, without a new summons, to take over the claim in the action in the form it has at the time of his entry in the proceedings.[662] In the preparatory legislative works, it is emphasized that the procedural acts undertaken by the former plaintiff have the same legal consequences with respect to the new defendant as they had against the former.

517. The reason why the transferee is entitled to enter into the proceedings is that he will be bound by the judgment when the transfer occurs before or during the trial.[663] This extension of the res judicata effect is deemed necessary in order to protect legal security, which in itself is a reason why the transferee must have the right to enter into the action.

518. Thus, the plaintiff has the right to take over the claim and he may thereby adjust the earlier plaintiff's procedural acts only insofar as that plaintiff could have adjusted them.[664] According to the Expert Drafting Committee, there is one aspect in particular which ought to be observed in this context, namely that the defendant's legal position may not be prejudiced by the substitution of parties.[665] The interests of the plaintiff in this respect are secured, since transfer on the defendant's side and substitution of the defendant presuppose consent from the plaintiff.[666] However, irrespective of whether the transfer occurs on the plaintiff's or defendant's side, the transferee must accept the nature of the claim at the time of entering into the proceedings.[667]

519. Obviously, substitution on the plaintiff's side cannot prevent the new plaintiff from making such changes in the claim, which are necessary because of the transfer. Thus, he may change the claim in order to ensure that the performance demanded is owed to him and use the transfer as a ground for that claim.[668] In other respects, the new plaintiff may undertake amendments permitted in the Code.

520. If the transfer has occurred on the defendant's side, the plaintiff might wish that the transferee enters into the action in order to get a judgment ordering the transferee to hand over the property to him. If, however, the transfer has occurred on the plaintiff's side, the defendant might be interested in having certain objections related to him examined in a trial.[669] For this reason, it is stated that the transferee on application of the opposing party is obliged to join as a party in the action.[670]

662. RB 13:7 para. 1.
663. Gärde et al., *supra*, 140.
664. Ekelöf, *Rättegång II*, 153, Cf. NJA 1972, p. 439.
665. SOU 1938:44, p. 189.
666. RB 13:7 para. 2.
667. Lindell, *Processuell preklusion*, 374.
668. Ekelöf, *Rättegång II*, 153, 148, KRB 13:61.
669. Ekelöf, *Rättegång II*, 157, Gärde et al., *supra*, 140.
670. RB 13:7 para. 3.

521. In the commentaries, some interest has been focused on the situation where the original plaintiff counteracts the entrance of the transferee in the action. In this case, the prevailing opinion seems to be that the transferee can exclude the original plaintiff party from the proceedings.[671] If this is not possible, the transferee can enter into the action as an intermediate party or as an independent intervenor.[672] If the main hearing has commenced, only independent intervention is an option in this situation.

671. Ekelöf, *Rättegång II*, 157, Gärde et al., *supra*, 140.
672. Concerning an intermediate party and independent intervention, *see* paras 303 and 495 *supra.*

Part VI. Legal Aid and Legal Costs

Chapter 1. Legal Aid

522. On 1 December 1997, a new Legal Aid Act (RhL) came into force. The most important feature in this Act is that legal aid has been made subsidiary to private legal insurance.[673]

523. The main reason behind this change was to save money for the state because of declining state income.[674] As an additional reason for the change, it was said that the legal aid system of rules was complicated and hard to grasp, the latter mainly because the provisions on legal aid and legal insurance ran parallel.[675] According to the old RhL, legal aid could be used to cover the party's own litigation costs, while legal insurance could be used to pay the counterparts litigation costs. This is no longer possible. Thus, it is obvious that the applicant carefully must examine his chance to win the case. Normally legal insurance cover costs between SEK 75,000 and SEK 250,000.

524. Some commentators criticized the new Act, saying that certain individuals did not have legal insurance in their home insurance.[676] The Government replied that this was true only with respect to 5% of the population. The subsidiary principle also means that legal aid will not be granted if the applicant does not have legal insurance, but should have had it.[677] An exception from this provision can be made only if there are particular reasons with respect to the nature and significance of the legal matter. Today, only about 2% of the population does not have legal insurance included in their home insurance. According to an investigation made by the National Court Board, the overall impression is that the reform has worked well.

525. With respect to the application of this rule, it is said in the preparatory works that legal aid must not be granted if the applicant has a home insurance, but deliberately decided not to include legal insurance in it.[678] Obviously, a person with

673. Section 9 in the Legal Aid Act.
674. The cost for legal aid 1994/95 was SEK 361 million.
675. Prop. 1996/97:9 s. 81.
676. *See, e.g.*, Gustafson, Advokaten 1995, p. 4 and Marteleur-Agrell, Advokaten 1996, p. 3.
677. Section 9 para. 2 the Legal Aid Act.
678. Prop. 1996/97:8, p. 209.

no home to insure is not required to have a home insurance. In addition, particular reason can be present, e.g., in disputes about custody or access to a child.[679]

526. A person who is close to or within the range of the upper half of the breaking point in order to be entitled to legal aid (SEK 260,000), shall normally be deemed to have the financial ability to insure himself. This is true also with respect to a person who has a yearly income which increases to SEK 105,000 after the reduction of child support.[680]

527. It has been mentioned above that a requirement for legal aid is that the applicant's income does not exceed SEK 260,000.[681] Further requirements are that the applicant needs legal aid and that this need cannot be fulfilled otherwise and that it, with respect to the nature and consequence of the legal matter, the disputed value and other circumstances, is deemed reasonable that the state contributes to the legal costs.[682]

528. Normally, there is no need for legal assistance if the applicant is a member of an organization, which helps him. Furthermore, a party might not need a lawyer, but can present the case himself. This must be assessed with respect to his physical and psychological qualifications and to where the dispute will be examined. The need for legal aid is namely considered to be less important if the dispute will be adjudicated in an administrative court and not in an ordinary court.[683]

529. Furthermore, it is always necessary to assess if it is reasonable to grant legal aid. This assessment shall be focused on the circumstances in each individual case.[684] The provision about assessment is laid down in order to prevent abuse of legal aid.

530. Guidelines regarding how to apply the provision can be found in the preparatory works to the old RhL where – with respect to a similar rule – a number of type cases were set out where legal aid should not be granted. For example, if the claim clearly rests on a misinterpretation of the law, where the evidence supporting the claim is poor, where the dispute relates to small economical values compared with the legal expenses, or where a relevant claim cannot be satisfied because the opposing party lacks assets.[685]

531. There are cases where legal aid may not be granted. These are exhaustively enumerated in the RhL. They can be divided into two groups.

679. *Ibid.*
680. Renfors & Sverne Arvill, *Rättshjälpslagen och annan lagstiftning om rättsligt bistånd. En kommentar.* 2:a uppl 72 (2006).
681. Debts and child support are deducted from the income when calculating the value SEK 210,000
682. *See* ss 6–9 the Legal Aid Act.
683. Prop. 1996/97:8, p. 115.
684. Prop. 1996/97:9, p. 121.
685. Prop. 1972:4, pp. 93 and 248.

532. The first contain matters which are very common and not regarded important enough to fall within the scope of legal aid, e.g., report on income tax return, a marriage settlement, will or deed of gift.

533. The second group addresses either the nature of the case or the applicant. Thus, legal aid may not be granted if the issue concerning legal aid can wait until another legal matter, supported upon essentially the same ground, has finally been adjudicated. This rule is primarily meant to be used when several actions are instituted at the same time in a large number of similar cases and the outcome of all of them depends on the outcome of one of them. In such situations, legal aid will be granted only in the 'test case'.[686]

534. Another example relating to the disputed matter is that legal aid may not be granted in legal matters concerning compensation for traffic injuries pursuant to the Traffic Injury Act, or concerning indemnity that can be paid out from liability insurance. However, legal aid may be granted to the injured person if the legal matter is pending in court or relates to other damage than a personal injury. The rationale behind this limitation is not to give public support to something that ends up benefiting the insurance companies.

535. As far as the applicant is concerned, legal aid may not be granted for claims, which have been transferred to him, if the transfer can be assumed to have taken place in order to obtain an advantage when the application for legal aid is assessed.

536. In section 11 of the RhL, a number of cases are enumerated where legal aid may be granted only if there are special reasons. If the legal matter is related to divorce, child support, taxes, fees or security measures for payment of custom, or an issue that shall be examined by a single judge pursuant to 1:3 d in the Code, or shall be examined abroad, special reasons must exist. In order for special reasons to be deemed present in divorce cases, it is required that the case is more complicated than normal and that the problems cannot be resolved in three hours with legal assistance. Legal advice for one hour shall thereby not be included.[687]

537. In addition, with respect to child support special reasons are required. If the need of the child is satisfied by the support paid by the public where the obligated parent does not pay (*bidragsförskott*), legal aid may not be granted. However, special reasons can exist where the need of the child increases the sum of the public paid support and in cases where the child is not entitled to such support.[688]

538. A person who does not have his residence in Sweden, regardless of his nationality, can never be granted legal aid for a legal matter that will be examined abroad. However, the Government can decide that foreign citizens or those who

686. Cf. Prop. 1981/82:28, p. 20 and Prop. 1986/87:86, p. 119.
687. Prop. 1996/97:9, p. 137.
688. Prop. 1996/97:9, p. 137.

have their residence abroad shall have the same status as Swedish citizens. By the decree (1988:123), certain foreign citizens have been granted equal status with Swedish citizens with respect to the right to be awarded legal aid, *inter alia* this is true for citizens within the EU.

539. A tradesman normally cannot be granted legal aid while, however, legal matters in respect of the tradesman's personal relations are not affected by the limitation in question. The reason underlying this rule is that legal aid should be regarded as a social benefit, intended to give protection in the occurrence of unexpected events. For a tradesman, legal expenses are just another running cost included in the trade and, in addition, such expenses can be insured against.

540. The possibility for a tradesman to be granted legal aid has been limited compared with the old RhL. In addition to the requirements laid down in sections 6–9, special reasons must exist. Furthermore, the notion 'tradesman' has been narrowed by being related to its meaning in consumer law, where it refers to every person managing such a business of economic value that it should be deemed as a trade. As a rule of thumb, it is said in the preparatory works that legal aid should not be granted if the yearly balance of the business exceeds SEK 500,000 or if more than two persons are employed.[689]

541. If legal aid has been granted the public pays the applicant's expenses for legal assistance, evidence (in an ordinary court, the Labour Court or the Market Court), examination expenses, mediation and certain fees.[690] Expenses for appearance (travel accommodation) are no longer reimbursed, but have to be paid by the applicant himself if he is not so poor that he cannot afford it. In such cases, the public, regardless of whether legal aid is granted, pays these expenses or not.[691]

542. As far as legal expenses for legal assistance is concerned there is a limit. The public does not pay for more than 100 working hours, i.e., SEK 120,000, tax included (*mervärdesskatt*). In order to avoid offensive results, e.g., if the limit is reached during the main hearing, it can be exceeded, but only under particular circumstances.[692] Also, with respect to expenses for examining the case a limit has been laid down, namely SEK 10,000.

543. According to the old RhL, the applicant had to contribute to the costs for legal aid by paying a basic amount and sometimes a maximum amount, the latter related to his income. These provisions were often complicated to apply and were hard to understand for the applicant. That is why the new RhL is simplified with

689. Prop. 1996/97:9, p. 128.

690. *See* ss 15–19 Rhl. If the applicant has been granted legal aid he does not have to deposit security for provisional attachment.

691. Concerning expenses for appearance, *see* Renfors & Sverne Arvill, 106.

692. *See* s. 34 Rhl.

respect to the calculation of the applicant's fee, which is based only on the expenses for legal assistance. In addition, the levels for the applicant's fee have been limited to six.

544. Legal aid is granted upon application from the person who seeks it. If the disputed subject matter is pending in court, the court decides the issue of legal aid. In other cases, the Legal Aid Authority will grant legal aid. As an assistant may be appointed to an advocate, an assistant lawyer in an advocate's office or someone else fit for the assignment. If the applicant himself has suggested someone, he shall be appointed if such an appointment will not increase the costs in an unacceptable way, or in other respects special reasons exist against making the appointment. The hinder for the applicant to get an assistant who lives far away has been removed.[693]

545. A legal assistant may be dismissed only for just reasons.[694] A change of legal assistant may occur only if specially permitted and if special reasons exist.[695] If a legal assistant has previously been dismissed on request of the applicant, a new legal assistant may be appointed only if there are special reasons, e.g., the legal assistant is sick or a very serious conflict has arisen between the legal assistant and the client.[696] Another advocate or legal assistant may substitute a legal assistant if the expenses thereby will not considerably increase.

546. A legal assistant is entitled to reasonable compensation for the work, time and effort laid down and other expenses incurred by the assignment. Concerning reasonable compensation, the nature of the case and the time spent on the assignment shall be considered, as well as the skill and care demonstrated during the performance of it.

547. The National Court Administration fixes the tariffs regulating the size of the compensation. Compensation to the legal assistant shall be decided in conjunction with the final judgment or order rendered by the court on the disputed matter or when the legal aid matter otherwise is finalized.

548. In principle legal aid shall discontinue if: (a) the legal fee is not paid; (b) the information given by the applicant is incorrect and legal aid would not have been granted if correct information had been presented by the applicant; (c) the applicant has intentionally or with gross carelessness presented false information, which has been aimed at decreasing or avoiding the legal aid fee; (d) the applicant's economic situation has changed in such a way that he is no longer entitled to legal

693. *See* Prop. 2008/09:232.
694. In NJA 1990, p. 264, dismissal was refused, but the legal assistant was nonetheless considered to be obliged to continue his assignment as assistant and supervise the interest of the client.
695. In NJA 1982, p. 685 the issue of change of legal assistant was considered without paying any attention to whether the conflict between the party and the assistant was caused by the assistant's way of performing the assignment.
696. Renfors & Sverne Arvill, 135 et. seq.

aid; (e) a legal assistant has been dismissed and not replaced; or (f) it cannot be deemed reasonable that the public continues to contribute to the legal expenses. Of course, the legal aid shall also discontinue when the limit on 100 working hours has been reached.

Chapter 2. Legal Costs

§1. Expenses Compensated as Legal Costs

549. If expenses incurred during the proceedings are regarded as litigation expenses, the losing party must reimburse them to the winning party, if they have been necessary to secure the latter's rights and can be deemed reasonable. Pursuant to the Code, the following expenses are regarded as litigation expenses:[697]

(1) expenses for the evidence in the case;
(2) expenses for a party's appearance in the action, and his or her work and loss of time; and
(3) expenses for the preparation and presentation of the action, including counselling fees.

550. Concerning expenses for evidence, different rules apply with respect to different sorts of evidence. Compensation of a witness called by the party shall be paid by that party. If the court called the witness on its own motion, the compensation in dispositive cases shall be paid to him by the parties jointly and severally, and in non-dispositive case out of public funds. Compensation paid by a party shall include reimbursement of necessary expenses for travel and maintenance and for loss of time in an amount deemed reasonable by the court.[698] Compensation will be paid only on request of the witness and may not exceed the required amount. However, the court can decide that the compensation shall be less than required, although the party who has called the witness accepted a higher amount, because compensation to a witness is a legal expense, which the adversary can be obliged to pay.

551. Compensation paid out of public funds shall be determined by the court pursuant to regulations issued by the Government.

552. Anyone other than a party who has produced a document or brought an object for examination is entitled to reasonable compensation.[699] With respect to compensation paid to an expert, different rules apply, depending on whether or not the expert has been appointed by the court. An expert appointed by the court (official experts) has the same rights as a witness to compensation for the appearance in court and in addition, he is entitled to reasonable compensation for the assignment. If the case is dispositive, compensation to the official expert shall generally be paid jointly and severally by the parties. If only one of the parties has called for the official expert, that party is obliged to pay his compensation. In non-dispositive cases compensation to an official expert shall be paid out of public funds.

697. RB 18:8. *See* H. Bellander, Rättegångskostnader. Om kostnadsbördan i dispositiva tvistemål. Uppsala 2017.
698. RB 36:24.
699. RB 38:7 and 39:5, commented in paras 660 and 676 *infra*.

553. With regard to a private expert, i.e., an expert called by a party, the same compensation rules as for witnesses shall be applied.[700] If a party has paid compensation to a private expert or a witness in an amount higher than the court subsequently deems appropriate, the excess amount can be claimed as a legal expense from the opposing party.[701]

554. If a party has been granted legal aid, the expenses for evidence are included in the legal aid.

555. In addition, as far as compensation to a witness and an expert are concerned, there are special provisions in the Decree on Compensation to Witnesses. Compensation for expenses concerning other kinds of evidence is not specially regulated, but shall be a reasonable amount.

556. Regarding compensation paid to the party for time and effort, it is assumed that his expenses are directly caused by the preparation and presentation of the action.[702] He is not entitled to compensation for suffering, inconvenience or losses directly caused by the trial itself.[703] Work done by the party's personnel can also be compensated.[704]

557. Settlement negotiations may be compensated, although they have not been of any manifest importance for the preparation and presentation of the action.[705] It might be possible to be compensated for settlement expenses as legal costs, although the negotiation has not referred to an issue upon which the court has adjudicated. Nonetheless, the negotiated issue must be related to such an issue.[706]

558. Compensation for legal costs shall also include interest pursuant to the Interest Act (SFS 1975:635), at 6% from the date of adjudication until payment is made. A claim for a collecting fee is not regarded as a legal cost, but as an ordinary civil law claim.[707]

559. There is a special rule in the Code concerning legal costs in small claims cases, which was enacted in 1987 when the Act on Simplified Judicial Procedure became a part of the Code. According to the Small Claims Act, the value of the disputed subject matter and the legal costs should be proportional to each other. This was achieved through rather restrictive rules on legal costs. These rules have essentially been transformed into a new rule, which provides that compensation for legal expenses in 'small claim cases' is limited to expenses for advice pursuant to the

700. *See also* para. 671 *infra*.
701. *See* about this debatable issue NJA II 1953, p. 514, Welamson SvJT 1964, p. 425 and Edelstam, 350 et seq.
702. SOU 1938:44, p. 238.
703. *Ibid.*
704. *Ibid.*
705. NJA II 1973, p. 337.
706. *Ibid.*
707. *See* the Fee Collecting Act and the decree on collecting fees. Cf. Prop. 1980/81, p. 93.

RhL, expenses for the application fee, travel and maintenance for the party or his legal representative attending the session or, if personal appearance has not been ordered, expenses for travel and maintenance for an attorney, expenses for witness's evidence and translation of documents. Compensation will be paid out only to the extent the expenses were reasonably incurred for the protection of the party's interests.[708]

560. Thus, in small claim cases, compensation is not paid for a legal assistant, nor is interest for litigation expenses allowed.[709] However, the rule allows certain adjustments if a party intentionally or carelessly caused the other party extra legal costs.

§2. The Provisions in the Code on Distributing Legal Costs

561. Beside the provisions on legal costs in civil cases in Chapter 18 of the Code, there are certain compensation rules for particular cases. However, these regulations, as well as the compensation rules that apply to summary proceedings, will not be discussed in the following account. Rather, a description of the provisions in the Code will be offered.

562. It should be mentioned that with respect to foreign plaintiffs, there are certain special rules concerning litigation costs in the Act on the Obligation for Foreign Plaintiffs to Furnish Security for Legal Costs (SFS 1980:307). These rules will be commented upon in the following paragraphs.

563. If a foreign citizen or legal entity who is not resident in the jurisdiction, wishes to institute an action in a Swedish court against a Swedish citizen or legal entity, on request of the defendant he shall furnish security for the legal costs which he can be obliged to pay, unless the foreigner does not have his residence or citizenship within the EU or European Economic Community area. The security shall not only cover the legal costs in the first instance but also, in the event of an appeal, the litigation costs in the appellate court.[710]

564. A claim for security must be asserted, at the latest, when the defendant makes his first appearance at court.[711] If he has legal excuse, the claim shall be asserted as soon the reason for the legal excuse has terminated.[712] After the claim for security has been presented, the court shall direct the plaintiff to provide the security within a certain time. An appeal may not be brought against a decision rendered by the district court directing the plaintiff to provide security. Instead, the

708. RB 18:8 a.
709. NJA 1981, p. 1006. *See also* NJA 1998, p. 387.
710. *See* NJA 1977, p. 349.
711. Cf. RB 34:2.
712. Concerning legal excuse, *see* para. 223 *supra*.

plaintiff is entitled to call for an examination of the validity of the directive in conjunction with an appeal against a decision for which the directive has been applied.[713] If, however, the decision rendered by the district court means that the defendant's claim is dismissed totally or partially on the merits, the defendant is entitled to appeal against it after formal notice of exception.[714] If the plaintiff does not furnish security accepted by the adversary or the court, the action shall be dismissed.[715]

565. The security shall consist of a pledge or a personal guarantee. The latter shall be issued as if it was issued for the guarantor's own debt. If two or more individuals undertake it together, they shall be severally liable. If the defendant does not accept the security, it shall be examined by the court. With the consent of the defendant, another type of security may be furnished. The security shall be kept by the court or by someone appointed by the court.

566. The principal rule in the Code regarding legal costs is that the party that loses shall reimburse his adversary for his litigation expenses, if nothing to the contrary is provided.[716] The purpose of this rule is to ensure that the winning party gets compensation for expenses incurred while seeking to protect his rights.[717] Furthermore, the preparatory legislative works state that knowing that one must pay one's own as well as one's adversary's legal expenses will prevent one from instituting an unfounded action.[718] Another purpose underlying this rule is to give an impact to civil law rules.[719]

567. In principle, the rule in question is probably also applicable to disputed claims in bankruptcy proceedings.[720] It certainly applies to appeals from proposals to distribute money to the creditors in such cases.[721] Moreover, it applies in actions concerning fees to an official receiver,[722] and it applies to matters pursuant to the Act on Processing of Court Matters (ÄL).[723]

568. However, there are certain exceptions to the principle that the losing party shall reimburse the winning party for litigation expenses. In an action concerning a

713. *See* RB 49:3 para. 2 and Pålsson, *Svensk rättspraxis*, 134.
714. RB 49:3 para. 2. *See also* NJA 1977, p. 349 and Pålsson, *Svensk Rättspraxis*, 134.
715. However, security must not be furnished in: actions disposed in accordance with the Act on Litigation in Labour Disputes (SFS 1974:371); actions instituted at Land Courts which do not refer to controversies concerning the rent for leased land or apartments or concerning rights in tenant owner's apartments; actions pursuant to 11:7 in the Water Act (SFS 1918:523); actions concerning bills of exchange and cheques; actions instituted at the administrative courts or the Commercial Court. Security is also not required when a counter-claim is brought into an action.
716. RB 18:1.
717. SOU 1938:44, p. 231.
718. SOU 1938:44, p. 231.
719. Jacobsson, *Parts kostnad i civilprocess*, 58 and Ekelöf, Boman & Bylund, *Rättegång III*, 180.
720. *See* NJA 1961, p. 84.
721. *See, e.g.*, NJA 1972, p. 633 and 1969, p. 423.
722. *See, e.g.*, NJA 1969, p. 337.
723. Cf. NJA 1979, p. 164.

matter that, by law, may not be resolved without judicial confirmation, the court may direct that each party shall bear his own expenses.[724] That each party shall bear his own expenses is usually called set-off. However, the use of the notion 'set-off' in this context (concerning litigation expenses) differs from the use of the notion in respect to substantive civil law, since it does not mean that the claims shall be discounted against each other, but that each party shall bear his own legal expenses.[725] The application of the principal rule assumes that the court examines whether the claimed change in the legal relationship presented in the action could have been achieved by a private settlement.[726] An example of a common situation that requires the court's confirmation is divorce.[727] There are also particular rules in family law cases; in paternity cases, where a Social Welfare Committee acts as a legal representative and in cases concerning custody of or access to a child, each party shall normally bear his own expenses.[728] There are also special set-off provisions regarding child support.[729] As implied, the rule in question is optional. Thus, the court may direct that the legal expenses shall be set-off, but are not obliged to do so. Pursuant to the preparatory legislative works, the expenses should be set-off if the defendant immediately consents to the claim or for which the relationship between the parties before or during the action gives reasons, but the normal situation should be that the winning party is compensated for his litigation expenses.[730] It appears from case law that the rule is applied in this way.[731]

569. The second exception to the principal rule provides that if the winning party is found to have initiated the action without provocation from his adversary, or otherwise to have deliberately or negligently caused unnecessary litigation, he shall reimburse his adversary for his litigation expenses or, if the circumstances so justify, each party shall bear his own expenses.[732] It should be noted that this rule does not refer to careless behaviour in the proceedings, but rather to situations in which the claim should never have been instituted. In the preparatory legislative works, the following example shows how the rule is meant to work: The winning party intentionally or by gross negligence can have caused an unnecessary trial if he neglected to inform the adversary about a circumstance which clearly demonstrates that he would win any possible litigation and of which the adversary did not know nor ought to have had knowledge about. For example, when an estate of a deceased person institutes an action on payment and the debtor waits until the trial to prove with a receipt that he has paid the debt, and it had not been possible to obtain this information from the deceased accounts.[733]

---

724. RB 18:2.
725. Jacobsson, *Parts kostnad i civilprocess*, 49.
726. *Ibid.*, 175.
727. *See* ÄktB 5:1–2.
728. *See* FB 3:11 and 6:22.
729. FB 7:19.
730. SOU 1938:44, p. 231.
731. *See, e.g.*, NJA 1973, p. 35; 1963, p. 423; 1967, p. 252; 1951, p. 223; 1961, p. 631; 1973, p. 654 and KRB 18:10.
732. RB 18:3 para. 1.
733. SOU 1938:44, p. 232.

570. However, if the debtor in this example waits until the main hearing to present the receipt, it might be disregarded by the court, pursuant to the rules on preclusion, in which case the debtor will lose the case and be obliged to pay the creditor's litigation expenses.[734] It might also be possible to apply 9:1 of the Code if, for example, the debtor intentionally has withheld the receipt.[735] Case law relating to this rule offers, *inter alia*, the following examples of its application: in one case, the legal expenses were set-off after a settlement offer had been rejected and the obligation to pay contested.[736] In another, the principal rule (18:1) was applied when a settlement offer was partly rejected.[737] Furthermore, the litigation expenses were set-off when a creditor was regarded to have had reason to believe that the debtor was bankrupt.[738] In addition, in an action concerning inspection of leased land, there were several claims asserted by the plaintiff, which were all immediately accepted. The litigation expenses were set-off, *inter alia* because no extra costs were incurred as a consequence of the adversary's view on the consented claims.[739] Moreover, in an action concerning liability for careless driving, the defendant admitted the amount of the claim as per se reasonable, but contested paying more than half of it. The defendant's legal expenses were fully compensated.[740] Finally, a man who, in the appellate court, changed his view in respect to the amount of a support in favour of the plaintiff was deemed to have caused an unnecessary trial.[741]

571. In the second paragraph of the elaborated rule, the third exception to the principal rule refers to the losing party: if he neither knew nor should have known of determinative circumstances prior to the commencement of the action, the court may direct that each party shall bear his own expenses.[742] The notion 'circumstance' in this rule refers only to legal facts.[743] The preparatory legislative works recommend that the courts use this rule with great caution. Thus, the losing party himself should normally bear the consequences for lacking knowledge of a circumstance decisive to the outcome.[744] As an example in the preparatory legislative works on how to apply this rule, reference has been made to a dispute concerning a contested will, where the beneficiary of the formally valid will loses the case, after it has been established that the testator was not mentally sound when drawing it up, something of which the beneficiary had no knowledge.[745] Case law offers, *inter alia*, the following examples to illustrate the application of this rule: the defendant contested a claim after a medical certificate concerning the plaintiff's mental health

734. Lindell, *Processuell preklusion*, 141.
735. *Ibid.*
736. NJA II 1937, p. 167, *en banc*.
737. NJA 1955, p. 329.
738. NJA 1966, p. 445.
739. NJA 1957, p. 202.
740. NJA 1972, p. 551.
741. NJA 1977, p. 707. Cf. 1984, p. 469. *See also* NJA 1980, p. 366 (I); 1982, p. 366, 1983, p. 635 and NJA 2007, p. 571.
742. RB 18:3 para. 2.
743. SOU 1938:44, p. 232.
744. *Ibid.*
745. *Ibid.*

had been presented in the action. The legal expenses were not set-off, since the defendant, even when the action was instituted, must have been aware that it was uncertain whether the other party had entered into the disputed contract under the influence of mental illness.[746] In another case, a man had registered himself as the owner of a car which his wife had bought on a hire-purchase plan. As the wife did not fulfil her obligations pursuant to the plan, the purchaser instituted an action against her husband, since he was registered as the owner of the car. He was not considered to have caused an unfounded trial by registering himself as the owner of the car. The litigation expenses were set-off.[747]

572. Furthermore, the state instituted an action through the Enforcement Service concerning the debt of a trading company of which the defendant was part owner. After it had been demonstrated that the information collected from the Trading Register had incorrectly shown that the defendant was part owner of the company when the debt was incurred, the action was dismissed on the merits. The Supreme Court regarded it as more reasonable to hold the state responsible for the defendant's litigation expenses than that the defendant should bear any of her own expenses.[748]

573. According to a rule enacted in 1990, the compensation to the party winning the case will be limited if he has instituted an action by summons and the action should preferably have been adjudicated in summary proceedings.[749]

574. The issue on how to distribute the legal costs when there are several claims in an action, and the parties alternatively win and lose or when a claim is only partly accepted, is regulated as follows: if, in a multi-claim action, each party is both winner and loser, either each party shall be required to bear his own expenses or one of the parties shall be awarded an adjusted compensation for his expenses, or, to the extent that the expenses attributable to different parts of the action are separable, the liability to compensate for expenses shall be determined by the outcome of each part. However, if the partition of the case that the party has lost is of only minor importance, he may receive full compensation for his expenses. This rule shall correspondingly apply if only a part of a party's claim is granted.[750]

575. Thus the rule in question offers four kinds of solutions:

(1) the liability to compensate for expenses shall be determined by the outcome of each part of the action;
(2) litigation expenses are fully compensated;
(3) the litigation expenses are set-off; or
(4) the litigations expenses are adjusted.

---

746. NJA 1972, p. 77. Cf. NJA 1962, p. 658; NJA 2006, p. 599 and NJA 2009, p. 342.
747. RH 1981:130.
748. NJA 1968, p. 268.
749. Concerning summary proceedings, *see* paras 694 et seq. *infra*.
750. RB 18:4.

576. The first alternative provides that the expenses for the different parts of an action can be separated, something that is seldom possible.[751] Therefore, the option will stand between set-off, adjustment or full compensation.[752] The choice must take place regarding the basic principles guiding distribution of liability for litigation expenses.[753]

577. In case law, certain rules of thumb have been developed with respect to the question of whether set-off or adjustment should take place. One such rule of thumb is that the court considers the expenses related to each claim in the action and which of the parties has been favoured by the outcome of it. This principle was applied in NJA 1978 p. 307, in which the dispute concerned compensation for different damages caused by faults in purchased property. One of the claims, for SEK 3,000, was dismissed on the merits while the other, for SEK 12,000, was accepted for only one-quarter of the sum claimed. The plaintiff was awarded full compensation for his litigation expenses, because the action had essentially been focused on the issue of whether liability to pay indemnification existed. Thus, no attention was paid to the extent to which the plaintiff's claims had been respectively accepted or not accepted.[754] This method can also be used when only one claim is partly accepted.[755]

578. Sometimes it is not possible to sever expenses related to different parts of an action. For example, this is the situation when an issue presupposes a discretionary evaluation. The Supreme Court has, in a judgment rendered *en banc*, NJA 1973 p. 623, thereby applied the principle that in such a case, the distribution of the litigation expenses should be made in direct proportion to the outcome. This means, for example, that if the plaintiff's claim is almost fully accepted, he will be granted adjusted compensation, while the defendant will achieve the corresponding benefit if less than half of the plaintiff's claim is accepted. If half of both parties' claims are accepted, the legal costs will be set-off.[756] An application of the rule in this manner contributes to private settlements in such a way that the creditor, during settlement negotiations, does not claim too much and conversely, that the debtor does not consent to a very small part of the claim. The occurrence of one of these options will prejudice the party because of its impact on the compensation for litigation expenses.[757]

579. A party whose claim is dismissed without reaching the merits is deemed the loser.[758] This does not necessarily mean that he must reimburse the other party for

751. Ekelöf, Bylund & Edelstam, *Rättegång III*, 307.
752. KRB 18:19.
753. H. Bellander, 323 et.seq.
754. *See* Ekelöf, Bylund & Edelstam, *Rättegång III*, 307 and in footnote 2: KRB 18:22.
755. Ekelöf, Boman & Bylund, *Rättegång III*, 201. *See* NJA 1978, p. 383.
756. Lindell, *Civilprocessen*, 659.
757. *Ibid.*
758. RB 18:5 para. 1.

his litigation expenses. If only a small part of the action of minor importance is dismissed, the party whose claim is dismissed might be compensated for his own expenses.[759]

580. If a party withdraws his claim or it is written-off because of his failure to appear, he shall reimburse the other party for his expenses, unless special circumstances indicate that a different resolution is appropriate.[760] The most important example of 'special circumstances' is that the plaintiff withdraws his claim after it has been satisfied by the other party. If a claim is withdrawn because its purpose has been forfeited, but it would have been accepted if examined, it might be reason to set-off the litigation costs.[761] If the plaintiff withdraws a claim because of knowledge of a circumstance, which would prevent a judgment in his favour, it is sometimes possible to set-off the litigation expenses.[762] In certain cases, the rule in question has been applied when the purpose of the action has been satisfied by a measure undertaken by a third person.[763] Withdrawal of an action concerning divorce is normally deemed to be caused by special reasons.[764]

581. If the parties settle their dispute by private agreement, each party shall bear his own expenses, unless a contrary provision is found in the settlement agreement.[765] This rule, and not the one mentioned above (18:5 paragraph 2) is to apply when the parties request that the court confirm their settlement agreement by judgment or to the part admitted by the defendant.[766] The court shall not examine whether the settlement corresponds to the parties' substantial rights.[767]

582. If compensation for litigation expenses is to be furnished by several parties on the same side, such parties are jointly and severally liable for the expenses.[768] It is thereby assumed that the parties have had essentially the same position in the action and jointly caused the expenses at issue.[769] Although the general rule is that, the parties are severally liable for the expenses,[770] to the extent that items of evidence are chargeable to a portion of the action involving only one of the co-parties, only he shall be charged.[771] As an example of this situation, the preparatory legislative works mention the case of a creditor who has sued the debtor as well as the guarantor in the same action where the creditor must present special evidence regarding the validity of the personal guarantee. In such a case, the guarantor shall

759. Gärde et al., *supra*, 206.
760. RB 18:5 para. 2.
761. NJA II 1943, p. 231. *See, e.g.*, NJA 1972, p. 12.
762. In that case pursuant to RB 18:3 para. 2, *see* NJA 1962, p. 658.
763. *See, e.g.*, NJA 1975, p. 155; 1980, p. 53 and 1983, p. 576.
764. *See* NJA 1978, p. 722.
765. RB 18:5 para. 3.
766. KRB 18:28.
767. Gärde et al., *supra*, 207.
768. RB 18:9 para. 1, p. 1.
769. NJA II 1943, p. 236.
770. *See, e.g.*, NJA 1989, p. 64.
771. RB 18:9 para. 1, p. 2.

be charged for the expenses of this evidence.[772] The corresponding rule applies if one of the co-parties has occasioned items of evidence by carelessness and oversight as described in 18:6 of the Code.[773] When, pursuant to 18:7 of the Code (*see* paragraph 265 above), a person is obliged to reimburse litigation expenses together with a party, he and the party are jointly and severally liable for the expenses.[774]

583. When party substitution occurs on the plaintiff's side, the original plaintiff and his successor are jointly and severally liable for expenses incurred prior to the substitution; after substitution, the successor bears sole responsibility. The successor of an original defendant is solely liable for the litigation expenses.[775] Note that transfer on the defendant's side cannot occur without the plaintiff's consent, in which case his interests are protected in this respect.

584. As far as the possibilities to distribute the mutual liability between severally liable co-parties are concerned, the Code provides the following solution: when two or more persons are jointly and severally liable for litigation costs, the court may, on request of one of them, specify the portion of the expenses that each should finally bear or authorize complete indemnification of one (or more) by the other.[776] An issue concerning the distribution of the litigation expenses among several parties who are mutually liable can also be put forward in an appellate court.[777] According to the preparatory legislative works, the distribution among the parties ought to be made with regard to each party's part in the disputed subject matter.[778]

585. Regarding an intervenor who lacks party standing to furnish compensation for litigation expenses and his right to be compensated for his litigation expenses, the rules concerning parties shall apply correspondingly. However, the intervenor is only liable for the special expenses incurred by his intervention. The party supported by the intervenor may not be directed to furnish compensation for such expenses.[779]

586. Some litigation expenses may not be directly related to any measure undertaken by a party. The answer in the Code concerning liability for and distribution of such expenses is that if disbursement for evidence or any other measure by order of the court shall be paid out of public funds or by the parties jointly and severally, Chapter 18 of the Code applies in respect of liability to provide reimbursement for

772. NJA II 1943, p. 236.
773. *See* paras 261–262 *supra*.
774. RB 18:9 para. 3.
775. RB 18:10. Concerning substitution of parties, *see* paras 516–521 *supra*.
776. RB 18:11.
777. NJA 1989, p. 64.
778. NJA II 1954, p. 238. Exceptions from this recommendation should follow the principles laid down in RB 18:9 para. 1.
779. RB 18:12.

such litigation expenses. Thus, if a party is liable to reimburse his adversary for litigation expenses, he must also reimburse expenses paid out of public funds. If the litigation expenses have been set-off, each party must generally equally reimburse expenses paid out of public funds.[780]

587. If a party has caused extra expenses by carelessness, he shall solely bear liability for those expenses.[781] Expenses paid out of public funds for bringing a party before the court shall always be paid by that party.

588. Regarding the disposition of issues concerning litigation expenses, a party desiring to be reimbursed for litigation expenses shall make a request for, and present a list of, his expenses to the court before the termination of the proceedings.[782] If such a request is not presented, the party forfeits the right to be reimbursed for expenses incurred in that court. Of course, the list of expenses must be so thorough that it is possible to determine whether the compensation requested is reasonable. However, despite the absence of a request, the winning party is entitled to interest and a copy of the judgment or final order of the court at his adversary's expense.

589. When finally disposing of an action, the court, on its own motion, shall simultaneously examine issues concerning the application of the rules on legal costs, if such an examination is necessary because of special circumstances.[783] This rule was changed in 1987, when it was laid down that the court is responsible for a correct application of the rules on legal costs. Previously, the parties relied on an examination by the court on its own motion, but this never took place. The parties must establish the framework of the examination by their claims. Thus, if a party should consent to pay the compensation claimed by the adversary, assuming that he wins the case, it is, according to the preparatory legislative works, hard to maintain that the court generally has the right to distribute the costs in another way, or to grant the adversary a smaller amount. Nonetheless, the court should, on its own motion, decide on the distribution of the litigation expenses within the confines of the amount demanded.[784]

590. Decisions on matters concerning litigation expenses shall be pronounced when the court renders its final judgment. The decision shall be brought into the judgment or final order. When a partial or an intermediate judgment is entered, it

780. NJA II 1943, p. 239.
781. NJA II 1943, p. 239.
782. Provided that the party has been given reasonable time to present his claim, *see* RB 32:1 and NJA 1984, p. 179. This rule is applied analogously in respect of claims for reimbursement of litigation expenses presented by legal assistants pursuant to the Legal Aid Act; *see* for example NJA 1980 p. 60. If the claim has been presented in due time, additional information related to the claim can be presented later on.
783. RB 18:14 para. 2. However, RB 18:11 only applies on request of the party.
784. Prop. 1986/87:89, p. 121.

may depend on the circumstances whether or not the court shall simultaneously decide upon the litigation costs in that part of the case or wait until the final judgment.[785]

591. Concerning liability for litigation expenses in an appellate court, litigation expenses incurred in the lower court shall be based upon the final outcome of the action.[786] If, for example, the plaintiff in the district court has been granted SEK 6,000 as indemnification, and the defendant in his appeal contests the obligation to pay any indemnification and the appellate court reduces the indemnification amount to SEK 4,000, the appellate court shall distribute the litigation expenses as if the judgment rendered by the district court had the same content.[787]

592. The obligation to reimburse litigation expenses in an appellate court shall be decided with respect to the outcome of the action in that court. Thus, the outcome of the action in the lower court does not affect the distribution of costs in an appellate court. If, for example, the plaintiff's claim in a dispute concerning indemnification is dismissed on the merits in the lower court but accepted in the appellate court, the defendant must reimburse the plaintiff his litigation expenses incurred both in the lower and in the appellate court.[788] When examining to what extent a party has won or lost in an appellate court, only claims asserted in the appellate court should be of relevance.

593. The rules in Chapter 18 of the Code shall also apply to an issue separately appealed to a higher court.[789] If an action is remanded to a lower court, the issue of expenses incurred in the higher court shall be determined by the lower court when it rehears the case.[790]

785. NJA II 1943, p. 240.
786. RB 18:15 para. 1.
787. Ekelöf, Bylund & Edelstam, *Rättegång III*, 320, KRB 18:66.
788. Ekelöf, Bylund & Edelstam, *Rättegång III*, 321.
789. RB 18:15 para. 2.
790. RB 18:15 para. 3.

Part VII. Evidence

Chapter 1. The Objects of Proof

594. Objects of proof can be legal facts, evidentiary facts, auxiliary facts, and laws of general experience and the content of the law. The meaning of these important concepts will be explained below.

595. The term 'legal fact' (*factum probandum*) refers to a fact to which a legal norm attaches certain legal consequences. However, this term is used with several different meanings. In order to understand these meanings, some brief remarks will be made regarding the construction of norms. A legal rule is generally formed in such a way that it refers to certain conditions, (prerequisites) which solely or together are either necessary or sufficient for the occurrence of a legal consequence. Therefore, it is generally possible to rewrite a legal rule in the form of a conditional statement: 'if *X* and *Y* exist, the court shall do *Z*'. In this context, the notion 'legal fact' can refer to the whole 'if-sentence', to elements in it, to the actual circumstances constituting such an element in it, or to the whole disputed event corresponding to the prerequisites in the 'if-sentence'. The term 'abstract legal fact' or the term 'prerequisite' is sometimes used to denote the legal rule, while the term 'concrete legal fact' denotes facts which have occurred. Generally, facts of the latter type will be objects for proof taking.[791]

596. The term 'evidentiary fact' (*factum probans*) denotes a circumstance which is of importance as proof of a legal fact. Even an evidentiary fact sometimes must be proved, in which case a chain of evidence will develop, but the final theme of proof (evidentiary theme) is always a legal fact. The term 'auxiliary fact', which is sometimes used, refers to a circumstance affecting the weight of evidence. Such a fact is, by itself, considered to lack evidentiary value for the theme of proof, but it can either strengthen or weaken the value of the evidentiary fact to which it is connected. If, for example, a witness has observed something at a distance and in darkness, the testimony is an evidentiary fact, and the distance and darkness are auxiliary facts.[792]

791. Lindell, *Sakfrågor och rättsfrågor*, 27.
792. Concerning these terms, *see* Ekelöf, Edelstam & Heuman, *Rättegång IV* 18 et seq. (2009). and A. Stening, *Bevisvärde* 45 (1975).

597. According to the principle *iura novit curia*, legal norms do not normally have to be proved. Pursuant to the preparatory legislative works, this principle does not prevent the parties from presenting evidence on how to interpret rules in force or on the content of customary law, but such evidence can only guide the judge. Thus, he is free to search for the meaning of the law in other ways.[793] Although a judge is not obliged to have knowledge about foreign law, if he has such knowledge he may use it. However, in such cases it can be concluded from the rules on procedural guidance that he should inform the parties of his knowledge, in order to give them an opportunity to state their opinions on the question at issue.[794] If foreign law is to be applied, and its content is not known to the court, the court may request one or both parties to present proof thereon.[795] Usually, evidence concerning the content of foreign law is obtained with the help from the Foreign Ministry's legal department. A request to a party to present evidence about the content of foreign law does not imply that failure by the requested party to present the evidence at issue will lead to a dismissal of the action on its merits.[796]

598. Laws of general experience ('frequency propositions' or 'commonplace generalizations') sometimes must be proved. Normally the judge, at the evaluation of evidence, uses his own knowledge in this respect, but sometimes an expert must provide the relevant knowledge.

793. NJA II 1943, p. 446.
794. *See* paras 357 et seq. concerning procedural guidance.
795. RB 35:2 para. 2, p. 2. *See also*: Ekelöf, Edelstam & Heuman, *Rättegång IV*, 305 et seq. Sweden has ratified the European Convention (London 7 Jun. 1968, changed by an additional protocol in Strasbourg 15 Mar. 1978) on Information About the Content of Foreign Law. Cf. the decree (1981:366) on the right to request information about the content of foreign law in certain cases.
796. NJA II 1943, p. 447.

Chapter 2. Circumstances Which Make Proof-Taking Unnecessary

599. A circumstance that is generally known does not require evidence.[797] The term 'circumstance' in this context refers to concrete facts as well as to laws of general experience. It has been maintained that, with respect to generally known facts, the court should not apply the principle of immediacy, provided that the term 'generally known fact' denotes only such facts that everyone knows with certainty.[798] In the preparatory legislative works, it is said that circumstances observed by the judge, when performing his office, should be regarded in the same way as generally known circumstances.[799] Obviously, this statement does not refer to observations related to the action in question, but to others, for example that the judge knows that a person instituting an action is bankrupt.

600. The plaintiff can renounce his claim, which means that he does not object to the claim presented by the defendant. The defendant can also consent to the claim presented by the plaintiff. In a dispositive case, a renunciation or consent constitutes a binding procedural act by the party, in which case judgment based on it may be entered without any examination of the court. However, in a non-dispositive case, the court must examine the merits on the action before entering judgment based upon a party's consent to or renunciation of a claim.

601. As far as admissions are concerned, the Code provides that if a party admits a certain fact during the proceedings in a case that is amenable to out-of-court settlement, his admission constitutes full proof against him. If the party withdraws his admission, the court shall determine, in view of the reasons for the withdrawal and other circumstances, the probative effect, if any, of the admission.[800] If in an appellate court a party withdraws an admission made in the district court, he is deemed to have presented a new circumstance, which then might be precluded.[801]

602. A binding admission must be disadvantageous as to the admitting party and must be presented in the action. It can refer to the existence as well as to the legal consequences of a legal fact.

603. According to the prevailing opinion, an admission can also refer to an evidentiary fact.[802] Such an admission is valid as long as it does not involve an issue concerning the evaluation of evidence. This regulation means, *inter alia*, that laws of general experience cannot be admitted.[803] Whether an admission can also include

797. RB 35:2 para. 1.
798. B. Lindell, *Notorietet och kontradiktion* 57 (2007).
799. NJA II 1943, p. 446.
800. RB 35:3.
801. NJA 1975, p. 603. *See* Lindell, *Processuell preklusion*, 364 et seq.
802. Ekelöf, Edelstam & Heuman, *Rättegång IV*, 70 et seq.
803. B. Lindell, *Partsautonomins gränser*, 121.

auxiliary facts is debatable.[804] Some scholars maintain that the court must also accept a false admission, i.e., an admission, which does not correspond to reality or an admitted legal consequence, or qualification that is not recognized by law. The reason for accepting such an admission is that the court is obliged to confirm a settlement by judgment, even if it contains such a false admission. Obviously, this view emanates from the principle of party disposition; when the parties can deal freely with the disputed subject matter outside the courtroom, they should be able to make the corresponding substantive dispositions at trial.[805] However, it has been argued that if the courts should accept clearly false admissions, their reputation would be prejudiced.[806] It should be mentioned that this problem is also relevant to a false consent or renunciation.

604. It appears from the Code that if the court finds that a circumstance that a party desires to prove is irrelevant to the case, or that a claimed item of evidence is unnecessary or evidently would be of no probative effect, the court shall reject that proof.[807] Pursuant to this rule, the court may also reject an offered item of evidence if the proof may be presented in another way with considerably less trouble or cost. Thus, if a legal fact lacks relevance, the court shall reject evidence supporting it. A claimed item of evidence might be unnecessary if the circumstance to be proved by it is not disputed. In addition, an item of evidence would lack probative effect if convincing evidence already exists.[808] However, it appears from the preparatory legislative works that the court shall be cautious in rejecting evidence.[809]

605. The issue of whether or not illegally obtained evidence may be presented in a Swedish court is not directly addressed in the Code or elsewhere. However, the starting point is deemed that all kinds of evidence may be presented in a trial, because of the principle of free evaluation of evidence laid down in the Code.[810] There is only one precedent case on the issue, NJA 1986 p. 489, where the circumstances were as follows: Lars travelled by motorcycle between two of the larger Swedish cities, Malmö and Lund. When Lars arrived in Lund he came to the attention of the police. Among other things, his motorcycle fell over when he tried to park it. The police suspected that Lars was under the influence of alcohol and took him to a hospital for a blood test. A laboratory assistant took the blood test, although the relevant rule in the Code clearly states that a doctor or an authorized nurse must take a blood test. The blood test showed that the concentration of alcohol in Lars's blood was over the permitted maximum. Lars was convicted on all instances. The majority of the Supreme Court stated, *inter alia*, that there were no obstacles against

804. Hassler, *supra*, 373 argues that neither evidentiary nor auxiliary facts may be admitted, *but see* L. Heuman, *Åklagarens processhandlingar*, 371, in SvJT (1982) 353–381, who accepts admissions of auxiliary facts.

805. *See* Boman, *Åberopsbördan*, 60 and Lindell, *Partsautonomins gränser*, 54 et seq.

806. S. Larsson, *Studier rörande partshandlingar* 19 note 4 (1979) and Olivecrona, *Rätt och dom*, 194.

807. RB 35:7.

808. *See* Lindell, *Processuell preklusion*, 37 et seq. and L. Heuman, *Skriftligt hovrättsförfarande i brottmål*, 98 (1983).

809. NJA II 1943, p. 451.

810. SOU 1984:54, p. 205.

relying on the blood test, although it was not carried out entirely in accordance with the procedural law. The court found that no fundamental principle of the Swedish legal system had been set aside in such a way that the blood test could not be admitted as evidence. However, the court stated that high demands should be placed upon the evaluation of such evidence.[811]

606. Thus, the Swedish standpoint on this issue is that, in principle, all kinds of evidence presented to the court are to be included in the material that the court uses to form its judgment. If there is no explicit rule, which excludes illegally obtained evidence, the presumption is that it will be admitted.[812]

811. *See* K. Thelin, *Grundlagen och blodprovet – prov utan värde*, SvJT 129 et seq. (1987); L. Welamson, *Svensk rättspraxis. Civiloch straffprocessrätt 1980–1987*, SvJT 579 (1989) and B. Lindell, *The Exclusion of Evidence in Criminal Cases in Sweden*. Swedish National Reports to the XIIIth International Congress of Comparative Law 301 et seq. (1990).

812. *See also* Ekelöf & Boman, *Rättegång IV*, 180 and L. Heuman, *Otillåtna inskränkningar av bevisföringen och bevisvärdering*, Advokaten 42 and 51 (1986). *See also* NJA 2003, p. 323.

Chapter 3. The Burden of Alleging Legal Facts and the Burden of Proof

607. The burden of alleging legal facts shall be applied only in dispositive cases.[813] It means that the court may not base its judgment on a legal fact that has not been alleged. As far as evidentiary facts are concerned, they normally need not be alleged. This is obviously true with respect to, *inter alia*, the behaviour of a witness at trial; a party need not, for example, allege that the witness avoids eye contact or seems to be embarrassed, although this behaviour might have evidentiary value. However, when it comes to more important items of evidence, the parties should state them in order to avoid surprises.[814] The evidentiary theme and the means of evidence shall be stated during the preparation.[815]

608. Normally, the burden of alleging legal facts follows the burden of proof, which means that the party who bears the burden of proof also bears the burden of alleging legal facts. However, as implied, there are exceptions to this rule.[816]

609. As far as who bears the burden of proof and the required degree of proof for the evidentiary theme are concerned, substantive law is usually silent.[817] How to allocate the burden of proof in such cases and decide the required degree of probability has been much debated in Sweden.

610. Olivecrona maintained that the purpose underlying the substantive rules applicable to the dispute should be decisive in this respect.[818] This idea was adopted and developed by Ekelöf, who recommended that a teleological construction and application of the provision at issue should determine who bears the burden of proof and the required degree of probability. Regarding the latter, Ekelöf argued that the required degree of probability should normally be confirmed on a scale with four degrees of probability: 'plausible' (the lowest), 'probable', 'confirmed' and 'obvious' (the highest, applicable in criminal cases).[819] Other scholars have argued that the probability requirement ought to be more flexible and that the preponderance of evidence should be the starting point in a debate on how to distribute the risk for an erroneous outcome of the disputed subject-matter.[820]

611. The different views on how to allocate the burden of proof, when case law and substantive law are silent on the matter, and how to fix the required degree of proof, are linked to different attitudes toward the ideological issue concerning the

813. RB 17:3, p. 2. *See also* para. 63 *supra*.
814. Lindell, *Processuell preklusion*, 245.
815. RB 42:2, p. 3; 42:6 and 42:7, p. 4 and Lindell, *Processuell preklusion*, 244.
816. *See* Boman, *Åberopsbördan*, 263.
817. To the extent substantive rules entail regulations on this subject, these often consist of presumptions, which either reverse the burden of proof or lower the required degree of proof.
818. K. Olivecrona, *Bevisskyldigheten och den materiella rätten* 130 (1930).
819. Lindell, *Civilprocessen*, 537.
820. P.O. Bolding, *Bevisbördan och den juridiska tekniken* 94 (1951) and the same author in *Går det att bevisa* 95 et seq. (1989) and Lindell, *Sakfrågor och rättsfrågor*, 284.

function of the judicial system. Both Ekelöf and Olivecrona stress that the purpose of litigation is behaviour modification, while, for example, Bolding and Lindell stress that its main purpose is conflict resolution.

612. According to the behaviour modification theory, the required degree of proof should normally be rather high. Thus, in actions concerning payment of a debt, it ought to be 'confirmed', in order to impose pressure on debtors to pay. The idea is that the requirement of a high degree of proof shall make debtors realize that there is no point in presenting unfounded or ill-founded objections to a claim, hoping to escape payment. This pressure on the debtors is assumed to improve their willingness to pay, and if it does, the creditors will be willing to arrange credits, something which will benefit the economic life of society. The argument that a debtor runs the risk of paying the same debt twice if the required degree of proof is high is met with the argument that some debtors must be sacrificed on the altar of credit in order to achieve behaviour modification.[821]

613. The theory of conflict resolution does not coincide with this way of arguing. Certainly, a higher level of proof creates pressure on debtors to voluntarily pay, thereby avoiding unnecessary trials. However, the opinion that litigation is capable of influencing the morality of a person is exaggerated and may even appear offensive in resolving individual cases considering its impact on behaviour modification in general. Instead, the goal must be to do justice in the individual case. If, therefore, there are no special reasons supporting placing the risk for an erroneous outcome on a particular party, that risk ought to be distributed equally between them. This means an application of the rule of preponderance of evidence, that is to say that the party who presents the strongest evidence will win the case, however small the preponderance of evidence might be.

614. As far as case law is concerned, it is difficult to say how high the requirement of the degree of proof is in different types of actions. The reason is that terms such as 'confirm' and 'probable' are both vague and ambiguous. They can mean either that the evidentiary theme has been proved, in which case nothing can be concluded about the particular degree of proof that has been applied, or they can refer to a special degree of required proof. However, at least one thing can be said for sure: the required degree of proof is lower in actions where there are difficulties of proving the theme, *inter alia* in actions where the plaintiff must prove causal relations.[822]

821. Ekelöf & Boman, *Rättegång IV*, 91 (6th ed.).
822. *See, e.g.*, NJA 1952, p. 104; 1959, p. 318; 1977, p. 176; 1977, p. 549; 1991, p. 622 and 1982, p. 421.

Chapter 4. Administration of Evidence

§1. Competence to Appear as a Witness

615. Anyone who is not a party in the case may be heard as a witness.[823] If a member of the court is called as a witness, he shall consider, on his oath as a judge, whether he knows anything that might be informative in the action. If he finds that he does, he may testify as a witness.[824] Through the reform A Modernized Procedure, the rule in 35:6 of the Code was changed so that the parties would become fully responsible for presenting the evidence in a non-dispositive case. Before the change, the court could in its own motion complement the evidence in such cases.

616. If testimony is sought from a person who is under the age of 15, is suffering from mental disease, simple-mindedness, or has any other mental illness or disturbance, the court shall determine, in accordance with the particular circumstances, whether he may be heard as a witness.[825] If the court decides that the person in question may be heard as a witness, an oath may not be taken nor may a sub-poena be used to make him give testimony. In addition, it is possible to examine the witness behind closed doors.

617. Persons who are subject to a duty of confidentiality outside the courtroom are not allowed to testify in certain circumstances. This includes, for example, people in the Foreign Ministry, the National Defence, the National Bank, doctors and lawyers.[826] These people are, of course, obliged to testify, but they may not be asked questions concerning matters that fall within their duty of confidentiality. This is also true if the trial is not held publicly. The court must apply the rule ex officio. The person on whose behalf the confidentiality is imposed can, however, waive his right in this regard.

§2. Limitations on the Obligation to Testify

618. The King and foreign diplomats who have diplomatic immunity are exempt from the obligation to testify.[827] Furthermore, a party's close relatives are not obliged to testify. This includes: (1) a person who is or has been married to the

823. RB 36:1.
824. RB 36:2.
825. RB 36:4.
826. RB 36:5.
827. As far as actions related to a foreign country are concerned the following Acts and Conventions are of importance: The EU Council (Decree No.1206/2001) on collaboration between the Member States with respect to proof-taking in commercial cases and matters, The Hague Convention (18 March 1970) on Proof-Taking Abroad in Cases and Matters of Civil or Commercial Nature and the Act (SFS 1946:817) on Proof-Taking at a Foreign Court. Annexed decrees are K (1947:847) on proof-taking at a foreign court and decree (2000:708) on the procedure when requiring proof-taking according to the above-mentioned Hague Convention; the Act (SFS 1946:816) on Proof-taking to a foreign court with the annexed decree K (1947:848) on particular regulations about

party; (2) a person who stands in ascending or descending relationship to the party; (3) a person who is related to the party by marriage or is brother or sister in-law; and (4) a person who is or has been married to a brother or sister to the party or is related in a similar way.[828] This rule does not release the witness from the duty to appear before the court, but after the relationship has been established, he or she may stand down. If the person in question is willing to testify, he or she will be treated as an ordinary witness. The rationale behind the rule is to protect the solidarity between relatives.[829]

619. An obligation to testify can be partially limited. Thus, a witness may decline to testify concerning a circumstance that might reveal that he, or a person related to him, has committed a crime or a dishonourable act. Furthermore, a witness may refrain from giving testimony that would involve disclosure of a trade secret, unless there are extraordinary reasons for examining the witness on the matter.[830]

620. It is sometimes difficult to say what kind of acts ought to be regarded as dishonourable. If, for example, a witness has promised someone to keep a secret, the rule will not apply, even if it could be regarded as dishonourable to reveal the secret.[831] Nor can the rule be assumed to apply to situations regarding a person's character, which might be regarded as dishonourable.[832]

621. The preparatory legislative works state that trade secrets include manufacturing methods, constructions, business relations or similar material, which can be regarded as something original, if the possessor of it has a reasonable interest in not revealing it.[833]

§3. The Procedure When Taking Witness Testimony

622. A person who must testify shall be served with a notice to appear in court. The notice to appear shall state names of the parties, the title of the case, and the time and place for the appearance of the witness. It shall also contain a summary

---

proof-taking to certain foreign states; the Act (SFS 1946:818) on Proof-taking to Certain International Bodies; the Act (SFS 1946:819) on Taking Oath to Secure Rights Abroad; The Hague Convention (25 Oct. 1980) on International Legal Aid; the Act (SFS 1985:988) on Immunity for Certain Witnesses etc. and the decree (KK 1974:122) on Immunity and Privilege for Certain Consulates.

828. RB 36:3.
829. Cf. Ekelöf, Edelstam & Heuman, *Rättegång IV*, 230.
830. RB 36:6.
831. Lindell, *Civilprocessen*, 475
832. G. Lagerbielke, *Om mened* 185 (1979). In NJA 1952, p. 262 a sexual relation outside marriage was regarded as a dishonourable circumstance in an action concerning judicial separation. In NJA 1985, p. 774 a person was regarded as not entitled to decline to give testimony concerning a circumstance which would reveal a criminal act against the tax law when the limitation period for the act at issue had expired.
833. NJA II 1943, p. 472.

description of the matter upon which testimony is sought.[834] Before his appearance to testify, the court may instruct the witness to refresh his memory on the subject of his testimony by examining accessible account-books, notes or other documents, or by inspecting a place or an object, if this can be done without considerable inconvenience to the witness.[835]

623. In the absence of special cause for his attendance, a witness may not observe the proceedings in the case prior to giving his testimony.[836] The purpose is to prevent the witness from being influenced by the proceedings, which could affect the content of his testimony.[837] However, the preparatory legislative works state that sometimes, for example if a case concerns a great number of items in an account and each item is separately examined at trial, it might be convenient to allow the witness to observe some part of the proceedings.[838]

624. Before examining a witness, the court shall ask him to state his full name, and if necessary, age, occupation and residence, and attempt to ascertain whether he has a relationship to any of the parties, or to the matter in dispute, that might be of importance in evaluating the reliability of his testimony, or whether any other circumstance exists that may be of importance in that respect. Any witness related to a party (*see* paragraph 620 *supra*) shall be advised that he is under no obligation to testify.[839]

625. The witness shall take the following oath before giving testimony: 'I (name) promise and assure upon my faith and honour that I shall speak the whole truth and will not conceal, add or change anything.'[840] However, an oath may not be taken by: (1) a person under the age of 15; or (2) a person who, owing to mental disease, simple-mindedness or any other mental disturbance, is found to lack insight into the importance of the oath.[841] Before hearing a witness, the court shall warn him of his duty to tell the truth and, when he has taken the oath, remind him of its significance.[842]

626. The party on whose behalf the witness has been called, if the court does not decide otherwise, shall commence the examination.[843] It appears from the preparatory legislative works that it might be more appropriate that the court leads the examination if, for example, a strong antagonism exists between the witness and the party who has called him, if a party is litigating without an attorney and lacks the

834. RB 36:7. The notice shall also refer the witness to the provisions in RB 36:20, 23 and 25, *see* para. 630 *infra*.
835. RB 36:8.
836. RB 36:9.
837. *See also* para. 384 *supra*.
838. NJA II 1943, p. 474.
839. RB 36:10.
840. RB 36:11.
841. RB 36:13.
842. RB 36:14. When there is cause the witness shall also be reminded of the provisions in RB 36:5 and 6.
843. RB 36:17.

ability to lead the examination properly or if the witness is very nervous.[844] In addition, it sometimes might be the best solution that the other party leads the examination if the witness makes statements, which are to the disadvantage of the party on whose behalf the witness has been called.[845] Leading questions are not allowed during this so-called principal examination.[846]

627. After the principal or primary examination of the witness, the other party shall be given an opportunity to question the witness if one of the exceptions mentioned above has not been applied. The purpose of the cross-examination is to check whether the testimony is reliable. Leading questions are allowed during the cross-examination.[847]

628. However, sometimes the most appropriate solution is that the court handles the cross-examination, for example if the party who normally should lead it is absent or lacks an attorney and cannot lead it by himself.[848]

629. After the cross-examination, the parties and the court may question the witness further. The party on whose behalf the witness has been called should be given the first opportunity to raise additional questions. This is called re-examination. If neither of the parties, or both, have called the witness, the re-examination shall be commenced by the court. The purpose of the re-examination is to give a witness, who during the cross-examination might have been influenced to state certain facts, an opportunity to reconsider his statements and change them if necessary.[849] With this purpose of the re-examination in mind, it is surprising that, according to the preparatory legislative works, leading questions may not be asked during re-examination.[850] However, this prohibition has at least one exception: if during the cross-examination it appears that the testimony is to the disadvantage of the party on whose behalf the witness has been called, leading questions may be allowed during the re-examination.[851]

630. A witness who fails to respond to a notice to appear shall be *fined*. Instead the court may order that the witness be brought to the hearing in custody, but this option is usually not initially used.[852] If a witness, without valid reasons, refuses to take an oath or to testify, or refuses to respond to a particular question or obey an order (*see* paragraph 624 *supra*), the court shall order the witness to perform his duty under penalty of a fine and, if the witness persists in his refusal, under penalty of detention.[853] However, in practice, detention hardly ever occurs. If a witness is

844. NJA II 1987, p. 203.
845. *Ibid.*, 204.
846. *Ibid.*
847. *Ibid.*
848. *Ibid.*
849. *Ibid.*, p. 205.
850. *Ibid.*, p. 204.
851. *Ibid.*
852. RB 36:20.
853. RB 36:21.

liable for such negligence or contumacy as mentioned, and a party has thereby incurred litigation costs, the court may order the witness to pay compensation for such costs.[854]

§4. Proof-Taking Outside of the Main Hearing

631. According to the Code it is sometimes possible to take witness evidence outside of the main hearing.[855] Such an examination may occur: (1) if a witness is unable to appear at the main hearing; or (2) it is found that the presence of the witness at the main hearing would occasion expenses or special inconvenience which are not reasonable with respect to the importance of an examination held at the main hearing. Point (1) is mainly meant to apply to the situation where a witness is unable to appear at the main hearing because of illness. The balancing of interests with respect to point (2) presupposes that the value of the claim is considered, as well as the importance of the testimony for the outcome of the action and, in addition, the impact on the evaluation of evidence that proof taking outside the main hearing would have.[856]

§5. Affidavits

632. According to the Code, testimony written down and presented to the court normally will not be accepted in ordinary proceedings.[857,858] This prohibition is based on the principle of free evaluation of evidence; if the court cannot see how the witness performs in court (i.e., how he reacts to certain questions, whether he makes any revealing facial gestures or shows embarrassment, etc.) then it (the court) is not in a position to judge the value of his testimony. Accordingly, the general rule is that evidentiary statements must be directly and orally presented to the court.[859] This is also an example of the principle of immediacy of evidence and of the best evidence rule.

---

854. RB 36:23.
855. RB 36:19.
856. NJA II 1987, p. 208. In NJA 1982, p. 372 a party claimed perpetuation of proof for the future (*see* paras 677–678 *infra*) concerning a witness, 74 years old. The crucial issue was whether to apply RB 41:1 or 36:19. The action was unusual since the preparation of the case had continued for eleven years. The proof-taking was required since there was a risk that the witness, considering his age, would die before the main hearing. RB 41:1 was not applied since this rule requires that an action has not been instituted. However, the Supreme Court applied RB 36:19 analogously, stating that this rule also covers situations where there is a risk that a witness will not appear at the main hearing.
857. The term 'affidavit' is used in the text to describe a paper written by a witness containing testimony not confirmed by oath.
858. Affidavits are accepted in summary proceedings and also at intermistic examinations, *see* AD 1982, p. 28 with respect to the latter issue.
859. RB 35:8.

633. However, there are exceptions to the general rule. These were made by the legislature when the Code was enacted. Thus, affidavits are admitted when it is specially prescribed. For example, when a party or a witness makes a statement in court that is inconsistent with an earlier statement given to the prosecutor or the police, or if a party refuses to make a statement in court, the earlier statement may be read in court.[860] In addition, it is permitted to read from documents that a party to the case referred to earlier, if he is not present at the trial.

634. In practice, the prohibition against affidavits is not applied to birth certificates, doctor's certificates and similar documents issued by a civil servant or another official functionary. The courts usually also accept certificates concerning the value of damaged or stolen property.[861]

635. However, the provisions in the Code concerning the principal rule on the prohibition of affidavits were relaxed in 1987 after a request from practising lawyers. Among others, the district courts during the legislative work pointed out some problems, which had arisen because of increasing international crime. It was not unusual that witnesses residing abroad were called to appear at Swedish courts for drug cases. If it was not possible to get the witness to appear at the Swedish court, the prosecutor during the preliminary hearings sometimes examined the witness abroad and subsequently presented the minutes from this examination to a Swedish court.[862] However, as it seemed doubtful whether this was acceptable pursuant to the wordings in the Code concerning affidavits, it was suggested that the rule at issue ought to be relaxed.[863]

636. Through the reform, A Modernized Procedure, the rule became even more generous (*see* point (4) below). Today there are exceptions to the prohibition against affidavits. An affidavit will be admitted when:

(1) it is specially prescribed;
(2) an examination of the witness cannot be held in or outside the courtroom or otherwise in front of the court; or
(3) there are special reasons with respect to the costs or the inconvenience an examination by or outside of the courtroom would entail, the advantages to be gained with such an examination, the importance of the evidence and other circumstances;[864](4) the parties agree about the use of affidavits and it is not deemed obvious that the use of affidavits would be inappropriate.[865]

637. Point (1) corresponds to earlier legislation, mentioned above. Point (2) is meant to apply when the deponent is deceased or so ill that he cannot be examined

860. RB 36:16 para. 2.
861. Ekelöf & Boman, *Rättegång IV*, 31.
862. Pursuant to RB 35:14.
863. *See* NJA 1987, p. 199.
864. RB 35:14.
865. Prop. 2004/05:131, p. 235.

in court.[866] Moreover, this exception aims at the situation where the deponent sojourns at an unknown place and cannot be expected to be found.[867] As far as point (3) is concerned, the advantage to be gained from an oral examination shall be related not only to the expenses for an examination in court, but also to the value of the claim and the time that can be spared if an affidavit is permitted.[868] The term 'the importance of the statement' is meant to refer to the impact of the statement on the outcome of the action. In addition, 'the importance of the case' is meant to be regarded in such a way that the court sometimes can be more generous in accepting affidavits in 'small cases' than in cases concerning large amounts, or in cases concerning severe crimes. It is pointed out in the preparatory legislative works that an alternative to an affidavit might be to examine the witness by telephone.[869] As far as point (4) is concerned, it is underlined in the preparatory works that the court should make the parties aware that an affidavit normally has a lower evidentiary value compared with appearance in the courtroom.[870]

638. The relaxing of the prohibition against affidavits is not meant to set aside the principle of immediacy of evidence. Nor does it imply that the court should accept a lower degree of proof. Oral examination of a witness in court will be the normal procedure even in the future.[871]

§6. Examination by Telephone

639. As has been mentioned above, the special rule about proof taking by telephone was omitted through the reform A Modernized Litigation.[872]

640. Today, the same prerequisites apply regardless of whether a person shall participate by appearing in person or by audio- and picture recording. However, the possibility to make a more secure assessment of the evidentiary value of a witness statement is higher if the person appears through video conferencing. Thus, if it is a more important witness, the telephone should not be used.

641. Finally, it should be stressed that proof taking by telephone assumes that the purpose of the oral examination will be essentially satisfied even though the telephone is used. Thus, the court must be able to evaluate the testimony in all relevant aspects.[873]

---

866. NJA II 1987, p. 201.
867. *Ibid.*
868. *Ibid.*
869. *Ibid.*
870. Prop. 2004/05:131, p. 236.
871. *Ibid.*
872. Cf. para. 350 *infra*.
873. *Ibid.*

§7. EXAMINATION OF A PARTY

642. In Chapter 37 of the Code, there are rules concerning examination of a party to obtain evidence. The chapter was reformed in 1987 to create a clearer distinction between the presentation of the facts in controversy and the examination of a party. Thus, an examination of a party, which is directly aimed at obtaining his standpoint on the disputed issue, does not fall under Chapter 37. Since the chapter mainly refers to Chapter 36, it only contains three paragraphs.

643. Before the reform, Chapter 37 only applied to an examination of a party under affirmation of truth. As far as the background to the reform is concerned, affirmation of truth was and is a primary means of evidence, meaning that it is at the free disposal of the parties. Thus, it is not used at the court's initiative when it is clear that items of evidence that were already presented are insufficient. However, only a short time after the Code came into force, the use of affirmation of truth was criticized, since the parties frequently used it to strengthen their positions and one could suspect that a considerable number of false statements were given under oath. Obviously, this is a criminal offence, but it is hard to prove.[874] In order to limit the use of affirmation of truth as much as possible, the option of examining a party with the purpose of obtaining evidence was therefore enacted by the reform in question.[875] Untrue statements given by a party examined with the purpose of obtaining evidence are not criminalized, since the party then neither takes an oath nor is heard under affirmation of truth. Although the Code provides that a party shall truthfully account for his allegation in the action, respond to the allegations of the other party and answer questions put to him, this rule does not impose any sanction on a party who lies.[876] Having discussed the background, a closer account of the rules will be given in the following paragraphs.

644. A party in a civil action shall be heard with the purpose of obtaining evidence, if he or the other party request such an examination.[877] An examination with the purpose of obtaining evidence should occur before any witness is heard, since a party might otherwise adjust his statements to the testimony of the witness.[878]

645. An examination of a party under affirmation of truth, with the purpose of obtaining evidence, is only permitted in civil cases.[879] Such an examination should be limited to circumstances of special importance. Before testifying, a party shall take this affirmation: 'I (name) promise and assure on my honour and conscience that I will speak the whole truth and will not conceal, add, or change anything.'

874. *See* para. 353 *supra.*
875. *Ibid.*, p. 211.
876. *See* RB 43:6 para. 1 and para. 353 *supra.* It should be mentioned that procedural fraud has not been adopted in the Swedish legal system.
877. RB 37:1.
878. RB 43:8 para. 2.
879. RB 37:2.

646. In the preparatory legislative works, it is said that it is appropriate that a party begins with making his statements without affirmation of truth and that he later on, if necessary, may confirm certain items of special relevance under affirmation of truth.[880] When the reform came into force, this method was already used by the courts, so in a sense the reform adjusted the law to reality.

647. A party who shall be examined obviously must be called to appear in person.[881] If a party fails to appear, a default judgment can be rendered in a dispositive case. In non-dispositive cases, the party can ultimately be brought to the hearing in custody. If a party, or for that matter a witness, should appear, but refuses to answer questions, such a refusal can be considered by the court when evaluating the evidence in the action.

648. Concerning the examination of a party, Chapter 37 refers to the rule on the same subject concerning the examination of a witness, and reference is made to what has been stated in paragraphs 626–629 *supra*. If the other party has requested the examination, it might also be best that his attorney leads the primary examination and that the other party leads the cross-examination.[882] An additional exception from the principal rule concerning examination of a witness, i.e., that the party on whose behalf the witness has been called shall commence the examination, is the situation where a party requests examination of the other party. In such a case, it has been regarded as appropriate that the other party starts the examination.[883]

649. In all other essential aspects, Chapter 37 refers to Chapter 36.

§8. Documentary Evidence

650. When a document is presented as proof at a trial, it is denoted as a documentary evidence. Its evidentiary value depends on the content of the document. Thus, a letter with fingerprints or blood on it cannot constitute documentary evidence, insofar as the evidentiary value is related only to the fingerprints, or the blood.

651. Documents are either public or private. The former can be official or secret, according to the Public Access to Information and Secrecy Act. Furthermore, there is a difference between 'intentional documents', i.e., a document produced in order to secure proof (e.g., a receipt), and 'occasional documents', e.g., a memory note. There are also certain other distinctions, but these will not be specifically addressed

880. NJA II 1987, p. 212.
881. RB II:5, 42:12 and 42:21.
882. KRB 37:6.
883. NJA II 1987, p. 210.

given its consent thereto; (2) a document for which the contents are such that anyone who has been concerned therewith may not be examined thereon; or (3) a document for which the production would disclose a trade secret, unless there is special cause.[897]

661. If provisions which differ from those prescribed in Chapter 38 of the Code have been issued concerning the obligation to produce a document, they shall apply.

§9. On-Site Investigations

662. For the examination of immovable property or objects that cannot conveniently be brought to the courtroom, or of the scene of a special occurrence, the court may hold a viewing at the *locus in quo*.[898]

663. However, the term 'viewing' as used in the Code is misleading, since the ability to see is not more important at viewing than it is when examining other types of evidence. In addition, sense organs other than the eyes can be used at viewings, for example the ability to smell and feel.[899]

664. A document can also be an object for viewing if the document per se, rather than its contents, is of evidentiary importance, for example when it is used to examine a specimen of a person's handwriting. It is thus obvious that the distinguishing quality of viewing is not the way in which an object is observed, but the object for the observation.[900] However, the borderline between documentary evidence and viewing sometimes is hard to find, for example when the contents of a document as well as the document as such might be important as proof. Nevertheless, the borderline issue is of no considerable importance, since the conditions required for an obligation to surrender an object for viewing are essentially the same as the obligation to produce documents.[901]

665. Objects that are easy to remove will be examined in the courtroom; otherwise the court may hold a viewing at the *locus in quo*. According to the principle of the best evidence, viewing at the *locus in quo* should preferably take place at the main hearing, which then may be held at the place for the viewing. The court can, on its own motion, issue an order on viewing in the courtroom or at *locus in quo* for all kinds of actions. Viewing may not be used to track documents or other removable objects.

666. Anyone possessing an object that can conveniently be brought to the courtroom and that can be assumed to be of importance as proof is obliged to make it

897. RB 38:8.
898. RB 39:1. There are special provisions regarding the taking of blood-tests. *See* the Act (1958:642) on Blood Examination when Examining Paternity.
899. NJA II 1943, p. 503.
900. Ekelöf, Edelstam & Heuman, *Rättegång IV*, 279.
901. *Ibid.*, note 1 c.

accessible for inspection at a viewing. The provision in the Code (RB 36:6) regarding the privilege of a witness to refuse to testify shall correspondingly apply to the privilege of a party, or any other person, to refuse to make an object available for inspection at a viewing. Regarding the duty to produce a document for inspection, the provisions concerning documentary evidence shall apply (RB 38:2).

§10. Experts

667. The court may call upon an expert if the appraisal and determination of a matter require special professional knowledge.[902] The difference between a witness and an expert is mainly that the former shall testify about his observations, while an expert provides the court with the laws of general experience necessary in order to draw correct conclusions with respect to the facts established in the action.

668. An expert sometimes makes statements about observed facts. In such a case, a difference between an expert and a witness is that the witness is called because he has observed something, whereas the expert might be asked to make an observation.

669. The court may obtain an opinion on the disputed matter from a public authority or officer, or from any person specially licensed to furnish opinions on the matter. The court may also commission one or more persons known for their integrity and their knowledge of the subject to offer an opinion. As far as disqualification of an expert commissioned by the court is concerned, essentially the same provisions are applied as for judges.[903]

670. Before appointing an expert, the court should invite the parties to state their views thereon. If the parties agree upon an expert he shall normally be used.[904] No person is required to perform like an expert, unless he voluntarily undertakes to do so, except for persons who in their official capacity are obliged to assist as experts and those specially licensed to furnish opinions.[905] To facilitate an expert's investigation, the court may, for example, order the examination of a person and may order that objects be made available for his inspection.[906] The court may direct that the parties be notified by the expert to attend such an inspection.[907]

671. Solely a party can also call an expert.[908] Such an expert will be regarded as an ordinary witness. Thus, it is not required that such an expert be impartial. As far as this expert is concerned, the court cannot, in contrast to the above-mentioned provision, facilitate his work by, for example, ordering proof-taking before the main

902. RB 40:1. *See* H. Edelstam, *Sakkunnigbeviset* (1991).
903. *See* RB 4:13.
904. RB 40:3.
905. RB 40:4.
906. RB 40:5.
907. RB 40:6.
908. RB 40:19.

hearing. Nor does a private expert take the oath prescribed for an expert appointed by the court: 'I (name) promise and assure on my faith and honour that I will perform the expert task assigned to me to the best of my ability.'[909] Thus, a private expert does not state his opinion under criminal liability. Moreover, he will be compensated as a witness. The party must, on request, reimburse him for expenses.[910] In spite of these rules, private experts are more common than experts appointed by the court, although it is clear that the legislator prefers an expert appointed by the court, who is deemed more reliable than a private expert is.[911]

672. Normally, an expert shall submit a written opinion in which he states the reasoning and circumstances upon which the conclusion in the report are founded. After the report is filed with the court, it must be made accessible to the parties, preferably before the preparation of the action commences.

673. An expert who has submitted a written opinion shall also be examined orally, if a party requests it, unless examination of the expert is plainly without importance, or if the court finds it necessary. However, with regard to a report obtained from a central administrative board, an academy or any other official society, neither the board or society nor any person who participated in preparing the report may be examined orally, unless such examination is found unavoidable. The reason underlying this exception is that an examination of an academy or other such body would occasion considerable expense and inconvenience, since reports from such bodies appear so often in courts.[912]

674. The costs of expert evidence normally constitute a part of the parties' litigation costs. These costs are divided in accordance with Chapter 18 of the Code.

§11. Perpetuation of Proof for the Future

675. The Code provides a possibility to take proof even though an action has not been instituted. It must be proof concerning a circumstance of importance to a person's legal rights. Furthermore, a risk must exist that the proof will be lost or difficult to obtain. Moreover, an action concerning the right at issue may not be pending and, finally, the proof that may be taken (in the lower court) must be a witness testimony, an expert opinion, a viewing or a documentary evidence. The purpose of the proof taking may not be to investigate a crime.[913]

676. The procedure is as follows: anyone desiring to take and perpetuate proof for the future shall apply to the court. The application shall state the fact expected

909. RB 40:9.
910. Cf. para. 553 *supra*.
911. *See* Ekelöf, Edelstam & Heuman, *Rättegång IV*, 288.
912. SOU 1938:44, p. 423.
913. RB 41:1. Cf. NJA 1884, p. 181 and 1935, p. 186 and KRB 41:6. Perpetuation of proof for the future may not be used if it directly aims at identifying the counterpart in a future action; *see* NJA 1984, p. 47, Cf. NJA 1982, p. 650.

to be established by the proof, the nature of the proof, the grounds claimed by the applicant in support of the proposed proof taking and, if possible, the other persons whose interests may be at stake.[914] The provisions on proof taking outside a main hearing shall correspondingly apply to the perpetuation of proof for the future.[915] The cost shall be paid by the applicant.[916]

914. RB 41:2.
915. RB 41:3.
916. RB 41:4.

Chapter 5. Evaluation of Evidence

677. The principle of free examination of evidence is laid down in the Code, which states that when assessing the evidence, the court is to consider all that has occurred in the action in order to determine what has been proved in the case.[917] The rule in question does not dictate how different pieces of evidence are to be evaluated. This freedom of evaluation constitutes the very essence of the free evaluation of evidence.[918] However, the freedom of evaluation entails that the rule at issue assumes the character of an ordinary material clause. Like a general clause, it allows scope for judicial discretion of appreciable significance. Yet, it diverges from a material general clause in that, *inter alia*, it pertains to facts and not to norms, the rules concerning burden of proof can be applied to the former but not the latter, and in the evaluation of evidence, a somewhat different material is used from that in applying norms.[919]

678. As far as the evaluation of evidence is concerned, the preparatory legislative works are meagre. However, some guidelines have been given. The evaluation at issue shall be objective, which means that it is to be supported on grounds acceptable to other reasonable individuals. In order to achieve this goal, the judge at the evaluation must use laws of general experience and general rules of deduction. In addition, this notion of objectivity brings with it a requirement for an account in the judgment concerning which facts were considered to have evidentiary value and how they were evaluated, together with a simultaneous requirement for analysis. The latter is of great importance for a party when appealing against a judgment.[920]

679. When evaluating evidence, the judge may only take into consideration that which emerged in the case. The evidentiary theme must express an assertion, about either a fact, a legal principle or a general law of experience. Moreover, the evidentiary theme obviously must be provable, and it must somehow be relevant to the evidentiary fact.[921] The fact that the evidentiary theme must express an assertion means that it must – in contrast to norms – be capable of being proven true or false. Consequently, the prerequisite, which expresses a value or is vague, must be reduced to a descriptive sentence. Indeed, value judgments are generally regarded as incapable of being true or false, and vague expressions, which cannot be directly said to articulate value judgments, may be too indeterminate to be included in an evidentiary relation.[922]

680. Laws of general experience are based on induction. In evaluating evidence, facts are subsumed under laws of general experience so that a statement concerning

917. RB 35:1.
918. Lindell, *Sakfrågor och rättsfrågor*, 96.
919. *Ibid.*, 100.
920. SOU 1926:32, p. 255, SOU 1926:33, p. 142 and SOU 1938:44, p. 377.
921. Lindell, *Sakfrågor och rättsfrågor*, 103.
922. *Ibid.*, 174 et seq.

probability can be made. At the subsumption in question, a variant of the subsumption model is used.[923] In addition, laws of general experience may be weak or strong, may refer to special areas where expert knowledge is needed, or may be common knowledge (of universal validity). Many laws of general experience are very vague, and may border on prejudice. It is important for the judge to be flexible in the evaluation of evidence so that prejudices do not impinge on the establishment of facts.[924]

681. The above-mentioned general guidelines concerning objectivity, laid down in the preparatory legislative works, have been developed in doctrine. In the same year that the Code came into force (1948), Ekelöf edited a book on civil procedure in which he introduced certain mathematical rules for calculating the evidentiary value of several items of evidence.[925] It might be seen as a paradox that new rules on how to value evidence were recommended at the same time as the formal rules of evidence were abolished.[926] However, Ekelöf wanted to construct a model for evaluating evidence in order to decrease the risk for extensive discretion. Certainly, such aspects of legal security are also behind the formal rules of evidence, but the difference between these and the model recommended by Ekelöf was considerable. According to Ekelöf, the judge should freely evaluate every item of evidence. However, the summing up of all evidence presented in the action should be performed in accordance with logical rules.

682. After the Code came into force, questions concerning how to evaluate evidence have been debated frequently in Sweden, particularly during the years between 1970 and 1990. The debate is still on going.[927] A brief account of this debate is given below.

683. There are two main models for evaluating evidence that have been debated in Swedish doctrine, namely the evidentiary value model and the evidentiary theme model.

923. *Ibid.*, 216.
924. *Ibid.*, 219 et seq.
925. P.O. Ekelöf, *Kompendium över civilprocessen, del II*, 348 (1948).
926. P.H. Lindblom, *Tes, antites och syntes*, SvJT 787 (1984).
927. *See* S. Halldén, *Indiciemekanismer*, TfR 55–64 (1973); A. Stening, *Bevisvärde*; R.W. Goldsmith & S.I. Andersson, *Bevisvärdemetoden versus temametoden vid juridisk bevisvärdering*, TfR 67–102 (1978); Ekelöf, Edelstam & Heuman, *Rättegång IV*, 184 et seq.; H.T. Klami, *On Truth and Evidence* (1986); *Rätt och sanning. Ett bevisteoretiskt symposium i Uppsala*, 26–27 maj 1989, ed. H.T. Klami (1990); B. Lindell *Sakfrågor och rättsfrågor*, Chs 4, 6 and 9; B. Lindell, *Några bevisrättsliga frågor*, TfR 221–241 (1989); T. Eckhoff, *Temametode og verdimetode i bevisvurderingen*, SvJT 321–339 (1988); Chr. *Diesen, Bevisprövning i brottmål* (1994); U. Zeidner, *Något om bevisföring vid tillämpning av samoch motverkansformeln*, SvJT 276–311 (1992) and H.T. Klami, M. Gräns & J. Sorvettula, *Law and Truth. A Theory of Evidence* (2000), C. Dahlman, Beviskraft: metod för bevisvärdering i brottmål (2018).

684. Ekelöf formulated the basic ideas of the evidentiary value model.[928] Others, mainly philosophers and mathematicians, among them the former Sören Halldén, subsequently developed the model. Halldén noted that, when evaluating evidence, the judge must consider an effect, called 'd', a hypothesis about a causal relation, called 'i', and a hypothesis about an initial cause, called 'h'.[929] The evidentiary value model focuses on the value P (i /d), that is to say the probability that the causal mechanism has worked.[930]

685. The requirement for a causal relationship between the evidence and the thing to be proved (which shall be referred to as the 'evidentiary theme') means, for example, that testimony must have been caused by the fact to be proved in order to be able to produce an evidentiary value.[931] Thus, if the testimony of a witness is all fantasy, but happens to correspond to something that has occurred, it lacks evidentiary value.[932]

686. As far as the evidentiary theme model is concerned in the Swedish doctrine represented by Bolding and Lindell, it focuses on the value P (h /d), that is to say the probability for the theme, presupposing that the theme exists. Thus, the evidentiary theme model focuses on the probability that the evidentiary fact proves the theme, but on the probability for the theme, considering the evidence presented in the action. This means, *inter alia*, that the theme probability model does not require a causal relationship between the evidentiary fact and the evidentiary theme.[933] Therefore, even if a testimony just happens to coincide with the evidentiary theme and there is no causality the evidentiary theme will have some original probability.

687. Thus, the difference between the models appears when it comes to the importance of the initial probability of the theme. The initial probability refers to the probability that the theme exists before any evidence has been presented in the action in support of it.[934] An assessment of initial probability is normally based on commonplace generalizations concerning how usual an event is in a certain population. It is sometimes very hard to assess and might end in pure guessing.

688. According to the evidentiary value model, the importance of the initial probability is minor, since it normally does not generate a causal relationship between the theme and the evidentiary fact.[935] Hence, the evidentiary value can be

---

928. Ekelöf has presented this model in German as well as in English, *see* '*Beweiswert*' in *Festschrift fur Fritz Baur*, 343 et seq., in ZZP (*Zeitschrift für Zivilprozess*) 1978, 64 et seq. and in *Library of Theoria no*. 15 (1983) 9 et seq.
929. Halldén, TfR (1973), 56.
930. *Ibid*.
931. Ekelöf & Boman, *Rättegång IV*, 133.
932. Halldén, TfR (1973), 56.
933. Bolding, *Bevisbördan och den juridiska tekniken*, 55 and Lindell, *Sakfrågor och rättsfrågor*, 145.
934. Ekelöf & Boman, *Rättegång IV*, 129 Stening, *Bevisvärde*, 42 and Goldsmith & Andersson, *supra*, 80.
935. Ekelöf & Boman, *Rättegång IV*, 129.

high, although the initial probability is low. The reverse is also true.[936] When using the theme probability model, the evidence presented in the action is, in a sense, laid above the initial probability. Thus, if the initial probability is high, the probability for the theme will also be high. However, according to the evidentiary value model, the initial probability might be of great importance for an individual piece of evidence, mainly when the initial probability is very high or very low.[937] From this, one can conclude that the impact of initial probability seems to be more or less the same pursuant to both models at issue. The only difference appears to be that, when using the evidentiary value model, the initial probability affects the evidentiary value of an evidentiary fact, while it affects the probability of the evidentiary theme according to the evidentiary theme model.[938]

689. Those who subscribe to the evidentiary value model have said that this model provides a stricter and more cautious model for evaluating evidence, a more limited task and a different treatment of information possessed by the judge before the trial than the evidentiary theme model.[939] It has been argued that these claimed advantages depend mainly on the fact that the evidentiary value model searches the probability that the evidentiary facts prove the evidentiary theme and thereby focuses on evidentiary relations, at which the evidentiary material presented in the action will be strictly divided into evidentiary facts, auxiliary facts and laws of general experience. With this operation, every item of evidence will be analysed with respect to laws of general experience possibly applying.[940]

690. Against these arguments, the objection has been made that a far-reaching analysis prevents the judge from reaching a comprehensive view of the evidence presented in the action, and that those who favour the evidentiary value model have not sufficiently considered that general laws of experience cannot only apply to individual pieces of evidence, but also to several items together. Consequently, if – as the evidentiary value model requires – every item of evidence and every auxiliary fact must be independently assessed, the evaluation of evidence risks becoming misleading.[941]

691. Finally, one more debatable difference between the two models will be pointed out. According to the evidentiary value model, we have no information on the theme's improbability if no contradictory evidence has been presented. Thus, if there is a law of general experience which says that *A* proves *B* in eight cases out of ten, we indeed know, according to the evidentiary value model, that in two cases out of ten the theme is not proved by *A*, but we know nothing about the actual improbability of the theme. The theme may or may not be present in the two cases, but nothing is known thereof for sure.[942]

---

936. Stening, *Bevisvärde*, 43.
937. *Ibid.*, 86.
938. Lindell, *Sakfrågor och rättsfrågor*, 168.
939. Goldsmith & Andersson, *supra*, 79 f.
940. Stening, *Bevisvärde*, 48 and 72.
941. Lindell, *Sakfrågor och rättsfrågor*, 247.
942. Ekelöf & Boman, *Rättegång IV*, 136, Stening, *Bevisvärde*, 36.

692. As is perhaps clear, the evidentiary value model works with a unilateral probability concept. Non-*A* is not regarded as an independent alternative to *A*. The reason for this probability construction is that the judge knows too little. There might be evidence, not presented in the action, which would be relevant if known. This uncertainty supports the judge not assessing the improbability of non-*A*, when there is no evidence to the contrary. According to the evidentiary theme model, however, one can conclude that the improbability of the theme is 0.2 when its probability is 0.8. It is thereby argued that although there is no concrete evidence about the improbability it should from logical reasons be assessed to be 0.2.[943]

943. Lindell, *Sakfrågor och rättsfrågor*, 150 and 353 et seq.

Part VIII. Special Procedures

693. In Part I, the structure of the Swedish court system was described and the special courts were also presented. In these courts, the procedure is conducted in accordance with special rules that compliment or displace the provisions in the Code. In addition, summary proceedings are regulated in a special act. Furthermore, certain special rules apply in family law cases, court matters and bankruptcy proceedings. The latter proceedings will be described in the following account. Hence, the special courts that have already been presented are not discussed below.

Chapter 1. Summary Proceedings

694. There are two forms of summary proceedings in Sweden, summary debt collection proceedings (*Betalningsföreläggande*) and assistance (*Handräckning*). The latter is divided into two groups, ordinary and special assistance.[944]

695. The summary collection procedure is available for collection of matured debts if settlement outside the courtroom is admitted. It can be applied to claims for damages, irrespective of whether the claim is contractual or not.[945] There is no monetary limit stated in the Act, thus the summary collection procedure also applies to very large amounts. However, the Act does not apply to non-dispositive claims, nor can it be used on declaratory claims.

696. Ordinary assistance may be used to oblige a previous owner or a person entitled to use and enjoy certain property, to vacate real estate or an apartment when the right to possess the property at issue has ceased to exist.

697. A frequent situation occurs when ordinary assistance is used and an owner of real estate wishes to obtain an execution title, which obliges a tenant to pay rent that is due and vacate the apartment after the right to possess it has ceased to exist. In the Act, there is a special rule on joinder for this situation, which makes it possible for the owner of the real estate to assert both claims in the same action, when they, as in the situation at issue, are supported on essentially the same grounds.

698. Ordinary assistance also applies when the plaintiff claims that the defendant is obliged to perform something other than payment of a debt. For example, it might concern an obligation on the part of the defendant to return property that he has leased, to deliver certain goods or to repair something. In addition, ordinary assistance can be used to prohibit the defendant from undertaking certain activities or to oblige him not to act in a certain way.[946]

699. Special assistance can be used to oblige the defendant to return to the plaintiff property that the defendant illegally possesses. For example, if a land owner has illegally blocked a road which for a long time has been used by someone else, special assistance applies. Moreover, it applies according to special provisions; for example, a land owner can apply for such assistance to get access to an apartment that he owns and that needs to be repaired.[947]

700. An application for summary proceedings shall be instituted at the Enforcement Service in the county where the defendant resides. The defendant's residence is deemed to be the place where he lives; with regard to the estate of a deceased person, it is the place where the deceased had his last residence. Concerning other

944. *See also* para. 230 *supra*.
945. LBH § 1.
946. Prop. 1989/90:85, p. 100.
947. *See* JB 12:26.

legal persons, the Act refers to Chapter 10 of the Code. However, an application may also be initiated at the Enforcement Service in the region where property belonging to the defendant is located or where performance otherwise is possible without inconvenience.

701. The application shall be written. The applicant shall state his claim and the grounds supporting it. If the application concerns a debt, the amount of the debt shall be stated, when it is due and the interest which is claimed.[948] The Enforcement Service may not immediately dismiss a defective application, but must direct the applicant to remedy the defect. If the applicant fails to obey such an order, the application shall be dismissed.[949] The Enforcement Service can dismiss an application concerning special assistance on the merits if it is plain that it is unfounded.

702. If the Enforcement Service accepts the application, the defendant shall be directed to answer within two weeks from being served with the application. If the defendant wishes to contest the application, he shall do so in writing. If he wishes, the applicant can thereafter request that the application be referred to the district court. This request must be made within four weeks from the date he was notified about the contested application. Otherwise, his application will be dismissed.[950]

703. The defendant can apply in writing for re-opening of a decision rendered in the summary proceedings. If the defendant has applied for re-opening within the prescribed time, the Enforcement Service shall refer the case to a district court competent to entertain it. Decisions rendered in the special assistance procedure can be appealed to an appellate court within three weeks from the day it was pronounced. The same applies if the applicant wishes to appeal against a decision rendered in the summary collection or ordinary assistance procedure.[951]

948. LBH §§ 9–11.
949. LBH § 20.
950. LBH §§ 25, 31, 33, 37.
951. *See* LBH §§ 52–58.

Chapter 2. Family Law Cases

704. Family law cases include cases involving paternity, custody, parental access to a child, maintenance, marriage and support to a spouse. Substantive rules on these subjects can be found in the Code relating to Parents, Guardians and Children (*Föräldrabalken* or FB) (enacted in 1949, last edition SFS 2019:838) and the Marriage Code (SFS 2019:235). These codes also contain some procedural provisions to be used instead of the rules in the RB. However, if special provisions are not to be found in the substantive family laws, the RB will apply.

705. In order to understand the procedural rules in family law cases, it is necessary to grasp the basic substantive rules. Consequently, these will also be briefly described.

§1. Paternity Cases

706. As far as marital children are concerned, the general rule is that the husband in the marriage is deemed the child's father. The same applies if the mother is a widow and the child is born within such time after the husband's death that the child could have been conceived with the husband before his death. However, the court shall rule that the husband is not the father of the child if:

(1) it is determined that the mother had sexual intercourse with a man other than her husband during the period when the child could have been conceived and, having regard to all circumstances, it seems probable that the child has been fathered by the other man;
(2) on the basis of the child's genetic make-up or on other special circumstances it can be ascertained that the husband is not the child's father; or
(3) the child was conceived before the marriage or whilst the spouses were living separately, and it is not probable that the spouses had sexual intercourse with one another during the period when the child could have been conceived.[952]

707. Paternity is determined either by a judgment or by an acceptance by the husband in the marriage of an admission of paternity made by another man. The admission of paternity must be made in writing and witnessed by two persons. In addition, it must be approved in writing by the Social Welfare Committee and by the mother or a guardian specially appointed for the child.[953] If the paternity is established by a judgment, the court will declare a man to be the father if it is through an examination showing that he is the genetic father. Furthermore, the court shall declare a man to be the father if he has had sexual intercourse with the child's mother or she has been inseminated with his sperm during the period when the child

952. FB 1:2.
953. FB 1:4.

could have been conceived and, with regard to all the circumstances, it is probable that he is the father of the child[954] to all the circumstances. However, paternity or parenthood is not determined if:

(1) the mother has undergone an insemination or fertilization outside the body according to Chapter 6 or 7, the Genetic Integrity Act (2006:351) or if the mother has undergone an insemination or fertilization outside the body at a competent institution abroad and the child has the right to information about the sperm donor;
(2) the mother at the treatment was a single woman according to Chapter 1, section 5 of the Genetic Integrity Act etc., and
(3) taking into account all circumstances, it is likely that the child is a result of the treatment.[955]

708. It shall be incumbent upon the Social Welfare Committee of the municipality where the child is registered to investigate who is the father of a child born out of wedlock.[956] In its investigation, The Social Welfare Committee shall obtain information from the mother and other persons who are able to supply particulars to the investigation. It should endeavour to arrange a blood test from the mother, the child and the child's putative father.[957] If the question of paternity can be decided with adequate certainty on the strength of the Social Welfare Committee's investigation, it should give the putative father of the child an opportunity to admit paternity.[958]

709. If a child has been born in wedlock, but the husband wishes to have a declaration that he is not the father, he must bring an action against the child regarding this, or if the child is dead, against his heirs.[959] If, however, the child wishes to have a declaration that the husband in wedlock is not his father, the child must institute an action against the man or, if he is dead, against his heirs.[960] Such an action may be brought before the court in the place where the child has his residence or, if the child is dead, in that court assigned to entertain actions concerning inheritance. In the absence of a competent court, the case shall be brought in the Stockholm District Court. If the party is under age, a guardian or custodian may act on his behalf.

710. If a child born out of wedlock institutes an action regarding the determination of paternity, the Social Welfare Committee shall act on his behalf. The

954. FB 1:5. *See* NJA 1998, p. 184 where an examination with DNA-technique was sufficient to prove paternity.
955. FB 1:3. There are provisions in FB 2:7, 2:8 and 2:9 with respect to Maternity in out of body conception, paternity for insemination or fertilization outside the body and parenting or fertilization outside the body.
956. FB 2:1 and 2:2.
957. FB 2:4, 2:6.
958. FB 2:5.
959. FB 3:1. Certain special provisions are to be found in paras 2 and 3.
960. FB 3:2.

mother of the child may always act on the child's behalf if she has custody. Furthermore, a specially appointed guardian may always act on the child's behalf.[961]

711. If the Social Welfare Committee is responsible for the determination of the paternity of the child, it shall institute an action against that man (or those men) who, according to the investigation, may be the father of the child.[962]

712. The court shall ensure that the question of paternity is properly investigated. In order to support this goal, anyone having the right to act on behalf of the child shall be given the opportunity to express his opinion in the case. However, an examination of a witness may not seek to determine whether the witness has had sexual intercourse with the mother at the presumed time of conception.[963]

713. If an action is withdrawn against one of several men, that party may be dismissed only if all agree. If the court, on the application of a defendant, has issued a summons against someone not earlier summoned in the action, the child's consent is also required.[964]

714. If a party appeals against a judgment concerning paternity, the appellate court shall examine the question of paternity in its entirety. If the appellate court finds that someone was not a party to the case and can reasonably be considered the father of the child, the judgment, on the application of one of the parties, shall be quashed and the case in its entirety returned to the court which first pronounced judgment on the case.[965]

715. It is possible to join an action concerning determination of paternity with an action to determine that the husband in wedlock is not the father of the child in a single action. If both cases are approved, but appeal is sought only from one of them, the appellate court shall likewise examine both.[966]

§2. Custody, Place of Living, Access to a Child and Maintenance

716. Custody. If the parents of a child are married to each other, the child is, from birth, in the custody of both; otherwise the child is in the custody of the mother alone. The child will be in the custody of both parents if they marry each other, unless the court has previously entrusted custody to one or two specially appointed guardians.[967] Joint custody remains after divorce if it is not dissolved.

961. FB 3:5.
962. FB 3:6.
963. FB 3:9.
964. FB 3:10.
965. FB 3:12.
966. FB 3:13.
967. FB 6:3.

717. The court shall order joint custody if the child is in the custody of one parent only and the parents so request, unless joint custody is manifestly incompatible with the child's best interests. Under certain circumstances, the parents can obtain joint custody simply by registration and notifying certain authorities.[968]

718. Upon application the court can order that custody shall be entrusted to one of the parents or be transferred from one parent to the other, if such a measure is in the child's best interests.[969] The court shall, when deciding on custody, pay special attention to the parent's ability to collaborate on issues which concern the child. The parents may agree on the matter if the Social Welfare Committee approves the agreement.

719. In actions concerning custody, place of living or access to a child, the court may request that the Social Welfare Committee or any other authority arrange a conversation between the parents to try to get them to cooperate and make an agreement (SFS 2001:453). If such an assignment is issued, the court can order the action to rest.[970]

720. The court shall assure that matters concerning custody, place of living and access to a child are properly investigated and shall always give the Social Welfare Committee an opportunity to be heard. The child may also be heard if there are special reasons therefore, and it is obvious that such an examination will not injure the child.[971]

721. Access to a child. It is the responsibility of the parents to ensure that the best possible provision is made for the child's access to the parent who is not living together with the child. This responsibility may also apply to some other person who is particularly close to the child.[972]

722. Questions relating to custody, place of living or access shall be instituted in the court in the place where the child has his or her residence. Proceedings concerning custody can also be instituted by an application if the parents agree about the matter, in which case a main hearing is not required. Otherwise, a summons is necessary. In custody proceedings, maintenance can be claimed for the child without a summons being issued.[973] The court can issue a provisional order without a main hearing, but after hearing the other party in an action concerning custody or access to a child pending a binding judgment. Such an order can be executed in the same way as a binding judgment.

723. Maintenance obligations. The parents are responsible for reasonable maintenance of the child, with regard to the needs of the child and the parents' total

968. *See* FB 6:4.
969. *See* FB 6:5 and 6:6.
970. FB 6:18.
971. FB 6:19.
972. 6:15.
973. FB 6:17.

financial resources. When the court decides upon the maintenance obligations it shall consider the child's own income and assets as well as his social benefits.

724. When the child reaches the age of 18, the maintenance obligations cease. However, if at that time the child is at school or returns to school before becoming nineteen, the parents are obliged to maintain the child until he is twenty-one, so long as schooling continues in an elementary or high school or other equivalent basic education.[974]

725. A parent shall fulfil his or her maintenance obligations by making payments to the child if the parent:

(1) neither has custody of the child nor lives permanently together with the child; or
(2) has custody of the child together with the other parent, but the child lives permanently only with the other parent.

726. Maintenance payments are determined by a judgment or an agreement between the parents. The custodian may represent the child in questions relating to maintenance payments, even if he or she has not reached the age of majority. An appointed guardian also has the right to represent the child. An agreement regarding maintenance payment can be made even before the birth of the child.[975]

727. When determining maintenance payments, the parent having the obligation to pay may retain a sum for his or her own or someone else's maintenance.[976]

728. A judgment or an agreement regarding maintenance can be adjusted by the court if prompted by a change of circumstances. In addition, a maintenance agreement can be adjusted by the court if the agreement is unreasonable with regard to the circumstances at the time it was completed as well as other circumstances. However, a decision under which maintenance already received shall be repaid may only be made if special reasons exist.[977]

729. An action concerning maintenance payments to a child is heard by the court in the place where the defendant has his residence. In the absence of a competent court, the action shall be instituted in the Stockholm District Court. Such an action can be instituted together with an action for divorce, paternity or custody.[978] A special rule makes it possible to join several actions concerning a person's obligation to pay maintenance in a single action. If the court is competent to entertain one of

974. FB 7:1.
975. FB 7:2.
976. *See* FB 7:3 and 7:4.
977. FB 7:10.
978. FB 7:12.

the actions, it is also deemed competent to entertain all of them, regardless of the rule that the court where the defendant has his residence is competent.[979]

730. The court can make a provisional order concerning maintenance as it sees fit. However, such an order may be issued only if there is reason to believe that a maintenance obligation exists. If an action concerning maintenance and a paternity action has been instituted simultaneously, a provisional order concerning maintenance may not be made if several men are summoned to appear. The court can rule on this issue without a main hearing but shall give the defendant an opportunity to state his opinion before an order is issued. A provisional order shall be re-examined when the case is finally adjudicated.[980]

§3. MATRIMONIAL CASES

731. Matrimonial cases include divorce cases and cases involving proceedings to determine whether or not a marriage exists. Proceedings to determine whether a marriage exists may only be instituted in a dispute between the woman and the man. However, such an issue may be considered in a dispute in which a person's rights depend on it. If both spouses want a divorce, they may make a joint application for this relief; otherwise, the case shall be instituted by an application for a writ of summons.

732. In a divorce case, the court may consider questions of maintenance, custody of, place of living and access to children, the right to continue to reside in the spouses' joint dwelling until property division takes place, and the prohibition of mutual visits between spouses. Claims relating to such matters shall be put forward in the application by which the proceedings for divorce are instituted.[981] However, if such proceedings have already been instituted, these claims may be put forward orally before the court or in writing, without a separate writ of summons. The question of the appointment of a property-division executor may also be considered as a part of the case.[982]

733. A judgment on divorce will be pronounced directly on the merits if the spouses do not have children under the age of 16, in which case a reconsideration period of six months is required. After the reconsideration period has expired, a new application for divorce is required in order that the court can render a judgment on divorce.[983]

979. FB 7:13.
980. FB 7:15.
981. The court can issue provisional orders on all these issues.
982. ÄktB 14:5.
983. ÄktB 5:1 and 14:6.

734. In matrimonial cases and cases concerning maintenance, a district court shall consist of a legally qualified judge and three lay assessors. However, the district court shall be competent when composed of one legally qualified judge to the same extent as in other civil cases. A Court of Appeal is in those cases normally competent with three legally qualified judges and two lay assessors.[984]

984. ÄktB 14:17 and 14:18.

Chapter 3. Court Matters

735. The Act on Processing on Court Matters (SFS 1996:242) applies primarily to matters concerning 'legal care' (*jurisdictio voluntaria*), i.e., judicial supervision of private arrangements ordinarily presented in a non-litigious context, e.g., adoption, the appointment of a trustee or a property-division executor. The district court shall deal with such matters, either on application, on its own motion, or after appeal. An application, which normally shall be in writing, shall contain the circumstances, on which it is based, the requested measure to be undertaken by the court and the evidence that will be presented. An incomplete or defective application can be dismissed.[985] The procedure is in writing, but sessions can be held.[986] At the proceedings, the provisions in the Code are subsidiary applicable. A default decision may not be rendered; instead, the matter will be written-off, if the applicant (or appellant) has been called to appear or face this consequence if he fails to appear. In other cases, the absence of the applicant or anyone else that has been called does not prevent the court from examining the matter.[987] Normally, the court is competent with one legally qualified judge.[988] A decision issued by the court can be re-examined and can be appealed.[989]

736. Sometimes it is not clear if the Procedural Code or the ÄL should apply. In those situations, it is determined that one must rely on the discretion of the court to decide which act to apply. In order to make this determination it is necessary for the court to find out if a single or multiple party relation is at hand. If the relation is a multiple party one, i.e., if the applicant has a counterpart, this is a strong indication that the present case is not a court matter, but instead concerns administration of justice, where the Procedural Code should apply. Sometimes another criterion is added: is the issue normally disputed by the parties? However, this criterion is weak since 'matters' quite often are in dispute.

985. *See* ÄL §§ 5–10.
986. ÄL § 13.
987. ÄL § 20.
988. ÄL § 3.
989. ÄL §§ 34–35 and 36–41.

Chapter 4. Bankruptcy Proceedings

737. Only a debtor who is insolvent can be declared bankrupt. 'Insolvent' means that the debtor lawfully cannot pay his debts as they mature and that this inability is not temporary.[990] A bankruptcy application shall be made in writing at the district court where the debtor should answer in civil cases in general.[991] Circumstances, which make the court competent, shall be stated, if they are not already known. A bankruptcy application made by the debtor should contain a list of debts and assets, including the name and address of every creditor. If a creditor makes the application, he shall give information about his claim and the circumstances that support it.[992]

738. As far as the competence to institute a bankruptcy application is concerned, a judgment that states the debtor's obligation to pay or a payment order rendered in summary proceedings are accepted, although the judgment or the order has not yet become irrevocable. A claim determined by an arbitration award also constitutes competence, if the arbitration award may be executed in accordance with certain rules in the Code of Execution.[993] In cases other than those mentioned, the creditor must prove his competence to apply for bankruptcy.

739. Since insolvency might be difficult to prove, there are some presumptions in the KL, which are aimed at making it easier for the creditor to prove that a debtor is bankrupt. Thus, an attempt by an execution officer to distrain the debtor of his property that has failed and occurred six months before the bankruptcy application, or a request to pay that has been ignored by the debtor, both constitute a presumption that the debtor is bankrupt. The burden of proof is then placed on the debtor, who must prove that he is solvent. If the debtor consents to the declaration of bankruptcy, such consent shall be accepted if there are no special reasons for not doing so.[994]

740. A creditor cannot have a debtor declared bankrupt if the debtor or someone else deposits a security according to certain provisions.[995] Preliminary seizure is also possible.[996]

741. Regarding the court's examination of a bankruptcy application, it is performed at a session before the bankruptcy court if it has been made by the debtor, but on the merits if made by the creditor. When the court declares a person (legal

990. KL 1:2.
991. *See* RB 10:1.
992. KL 2:3–4.
993. *See* UB 3:1, 3:15 and 16.
994. KL 2:7–9.
995. KL 2:10. According to the Act on Company Reconstruction (SFS 1996:764), the procedure on bankruptcy shall rest on the request of the debtor until the reconstruction has been finalized.
996. KL 2:11–13. It should be mentioned that in many cases an attempt is made to avoid bankruptcy by negotiating a composition.

or physical) bankrupt, it shall immediately decide the time and place for that session, at which the debtor shall take an oath concerning the debts and assets of the bankruptcy estate.[997] If an action between the debtor and someone else is pending concerning property belonging to the estate, the estate may take over the action.[998]

742. In the KL, there are rules which make it possible to recover property disposed of by the debtor a short time before the bankruptcy application.[999] In the first place, the administrator of the bankrupt estate may initiate recovery, but if he does not do so, a creditor may do so. The legal consequence of recovery is that the property at issue shall be returned to the bankrupt estate.

743. If the administrator so requires, the court can order a guarding procedure, in which a creditor notifies the court that he has a claim against the debtor. Such a procedure ought to take place if it can be assumed that claims without priority will be satisfied. Objections can be raised against a guarded claim.[1000]

744. If the assets of the estate are insufficient for paying incurred, expected bankruptcy costs, and other debts relating to the estate, the bankruptcy shall be written off.[1001] Otherwise, the remaining assets shall be distributed to the creditors.[1002]

745. A bankruptcy application is in many respects disposed of as a matter in the district court. For example, the appointment of a trustee is a matter, and in many situations the proceedings are in writing. However, the provisions in the Code are used where it seems adequate to apply them, if in doing so the rules in the KL are not contradicted. A decision concerning bankruptcy or to revoke such a decision can be executed immediately. Certain bankruptcy decisions can be appealed to an appellate court and – after review dispensation – to the Supreme Court. Other decisions are irrevocable.[1003]

---

997. KL 2:24.
998. KL 3:9.
999. KL 4:5–13.
1000. KL 9:1–12. Concerning a disputed remarked claim, *see* KL 9:13–19.
1001. KL 10:1.
1002. *See* KL Ch. 11.
1003. *See* KL Ch. 16.

Part IX. Preliminary Seizure and Enforcement of Judgments

Chapter 1. Preliminary Seizure

§1. Proceedings

746. In Chapter 15 of the Code, there are rules concerning interim enforcement measures that aim to secure the forthcoming enforcement of the judgment. The most commonly used interim enforcement measure is provisional attachment to secure the enforcement of a claim.[1004] Provisional attachment presupposes that:

(1) a person has shown probable grounds for a claim which is or may be presumed to be the subject of legal proceedings or adjudication in other similar forms; and
(2) it can reasonably be expected that the defendant, by absconding with or removal of property, or by other means, will evade payment of the debt.

747. The applicant's claim is due or will be due for payment before a judgment is entered. Probable grounds refer to the outcome of the action.[1005] The prerequisite adjudication 'in other similar form' refers to an examination by arbitrators, a viewing, the summary process and every other sort of examination, which can replace an examination by the court.[1006] Provisional attachment can also be granted when an arbitration award is attacked.[1007] In addition, it is possible for the court to grant provisional attachment concerning claims that shall be examined by a foreign court, if the judgment can be enforced in Sweden.[1008] The requirement that the claim will presumably be the subject of legal proceedings denotes a rather low degree of probability.

748. As far as the required degree for the sabotage risk in point (2) above is concerned, it is not required that the defendant intends to sabotage the impending performance; it is enough that the applicant shows that it is probable that the

1004. RB 15:1.
1005. P. Westberg, *Det provisoriska rättsskyddet i tvistemål*, bok 4 (2004), 100.
1006. Prop. 1980/81:84, p. 227.
1007. *See* NJA 1979, p. 698 (concerning the older tenor of the rule).
1008. NJA 1983, p. 814.

defendant's actions can have this effect.[1009] The threat to property, which would support provisional attachment, ought to be such that it can be regarded as reprehensible, such that it would entitle the applicant to take steps to recover alienated property.[1010] Affidavits may be used when provisional attachment is sought.

749. When granting provisional attachment, the court may order provisional attachment of so much of the property that the claim may be assumed to be covered in the event that part of the property is disposed. The claim includes the coming costs due for enforcement, but not the legal costs of the action.[1011] Generally, the court in its decision about provisional attachment shall not state what kind of property shall be included in the forthcoming performance, since this is a task for the Enforcement Service. Provisional attachment does not grant priority in a subsequent bankruptcy procedure. Property, which has been attached, can be subject to distraint for a third party's claim.

750. If a person claims a superior right to certain property, the same prerequisites apply as for a claim, as far as the required evidence is concerned.[1012] However, the prerequisites concerning the risk for sabotage are different; it shall reasonably be expected that the other party will remove, substantially impair or otherwise take possession of the property to the detriment of the applicant. The term 'superior right' refers to personal property and real estate, even if it is in the possession of a third party. In addition, it applies not only on ownership, but also to more limited rights, as for example the right to use certain property.[1013] It is very seldom possible to apply the provision to declaratory claims.[1014]

751. The court may impose an appropriate sanction to secure the claimant's legal right in situations other than those covered by the provisions mentioned above.[1015] According to this rather wide rule, it is required that the applicant shows reasonable grounds for asserting his claim, which is or may be presumed to be the subject of legal proceedings or adjudication in another similar form. If a risk of disposal of property exists, it must be reasonably expected that the opposing party will prevent or render difficult the exercise of the claimant's rights, or substantially diminish their value by carrying on a certain activity or performing or refraining from performing a certain act, or by other means. If these requirements are fulfilled, the court may impose an appropriate sanction to secure the claimant's legal rights. Such a sanction may entail prohibition or an order, on penalty of a fine, to respect the claimant's title, the appointment of a custodian, or other measures calculated to

1009. Ekelöf, Bylund & Edelstam, *Rättegång IV*, 28.
1010. Prop. 1980/81:84, 427.
1011. *Ibid.*, 228.
1012. *See* RB 15:2. As far as the borderline between 15:2 and 15:3 is concerned, *see* NJA 1987, p. 829. However, it has recently been laid down in the legislation that 15:3 also applies in situations covered by 15:1 or 15:2.
1013. Prop. 1980/81:84, p. 229.
1014. *Ibid.*, 428.
1015. *See* RB 15:3. *See, e.g.*, NJA 1990, p. 338.

prevent encroachment upon the claimant's legal rights. This provision is of importance mainly in cases where the claimant might institute an action concerning prohibition and situations where a declaratory claim or a performance claim will not be of relevance.[1016] An interim enforcement measure according to this rule might force the defendant to fulfil the plaintiff's claim during a pending action. Consequently, it can function as a substitute for an ordinary trial. Therefore, the court ought not to order a provisional measure, pursuant to the rule at issue, without strong reasons supporting it.[1017] This is also a reason why the rule is optional, which means that the court can balance different interests.

752. In order for the court to grant interim enforcement measures in those cases described above, the claimant must deposit with the court security to compensate the other party for the loss he may suffer.[1018] If the security has not been accepted by the other party, the requirements of the examination of the security are very strict.

753. The security shall consist of a pledge or a personal guarantee and must be possible to convert into cash. In addition, it must cover possible claims for damages.[1019] The latter shall be issued for a personal debt, issued by several individuals who shall be jointly and severally liable. If a bank or a similar financial institution deposits a security, a commitment to fulfil the security obligation will be accepted.[1020] A request in an appellate court to complete the security will not be accepted.[1021] However, if the claimant fails to deposit a security and has shown extraordinary cause for his action, the court may exempt him from the obligation to deposit a security.[1022] The state, municipalities, county authorities and municipal associations need not deposit a security.

754. If an interim enforcement measure has been granted and an action has not already been brought, the claimant shall, within one month of the order, bring an action before a court or, if the claim is to be entertained in another form, in accordance with the provisions pertaining thereto.[1023] An action that is to be entertained by a court shall be considered to have been brought when a summons has been initiated at the court. An action that is not to be entertained by a court or other authority shall be considered to have been brought when a request for examination has been addressed to the other party, or the procedure has been initiated by other means. The action at issue must refer to a judgment that is possible to execute,

1016. KRB 15:9.
1017. NJA II 1943, p. 186, Prop. 1980/81:84, p. 230, Ekelöf, Bylund & Edelstam, *Rättegång III*, 34.
1018. RB 15:6. *See, e.g.*, NJA 1994, p. 45.
1019. Prop. 1980/81:84, p. 234.
1020. UB 2:25.
1021. NJA 1986, p. 419.
1022. Such an issue was examined in NJA 1979, p. 317.
1023. RB 15:7.

unless such an action cannot reasonably be performed.[1024] If an action is not brought, the measure shall be immediately rescinded.

755. An interim enforcement measure shall be immediately terminated if security relating to the purpose of the measure is furnished or there is otherwise no longer any reason for the measure.[1025] In addition, if a claim is withdrawn or dismissed without reaching the merits, the measure shall also be immediately terminated. The question of termination is determined by the court in which the action is pending or, if no action is pending, by the court which first dealt with the issue. In other situations, the court shall determine whether the measure shall continue in effect while it adjudicates the case. If the case is approved, the measure should remain in effect until the judgment can be executed.[1026]

756. As far as interim enforcement measures are concerned, there is one final provision of importance, which, in some respects, is different from the provisions mentioned earlier. If it is apparent that, in an action concerning a superior right to property, one party has unlawfully infringed upon the other party's possession or has taken any other unlawful action with respect to the property, the court may direct that the possession be restored or other rectification immediately made.[1027] On the request of either party, the court may rescind an order imposed under this rule.[1028] This provision only applies if an action has been instituted. Sometimes a claimant can make a choice between this rule and the others stated above. However, it might be an advantage for him to choose the rule at issue, since he then need not deposit a security.

757. The following should be noted regarding the procedure for a measure regulated in Chapter 15 of the Code. A decision concerning an interim enforcement measure is issued by the court where the action is pending. If an action is not pending, the provisions in Chapter 10 of the Code apply.[1029] Thus, the rules aim to guarantee that an order concerning an interim enforcement measure shall be issued by the same court that examines the principal action.[1030] If a special court is to adjudicate upon the principal action, it shall also examine a question concerning an interim enforcement measure. In addition, if an ordinary court is not competent to adjudicate upon the principal action according to the rules in Chapter 10 of the Code, it shall be deemed to have such competence as if it would have been competent without the limitation of competence at issue.

1024. Concerning an exception when a performance claim cannot be brought, but the claim none the-less will be accepted. In NJA 1988, p. 13 provisional attachment was granted on a declaratory claim concerning joint-ownership.
1025. RB 15:8. *See, e.g.*, NJA 1993, p. 356.
1026. Ekelöf, Bylund & Edelstam, *Rättegång III*, 24.
1027. RB 15:4.
1028. RB 15:9.
1029. *See* Ch. 10 of the Code, commented on in Part II.
1030. Prop. 1980/81:84, p. 411.

758. The question of imposition of an interim enforcement measure may be determined only on request. If an action is not pending, the request shall be made in writing. The principle of party disposition is applied; thus, a request may not be granted unless an opportunity to respond thereto has been given to the other party. If needed, a special session can be scheduled. However, when delay entails risks, the court may act immediately, issuing an order, which remains effective until it directs otherwise.[1031]

759. Instead of applying for an interim enforcement measure, the creditor can try to safeguard his interests by initiating bankruptcy proceedings, since then the debtor will lose the capacity to deal with property included in the estate. However, bankruptcy presupposes that the debtor is insolvent. In addition, the debtor's assets will be divided equally between all his creditors at bankruptcy proceedings. Therefore, bankruptcy proceedings are seldom an advisable alternative to provisional attachment.[1032]

§2. Judicial Review

760. A question concerning a security matter is decided through an order, which can be immediately executed and which can be appealed to an appellate court. If a district court has rejected an application for an interim enforcement measure or terminated such a measure, an appellate court may immediately order that the measure shall be in force until otherwise decided. If a district court has granted an interim enforcement measure, an appellate court can immediately block it.[1033]

1031. RB 15:5.
1032. *See* paras 737–745 *supra.*
1033. *See* RB 50:8.

Chapter 2. Enforcement of Judgments

§1. Enforcement of Domestic Judgments

I. Proceedings

761. The Code of Execution applies to enforcement of a judgment or some other right to execution, which contains an obligation to pay, or any other obligation. In addition, it applies to provisional attachment or similar interim enforcement measures. An application for enforcement can be founded on the right to execution enumerated in the Code of Execution, which are:[1034]

(1) a judgment, order or decision rendered by a court;
(2) a settlement confirmed by the court; and a mediation agreement which has been declared enforceable by the court;
(3) an approved order of summary punishment;
(4) an arbitration award;
(5) an agreement concerning maintenance;
(6) a decision rendered by an administrative authority which, according to special regulations, may be enforced;
(7) a document which, according to special provisions, may be enforced; and
(8) an order or a decision, rendered by the Enforcement Service concerning the summary proceedings.

762. The Code of Execution distinguishes between public and private cases.[1035] The former category includes public claims, e.g., claims concerning fines and taxes.[1036] Such claims may be executed without a previous judgment. Characteristic of the public cases is that the Enforcement Service, which then functions as a party representative as well as a public authority, represents the state.

763. There are several different forms of enforcement, depending on the type of performance claimed in the proceedings. Attachment is the standard means of enforcing a monetary judgment, meaning that the debtor's assets are taken and sold.[1037] Salary can also sometimes be attached.[1038] As far as certain types of debts are concerned, namely maintenance and taxes, enforcement can occur through a special form of attachment (*see* paragraph 794 below). Another type of enforcement is eviction, meaning that the debtor is obliged to vacate real property.[1039] Furthermore, execution for surrender of personal property, as well as performance of an

---

1034. UB 3:1. An extensive commentary on the Code of Execution is *Utsökningsbalken. En Kommentar*, G. Walin, T. Gregow and P. Löfmarck, Millqvist, G., Persson, A.H., Utsökningsbalken. En kommentar (2009).
1035. Cases which are not public are private.
1036. *See also* para. 178 *supra.*
1037. *See* UB Chs 4–7.
1038. UB Ch. 7.
1039. UB Ch. 16.

order concerning provisional attachment should be mentioned.[1040] However, the following paragraphs will mainly deal with attachment, since it is the most common form of enforcement.

764. Enforcement can normally commence even if the judgment supporting the execution is not yet irrevocable.[1041] Otherwise, the defendant would be able to delay the enforcement by appealing against the judgment. However, since a judgment rendered in favour of the plaintiff can be reversed in an appellate court, the defendant's interests must also be considered. Consequently, the Code of Execution provides that attached property may not be sold without the consent of the debtor, until the judgment is binding.[1042] In addition, the debtor can prevent enforcement by depositing a security.[1043]

765. An application for enforcement can be oral or in writing, signed by the applicant or his attorney and instituted at the Enforcement Service in the region where the debtor resides. In addition, attachment may be sought in another region where the property is located or where enforcement seems suitable.[1044] However, as far as the summary proceedings are concerned, an order will be enforced ex officio, unless the claimant does not request otherwise.[1045] The applicant shall state the measure that he claims and refer to the title of execution. The applicant can withdraw his application or reduce his claim.[1046]

766. The Enforcement Service shall rapidly examine the application in order to find out if the debtor has property available to attach. The debtor is obliged to give information about his assets and can be directed to confirm the information he gives by taking an oath on his honour and conscience. In addition, a third person is obliged to give information concerning economic relations between himself and the debtor.[1047] If such a directive is not obeyed after a penalty of fine, the debtor or third person can be detained, if particular reasons for this exist.[1048]

767. As far as other means of compulsion are concerned, the enforcement officer may search a house, a room or a warehouse if necessary for the enforcement. In addition, he may enter a locked room. However, he may not enter an apartment when the occupant is absent, unless the occupant has been previously notified about the enforcement and it can be assumed that he is in hiding, or if other special reasons exist. In other respects, the enforcement officer may use force to the extent that such force can be justified regarding the circumstances. He may use violence against

1040. *Ibid.*
1041. UB 3:3–10.
1042. UB 8:4 para. 1.
1043. UB 3:6 and 2:25.
1044. UB 4:8.
1045. UB 2:1.
1046. Prop. 1980/81:8, p. 488.
1047. UB 4:14–15.
1048. UB 2:15–16.

a person only when facing resistance and only such violence can be regarded as justified with regard to the purpose of the enforcement.[1049]

768. The debtor shall be notified that attachment will occur, unless there is a risk that he will remove or destroy his property.[1050]

769. In order to attach property, the property must belong to the debtor and must be possible to transfer. However, some property, which fulfils these conditions, cannot be attached, because of the beneficiary rules. Such property includes:[1051]

(1) clothes and other items solely for the debtor's personal use;
(2) furniture, household utensils and other equipment, to the extent it is necessary for a home;
(3) working tools and other equipment, to a reasonable value, necessary for the debtor's trade or vocational trading, and, in addition, animals, fodder and such, necessary for living, also to a reasonable value;
(4) items with such an overwhelming personal value to the debtor that it would be manifestly unreasonable to enforce it;
(5) the lease to an apartment in which the debtor permanently lives or which is required for his trade, even if the lease can be transferred;
(6) a tenant owner's apartment where the debtor lives permanently, unless the debtor has not prejudiced the creditors by buying the apartment, or it would seem unreasonable to except it from enforcement with regard to the needs of the debtor and the value of the apartment;
(7) money, bank assets, other claims and supplies unless otherwise prescribed and the asset is reasonably required to support the debtor until an income, covering his needs, can be expected. However, enforcement cannot be postponed for more than a month.

770. In the Code of Execution, there are also some other exceptions from enforcement, with reference to other cases than those concerning the needs of the debtor, for example, regarding claims for damages and life annuity. It is the responsibility of the debtor to give the Enforcement Service information about his assets, so that it can consider what items should be excepted from enforcement.[1052] However, the Enforcement Service shall always, on its own motion, observe provisions set up to protect the debtor.[1053]

771. It is not unusual for the debtor to claim that certain personal property does not belong to him. Since a condition for attachment is that it shall be 'shown' that

1049. UB 2:17.
1050. UB 4:12.
1051. *See* UB 5:1.
1052. UB 5:14.
1053. Heuman, *Special process. Utsökning och konkurs*, *supra*, 140 et seq.

the property belongs to the debtor, this requirement of proof might cause evidentiary problems for the creditor. In order to avoid such problems, the Code of Execution contains certain presumptions. Thus, the debtor is regarded to be the owner of the property in his possession, if it is not shown that it belongs to another.[1054] However, there is a special provision if the debtor is married and permanently lives together with his spouse. In that case, the debtor is presumed to be the owner of the property, if it is shown neither that they own the property together, nor that the property belongs to the other spouse or to someone else. The same rule applies when the debtor permanently cohabitates with someone under 'marriage-like' conditions.[1055] It appears from the provision that the required degree of proof for joint-ownership in marriage is lower than that which applies pursuant to the presumption in the principal rule. The reason is that spouse's normally live together and own property of a considerable value. Thus, with a high requirement of proof it would very often be difficult to prove that either one of them owns certain property.

772. If personal property is attached according to the provisions mentioned above, even though a third person has claimed a superior right to the property at issue, the Enforcement Service may, if there are reasons, direct the third party to institute an action against the claimant and the debtor, within one month from receiving the order. The same applies if a third person has claimed a superior right after attachment has been performed. If the third person does not follow the order, his right to bring an action against the claimant is forfeited, unless the claimant has instituted an action against the third person.[1056]

773. Sometimes an attachment can be performed with reservations for a third party's right, for example, when personal property cannot be attached pursuant to the rules mentioned above (UB 4:17–19). As a rule, the Enforcement Service shall then direct the applicant to bring an action against the third person within a month after the order was served. If the applicant fails to obey the order, the attachment shall be suspended, unless the third party has instituted an action against the applicant within one month.[1057]

774. If the enforcement officer finds that the debtor has property available to attach, he shall decide which property to attach and shall list, evaluate and secure that property.[1058] The property will be secured by being taken into safekeeping, or – if it is allowed to remain in the possession of the debtor – by being marked and sealed. The attachment decision means that the debtor is not allowed to dispose of or use the property.[1059]

1054. UB 4:18 para. 1. However, concerning a registered ship or aircraft it is deemed to belong to the registered owner, if it is not shown that it belongs to anyone else, *see* UB 4:18 para. 2.
1055. UB 4:19.
1056. UB 4:20.
1057. UB 4:22. This provision does not apply to a registered ship or aircraft. The corresponding rule for a claim or another right which has been attached can be found in UB 4:23.
1058. UB 4:7, 6:1 and 6:9.
1059. UB 4:29.

775. As a rule, attached property may not be sold until the execution order has become irrevocable. Normally, it will be sold at an auction, arranged by the Enforcement Service, but sometimes it can be sold without such a public arrangement, if a higher amount can be reached.[1060] The Enforcement Service shall account for the sale as soon as possible. If the execution order has not become irrevocable at the sale, the proceeds from it may not be distributed until it has become binding. The same applies if the debtor has appealed against the decision concerning attachment or if there is a dispute regarding who is entitled to receive the money from the sale of the property.[1061]

776. It appears from the provisions in Chapter 7 of the Code of Execution that wages due to be paid may be attached, in which case the employer is obliged to withhold and send a part of the debtor's wage to the Enforcement Service (*Löneutmätning*). The Enforcement Service decides how much of the wages may be withheld every payday, and how much of it shall be reserved for the debtor.

777. Attachment of wages may be performed only to the extent the wages obviously exceed what is necessary to support the debtor and his family and to fulfil maintenance obligations. As a rule, wages may not be attached for more than six months altogether, during the same calendar year. In addition, attachment of wages during two calendar years may not be performed in such a manner that the wages are attached for more than six months in a row, or with only a short break. Wages should not be attached during vacation time.

778. In an execution case, the applicant or the defendant cannot be entitled to compensation for work, attorney's fees, or examination expenses. If the case is complicated, a party can be granted legal aid. The state shall be reimbursed for the costs to execute the judgment, which are initially recovered from the proceeds of the sale. If the proceeds are insufficient, attachment can be executed in order to obtain the remaining amount.

II. Judicial Review

779. Appeal against a decision rendered by the Enforcement Service can be brought only to certain enumerated district courts. On appeal, the provisions in the Act on Processing in Court Matters apply. Not only can the parties appeal, but also anyone who is affected by the decision. However, not all decisions rendered by the Enforcement Service can be appealed. Review dispensation is required for an examination in an appellate court.

780. When wages are attached, appeal is possible without any time limits. In most other situations, appeal must be brought within three weeks from the time

1060. *See* UB 9:2 and 9:8.
1061. UB 13:14.

when the decision was served on the applicant or defendant. However, a third person may appeal from such a decision without time limits.

781. In the appeal petition, which shall be brought to the Enforcement Service, the applicant shall state the decision against which he appeals, the change he claims and the ground supporting the claim for change. In addition, he shall state the evidence he wishes to present and what he wishes to prove with every item of evidence. The execution will continue even though an appeal has been brought. However, the appellate court can restrain execution without giving the adverse party an opportunity to be heard.

Chapter 3. Recognition and Enforcement of Foreign Judgments

§1. Rules Applicable in the Absence of a Treaty

782. In order to recognize and enforce a foreign judgment, support is required in a law or in subordinate legislation.[1062] An exception from this requirement is made for judgments supported on a prorogation agreement.[1063] However, in this respect, it should be observed that the Supreme Court in Sweden has not accepted a so-called silent prorogation agreement; that is to say the situation where the defendant participates in the proceedings without making any objections in respect to the court's competence.[1064] It should be mentioned that a judgment could, without being recognized, have an evidentiary impact on the facts that have been examined and concerning the content of foreign law.[1065]

§2. International Treaties

783. The Lugano and Brussels Conventions have been incorporated into Swedish law.[1066] Furthermore, the Brussels-I Decree came into force in March 2002. This Decree has in principal replaced the Brussels Convention. The importance of these Conventions and the Decree for the enforcement of foreign judgments is considerable. The main principle according to the Brussels-I Decree is that a judgment rendered in a state belonging to the EU, shall – with some rare exceptions – be recognized and enforced in other membership states. Enforcement in Sweden requires a special procedure which is regulated partly in the Conventions and the Decree and partly in national law. An application for enforcement shall be addressed to the Svea Court of Appeal.

784. Among other international Conventions ratified by Sweden regarding importance for recognition and enforcement of foreign judgments, *see*, e.g, the following:

- The Convention on Divorces and Judicial Separations (The Hague 1 June 1970).
- The European Convention on Recognition and Enforcement on Decisions Concerning Custody of Children and Restoration of Such Custody (Luxembourg 20 May 1980)
- The Convention on Recognition and Enforcement of Decisions Concerning Maintenance to Children (The Hague 15 April 1958).

1062. This is also true for other titles of execution than judgments.
1063. *See, e.g.*, NJA 1973, p. 628.
1064. NJA 1986, p. 119. This judgment has been criticized by Pålsson, *Svensk rättspraxis*, 155 et seq.
1065. *See* NJA 1894, p. 96; 1913, p. 326; 1935, p. 611; 1910, p. 594; 1982, c 27; 1986, p. 119 and Pålsson, *Svensk rättspraxis*, 148 et seq.
1066. *See* para. 228 *supra*.

- The Protocol Concerning the Competent Court and the Recognition of Decisions Concerning the Right to Obtain a European Patent (Munich 5 October.1973). This protocol is a part of the European Convention of Patents.
- The Act on Enforcement of Certain Foreign Decisions on Litigation Costs (SFS 1986:1042).
- The UN Convention on Children's Rights (1989). The Convention became Swedish law 1 January 2020 (SFS 2018:1197).

Part X. Arbitration

Chapter 1. Introduction

785. The Swedish Government issued instructions for the preparation of a new Arbitration Act at the beginning of 1992, in order to replace the Arbitration Act of 1929. The Committee entrusted to make the new draft presented their final Report in June 1994. When constructing the new draft, utmost attention was paid to the United Nations Commission on International Trade Law (UNCITRAL) Model Law. In substance, there are few essential differences between the new Arbitration Act (SFS 1999:116), hereinafter LSF, and the Model law. The new LSF came into force on 1 April 1999. Arbitration is a kind of private conflict resolution competing with the state governed administration of justice in the ordinary courts. There are two forms of arbitration, the *conventional* and the *legal*. Legal arbitration is founded on provisions in the law or other regulations.[1067] LSF applies only on conventional arbitration, that is to say if the parties have made an agreement to refer the conflict to arbitration and the arbitration agreement does not give any of them the right to attack the arbitration award.

786. LSF does not apply to future consumer disputes. Nor does LSF apply to future consumer insurance disputes.

787. The advantages of arbitration are that it is fast and secret and that the parties themselves can pick the judges that form the arbitration board. Another advantage is the flexibility. Arbitrators do not have to apply basic and fundamental principles in litigation, such as the principles of orality, immediateness and concentration. Instead, they can set up and adapt the procedure for each individual case. Furthermore, arbitration is less formal than litigation, which improves the atmosphere for conflict resolution. Disadvantages of arbitration are the high costs and the lack of guaranties of legal security.

788. LSF contains sixty sections, of which sections 1–6 refer to the arbitration agreement, sections 7–18 to the arbitrators, sections 19–26 to the procedure, sections 27–32 to the arbitration award, sections 33–36 to void and challengeable awards, sections 37–42 to the costs of arbitration, sections 43–45 to forum issues and time limits, sections 46–51 to international relations and, finally, sections 52–60 to recognition and enforcement of foreign awards. The LSF was subject to a review

1067. *See, e.g.*, JB 12:66.

in SOU 2015:37, 'A Review of the Arbitration Act', since it had been in effect for almost two decades. The result of this review led to some minor changes, which can be found in prop. 2017/18:257, *A Modernization of the Arbitration Act*. The most important changes because of the review are that the arbitrators' decision on jurisdiction can be reviewed by the Court of Appeal and the possibility to attack the arbitrators' jurisdiction at the district court has been limited. Furthermore, the parties have a greater opportunity to appoint new arbitrators in certain situations and a provision has been inserted about applicable substantive right to the dispute. In addition, the grounds for setting aside the award have been limited and the time for doing that has been shortened to two months. Finally, the possibility of using English in taking evidence in an action about setting aside the award has increased. Some linguistic changes were also made. The following disposition follows the disposition in the LSF.

Chapter 2. The Arbitration Agreement

789. An arbitration agreement is usually defined as a private contract with procedural effects.[1068] Civil law provisions apply to the *validity* of an arbitration agreement, meaning, *inter alia*, that the parties must have legal and procedural capacity and, in addition, have the right to undertake dispositions concerning the disputed subject.[1069] With respect to its *form* an arbitration agreement can be oral, but normally it is written, most often in the form of an arbitration clause in a contract.[1070] With respect to the content of an arbitration agreement, it must refer to a question amenable to out-of-court settlement. Thus, it may not refer to cases, which are not dispositive such as custody of, or access to, a child.

790. The parties must state to the arbitration agreement the issues to be examined by the arbitrators. Furthermore, the arbitration agreement must contain a declaration that the disputed issue is referred to the arbitrators for examination.[1071] As far as future disputes are concerned, it is obvious that the disputed issue cannot be stated in the arbitration agreement. Instead, it must be stated in the request for arbitration. A future dispute must emanate from a legal relationship referred to in the arbitration agreement, which must have come into being before the arbitration agreement was made. In addition, the legal relationship must be able to be separated from other existing legal relationships between the parties. In other words, it must be *individualized*. It follows from this requirement that the parties cannot refer all future disputes to arbitration. Nor can they refer future disputes of a certain kind to arbitration.[1072]

791. The requirement on individualization is based on reasons of legal security. The consequences of accepting arbitration agreements not relating to individualized legal relationships could be detrimental for the parties. However, the requirement that the legal relationship must be individualized does not mean that every clause in a contract must be individualized, even if it could be said that every clause constitutes a legal relationship. Thus, it is sufficient if an arbitration clause in a contract states that 'every dispute arising from this contract shall be referred to arbitration'. This clause is recommended by the Stockholm Chamber of Commerce (SCC) as a standard clause.

792. Ordinary civil law rules on interpretation apply with respect to the extent of an arbitration agreement. In the first place, the parties' intentions are of importance. If the intentions of the parties cannot be determined, the predominant opinion in Sweden is, *in dubio*, the interpretation, which gives the agreement the narrowest

1068. T. Cars, *Lagen om skiljeförfarande* 20 (2000); Kvart & Olsson, *Tvistlösning genom skiljeförfarande. En handledning till lagen om skiljeförfarande.* 2:a uppl., 38 (2006).
1069. Cars, 20. Kvart & Olsson, 38.
1070. P.O. Bolding & H. Stenberg, *Affärstvister och skiljedom. Exporträtt 4* 110 (1970). Kvart & Olsson, s. 38. The parties can make an arbitration agreement in front of the arbitrators in an arbitration procedure already commenced.
1071. Cars, s. 32; Dillén, 106.
1072. Heuman, 22.

extension, should take preference over any other interpretation.[1073] The reason is that an arbitration agreement restricts a party's right to institute an action at an ordinary court, and such a limitation should have clear and unmistakable support in the agreement.

793. A standard arbitration clause gives the arbitrators an extensive authority. Such a clause embraces all events between the parties related to the performance and completion of the arbitration agreement.[1074] As far as the retirement of relation is concerned, it must at least be a casual relation between the arbitration clause and the dispute, meaning that if an interpretation of the contract is necessary the arbitration clause will apply.[1075] In addition, the casual relation must have legal relevance. In order to assess the legal relevance *inter alia* it has to be considered if the dispute is typical for the type of contract in question.[1076] The requirement of a casual relation is a minim requirement.[1077]

794. The restrictive interpretation has support in precedent cases. In NJA 1949 p. 609, the seller in a purchase agreement between him and another tradesman had referred to certain standard delivery regulations, which *inter alia* contained an arbitration clause. Since the arbitration clause had not been sent to the buyer or otherwise brought to his attention, and – in addition – it could not be assumed he knew about it, an arbitration agreement was not deemed to be made between the parties. A similar motivation can be found in NJA 1969 p. 285 and NJA 1979 DT 22, where the arbitration clause also was brought forward against a tradesman. However, praxis was slightly changed through the case NJA 1980 p. 46. In this case, the reference to standard regulations containing an arbitration clause was accepted since the contract was made between tradesmen, although the main contract did not refer to these standard regulations.[1078] The Supreme Court motivated the change of praxis compared with the case from 1949 by saying that the use of standard conditions significantly had increased and that such regulations can be adjusted by applying section 36 in AvtL. Thus, the Swedish praxis today is that arbitration clauses not referred to in the main contract are void in agreements between a tradesman and a consumer, but valid in agreements between tradesmen.[1079]

795. A question which has been brought to the fore both in praxis and in the doctrine is if an arbitration agreement in a main contract also applies on an amendment to this agreement which the parties have agreed upon. An amended contract is connected to the main contract in some way, e.g., new clauses about delivery might have been put in. In these cases the arbitration clause in the main contract embraces

1073. Dillén, SvJT 1937, p. 692. Jarvin, *Årsskrift från Sveriges Handelskammares skiljedomsinstitut* 49 (1987).
1074. Cars, p. 37.
1075. *See* NJA 1948, s. 590 and – on the other hand – NJA 1941, p. 198.
1076. Bolding, 101.
1077. Bolding, 99 ff.
1078. Jfr RH 1989:1, RH 1989:51, RH 1989:83, RH 1982:102 and RH 1990 cf.
1079. Kvart & Olsson, 50. *See also* NJA 1984, p. 229 and NJA 1992, p. 290.

disputes arising from the amended agreement, if the contracts are deemed to be independent of each other. It is decided upon the discretion of the court if the contracts are independent.[1080]

796. The prerequisite 'issue' (*fråga*) also includes the existence or condition of a *certain factual relation*. Thus, an arbitration award can be rendered with respect to an independent legal or evidentiary fact.[1081] However, the factual circumstance at the same time must be within the scope of the legal relation stated in the arbitration agreement. This requirement limits the kind of circumstances, which can be the object for an arbitration award. If an arbitration board renders a judgment on an independent legal fact, this judgment will have a res judicata effect if the same legal fact would be of relevance in another dispute between the parties. If, however, an arbitration award is rendered on an evidentiary fact, no res judicata effect will appear since the parties can present new evidence in a new arbitration procedure.[1082]

797. The arbitrators may decide how to *legally qualify* a circumstance, e.g., they may decide that certain facts constitute 'force majeure'.[1083] However, the arbitrators may not render a judgment on an *abstract legal issue*. This means that they may not determine the meaning of a legal rule without there being facts that are disputed. Furthermore, arbitrators may *interpret agreements* and fill out gaps in a contract more extensive than according to civil law provisions. However, in order to do this the arbitrators must have direct or indirect support from the parties in the arbitration agreement or otherwise.

798. Arbitrators may also rule on the civil law effects of *competition law* as between the parties. However, the EU-court has rendered a judgment declaring that the membership states are obligated to set aside an arbitration agreement if it prejudices the competition rules laid down in Article 81 in the Rome Treaty. Such awards shall be deemed to be in conflict with the rules on *ordre public* in the jurisdiction in which the judgment was rendered.[1084]

799. If a party makes an objection that the arbitration clause in a contract is invalid, the arbitrators are competent to rule on their own jurisdiction.[1085] The reason why this provision is laid down in the LSF is to clarify that the arbitrators' competence stems from the arbitration clause, and that their competence remains if the validity of the contract is disputed. A party may institute an action in an ordinary court about the validity of the arbitration agreement, if the arbitration procedure has not commenced. The previous order under which a party could bring an action for

---

1080. *See* NJA 1910, p. 227; NJA 1919, p. 497; NJA 1922, p. 37; NJA 1964, p. 2; NJA 1972, p. 458 and NJA 1973, p. 480.
1081. Prop. 1998/99:35, p. 62.
1082. *See* Lindell, *Alternativ tvistlösning, särskilt medling och skiljeförfarande*, 149.
1083. Prop. 1998/99, p. 62.
1084. *See Eco Swiss China Ltd v. Benetton International N.V.*, C126/97.
1085. 2 § LSF.

the arbitration panel's jurisdiction in public court during an ongoing arbitration process is removed through the revision of the LSF. The reason for this is that this arrangement did not infrequently cause complications and time delays due to parallel processes regarding the validity and applicability of the arbitration agreement.[1086] Although the change in LSF has not completely eliminated the risk of parallel processes, this is considered to be reduced by the fact that the question of jurisdiction should now be tried in court more closely linked to the arbitration process.

800. Where the validity of an arbitration agreement, which constitutes part of another agreement, must be determined in conjunction with a determination of the jurisdiction of the arbitrators, the arbitration agreement shall be deemed to constitute a separate agreement.[1087] This is called the doctrine on *separability*. While section 2 gives the arbitrators the right to rule on their own jurisdiction, the doctrine on separability says that the arbitrators do not lose their jurisdiction if they would find that the contract with the arbitration clause is invalid.[1088] Obviously, this doctrine is related to the doctrine on jurisdiction (*Kompetenz-Kompetenz*), since a condition for the latter is that the arbitration clause is regarded as independent from the substantial contract.[1089]

801. The arbitrators may not entertain an issue, which is the object for a pending action, unless the action has been withdrawn.[1090] If, however, a party in an ordinary civil action, makes the objection that the parties have made an arbitration agreement, this is an objection concerning a *procedural hindrance*. Such an objection must be raised at the first appearance; otherwise, the right to raise the objection can be precluded. This is true also with respect to a set-off defence.[1091]

802. Special provisions in the LSF apply if the disputed issue has earlier been entertained in summary proceedings, i.e., summary debt collection (*Betalningsföreläggande*) and ordinary assistance (*Handräckning*). The foundation for this regulation is that the entertainment of undisputed claims on payment should not be aggravated unless there are strong reasons.[1092] The defendant keeps his right to make the objection that the parties have made an arbitration agreement until his first appearance in the referred or re-opened case.[1093] However, if the defendant has contested and the plaintiff claimed that the case should be referred to the district court, the plaintiff has lost his right to allege that the arbitration agreement is a procedural hindrance. This is true regardless of whether the defendant has contested the summon proceedings, alleging the arbitration agreement, or not contested it.[1094] In the

1086. Prop. 2017/18:257, p. 22, SOU 2015:37 p. 24.
1087. 3 § LSF.
1088. Broches, 74.
1089. Cars, 55; Kvart & Olsson, 61.
1090. 4 § LSF.
1091. SOU 1994:81, p. 97.
1092. Prop. 1998/99:35, p. 70.
1093. *See* NJA 1972, p. 331 and NJA 1982, p. 711.
1094. Prop. 1998/99:35, p. 70.

preparatory works, the reason for this provision is said to be that it then must be clear for the applicant that there is a real dispute.[1095] Consequently, if the defendant contests without giving reasons, the applicant must let the Execution Office write-off the case, while the defendant in his response can be silent about the arbitration agreement. Thus, he can apply for a re-opening of the decision rendered in the summary proceedings and wait until his appearance in the district court until he objects that there is an arbitration agreement.

803. A court may, during the pendency of a dispute before arbitrators or prior thereto, irrespective of the arbitration agreement, render a decision on *security measures*.

804. It has been deemed reasonable that a party shall forfeit his right to invoke the arbitration agreement as a bar to court proceedings, where the party has opposed a request for arbitration, failed to appoint an arbitrator in due time, or fails, within due time, to provide his share of the requested security for compensation to the arbitrators.[1096]

1095. *Ibid.*
1096. Section 5.

Chapter 3. The Arbitrators and Their Appointment

805. An arbitrator may not be under age or have an administrator according to Chapter 11, section 7 of the Parental Code, nor may an arbitrator be declared bankrupt. It is not required that an arbitrator is a Swedish citizen, that he or she is legally trained, or that he or she is experienced as an arbitrator or a judge.[1097] These requirements express a *minimum standard* that means that the parties are free to set up additional requirements. The main function of the competence rule is to *protect the parties*. If there were no rules on competence, e.g., an arbitrator suffering from a mental illness could not be separated from his assignment.[1098] It has been debated whether the arbitrators should adjudicate upon the controversy according to the present substantive rules in force or *ex aequo et bono*.[1099] At the turn of the century, it was, under the influence of continental doctrine, argued that the arbitrators could adjudicate in the latter manner. However, this opinion never has had any impact in practice.

806. An arbitrator shall be *impartial*. He shall be discharged on the request of a party, if any circumstance exists that may diminish confidence in his impartiality. According to section 8, such a circumstance shall always be deemed to exist:

(1) where the arbitrator or a person closely associated to him is a party, or otherwise may expect benefit or detriment worth attention, as a result of the dispute;
(2) where the arbitrator or a person closely associated to him is the director of a company or any other association which is a party, or otherwise represents a party or any other person who may expect benefit or detriment worth attention as a result of the outcome of the dispute;
(3) where the arbitrator has taken a position in the dispute, as an expert or otherwise, or has assisted a party in the preparation or conduct of his case in the dispute; or
(4) where the arbitrator has received or demanded compensation in violation of section 39, second paragraph. This provision is not exhaustive, but *exemplifying* and may not be interpreted *e contrario*.[1100]

807. A person who is asked to accept an appointment as arbitrator shall immediately disclose all circumstances, which might be considered to prevent him from serving as arbitrator. An arbitrator shall inform the parties and other arbitrators of such circumstances as soon as all arbitrators have been appointed and thereafter in the course of the arbitral proceedings as soon as he has learned of any new circumstance.[1101] The arbitrators shall apply this provision in their own motion. However, lack of competence does not make the arbitration award invalid. Furthermore, an

1097. Section 7.
1098. Kvart & Olsson, 69.
1099. Arbitration in Sweden, 126.
1100. Prop. 1998/99:35, p. 218.
1101. Section 9.

arbitrator's impartiality does not make the arbitration award invalid and, in addition, if a party does not challenge the award because of impartiality, the rule on preclusion in section 34 paragraph 2 will apply.

808. The parties can make an agreement to appoint partial arbitrators, but only if they know why the arbitrators are impartial.[1102] The provision about impartiality is mandatory only in that the parties cannot *beforehand* waive their right to allege impartiality or – for that matter – any other ground for challenging the arbitration award. The principle is because a party, during a pending arbitration procedure, can decide not to request that an arbitrator shall be discharged, even if the party knows about a circumstance that makes the arbitrator impartial.

809. A challenge of an arbitrator founded on a circumstance laid down in section 8 shall be presented within fifteen days commencing on the date on which the party became aware both of the appointment of the arbitrator and of the existence of the circumstance.[1103] The arbitrators – including the challenged arbitrator – shall adjudicate the challenge unless the parties have decided that another shall examine it. If the challenge is approved, the decision may not be appealed. If, however, the challenge is not successful, the dissatisfied party may file an application with the district court that the arbitrator be removed from his post. The application must be submitted within thirty days starting on the date on which the party receives the decision. The parties may agree that an arbitration institution shall conclusively determine the decision.[1104] If the parties have made an agreement to exclude or limit the application of the grounds for setting aside an award, they are deemed to also have agreed to set aside an examination pursuant to section 10.[1105]

810. The parties may determine the number of arbitrators and the manner in which they shall be appointed.[1106] The parties can do this in the arbitration agreement, but they might have confined themselves only to agree on how the arbitrators shall be appointed or simply referred to the procedure in the LSF. Thus, the arbitration agreement can be more or less detailed on this subject. If the parties have not agreed on the choice of the arbitrators, their number or the mode of their appointment, there shall be three arbitrators according to the LSF. One shall be appointed by each party and the third by the two arbitrators together. The latter then usually becomes the chairperson of the arbitration board.[1107]

811. Where each part is required to appoint an arbitrator and one party has notified the opposing party of his choice, the opposing party must, within thirty days of

1102. Prop. 1998/99:35, 219, Cars, 77, Kvart & Olsson, 73.
1103. Section 10.
1104. Section 11.
1105. Prop. 1998/99:35, p. 220.
1106. Section 12.
1107. Section 13.

receipt of the notice, notify the first party in writing in respect of his choice of arbitrator.[1108] Thus, an oral notification is not sufficient.[1109] In order to prevent obstruction a rule has been laid down which says that a part may not revoke the appointment without the consent of the other party. If the opposing party fails to appoint an arbitrator within the stipulated time or the arbitrators so appointed fails in this respect the district court shall make the appointment at the request of a party. This is true also where someone shall appoint an arbitrator other than a party or an arbitrator.[1110] If an arbitrator resigns or is discharged, the district court shall, upon request by a party, appoint a new arbitrator. Where the arbitrator cannot fulfil his duties due to circumstances, which arise after his appointment, the person who originally was required to make the appointment, shall, instead, appoint a new arbitrator. Thus, according to LSF, it is of no relevance in this respect how the arbitrator originally was appointed. The reason for this resolution of the problem is based on the assumption that the appointment of a certain person has not been of such importance for the parties that they would like that the arbitration agreement ceased to exist if he must be replaced.[1111]

812. The district court shall, upon the request by a party, discharge an arbitrator who has delayed the proceedings and appoint another arbitrator. The parties may decide that an arbitration institution shall finally determine this issue.[1112] According to the preparatory works, the question of when there is a delay must be examined with respect to what the parties have agreed upon or assumed about the time plan for the procedure.[1113] This provision is not dispositive.

1108. Section 14.
1109. Prop. 1998/99:35, p. 220.
1110. Section 15.
1111. Prop. 1998/99:35, p. 95.
1112. Section 17.
1113. Prop. 1998/99:35, p. 223.

Chapter 4. The Procedure

813. If the parties have not agreed otherwise, the arbitral proceedings are initiated when a party receives a request for arbitration. Normally, the request must be in writing and include an express and unconditional request for arbitration, a statement of the issue which is covered by the arbitration agreement and which is to be resolved by the arbitrators and a statement of the party's choice of arbitrator where the party is required to appoint an arbitrator.[1114] However, a party may accept a request that does not fulfil these requirements.

814. The LSF does not require that the invoking party specify the disputed issue in depth. It is sufficient that he state the question or questions upon which the arbitration award is required.[1115] Thus, he must not at these stage state specific claims and the grounds for these claims. However, the disputed issue must be specified to such an extent that it is possible to determine whether or not it is within the frame of the arbitration agreement and to reassure that arbitrators with the right qualifications can be appointed. In addition, because of the low requirements on the request it cannot found the basis for an assessment about *lis pendens* and res judicata. There are certain important legal consequences connected to the time for invoking arbitration, e.g., if a party, according to the law, must initiate proceedings within a certain time, this preclusion time will stop running from the tome in question.[1116] In order to stop the preclusion time the party invoking arbitration must have made his choice of arbitrator if he by himself shall appoint one or more arbitrators. The risk that a party will overlook this has been regarded as small.[1117]

815. As far as the arbitration procedure is concerned, there are few provisions in the LSF. The Act is based on the idea that formal rules in this respect counteract the advantages a flexible procedure gives, which is one of the reasons why parties prefer arbitration to ordinary procedure. Thus, the parties, as well as the arbitrators, have been given extensive leeway to decide about the procedure themselves, but it is unusual that the parties give the arbitrators instructions regarding the procedure.[1118] However, the LSF is not completely silent on the matter. It is provided that the arbitrators shall handle the dispute in an impartial, practical and speedy manner and they shall in this respect act in accordance with the decisions of the parties insofar as there is no impediment to do that.[1119] With respect to the question of how much – if at all – the arbitrators should intervene in the case to clarify the disputed issue the LSF is silent. However, there are good reasons why the arbitrators should

1114. Section 19 LSF. A request for arbitration must not be in writing, e.g., during a pending proceeding the parties can make a new arbitration agreement or extend the present agreement.
1115. Prop. 1998/99:35, p. 102. Jfr Cf. NJA 1955, p. 224.
1116. *See* the Prescription Act s. 5 para. 3.
1117. Kvart & Olsson, 88.
1118. L. Hagberg, *Evidence in Swedish Arbitral Procedure. Yearbook of the Arbitration Institute of the Stockholm Chamber of Commerce 1982*, 31 (1982). If the parties have agreed that the dispute shall be resolved under the rules of an arbitration institute they must also be deemed to have accepted the procedural rules of the institute.
1119. LSF s. 21.

be careful before this kind of intervention. The parties appoint them and the examination of impartiality is more individualized in arbitration than in ordinary proceedings.[1120]

816. The seat of arbitration shall be determined by the parties and where this is not the case by the arbitrators.[1121] The seat of arbitration determines the nationality of the arbitration award.[1122] In addition, it is of importance with respect to certain forum issues.[1123] This is the reason why the seat of arbitration must be stated in the arbitration award.[1124] If the seat of arbitration procedure is not stated in the arbitration award, the seat of arbitration is deemed the place where the arbitration procedure – according to the award – is said to have been rendered.[1125] According to the preparatory works, the previous notion 'place of arbitration' or 'seat of arbitration' has a judicial-technical meaning.[1126] This is true because the proceedings might have taken place in different places. However, there must be some connection to the place of arbitration which has been stated in the arbitration award, e.g., if the procedure has been purely written it is sufficient that the chairman has some connection to the place of arbitration.[1127]

817. The LSF gives both parties extensive possibilities to amend their claims.[1128] According to the preparatory works, the assumption is that the parties within the scope of the arbitration agreement may assert new claims and allege new legal facts to support these claims. Another guideline is that there must be very strong reasons to deny a party to make a set of claim or to deny a party to allege a legal fact, which would be precluded as res judicata if it would be alleged in a new procedure between the parties.[1129] To be more specific, the claimant shall, within the period of time determined by the arbitrators, state his claims in respect of the issue stated in the request for arbitration, as well as the circumstances which support his claims. After this, the respondent, within a certain time, shall state his position to the claims, and the circumstances invoked in support of them. Furthermore, the claimant may submit new claims and the respondent may submit his claims, if the claims fall within the scope of the arbitration agreement. However, this is permitted only if the arbitrators do not consider it inappropriate to adjudicate such claims with respect to the risk of *delay* or other circumstances. Subject to the same condition,

1120. B. Lindell, *Alternativ tvistlösning. Särskilt medling och skiljeförfarande*, 176.
1121. The wording 'Place of Arbitration' was changed to 'Seat of Arbitration' at the revision of LSF, *see* prop. 2017/18:257. The meaning of the prerequisite has not changed.
1122. LSF s. 52.
1123. LSF ss 43 and 44.
1124. LSF s. 31 para. 2.
1125. Prop. 1998/99:35, p. 225.
1126. *Ibid.*
1127. SOU 1994:81, p. 275.
1128. LSF s. 23.
1129. Prop. 1998/99:35, p. 226. An arbitration award is deemed to have approximately the same res judicata effect as an ordinary judgment. However, the arbitration agreement or the request for arbitration can make the res judicata effect more limited than in ordinary proceedings, *see* B. Lindell, *Alternativ tvitslösning*, 184.

each party may amend previously presented claims and may allege new circumstances in support of his case. This rule does not apply where the parties have decided otherwise.

818. The parties are entitled to present their respective cases in writing or orally to the extent the arbitrators find necessary. The notion 'necessary' means that the arbitrators can reject such material that can be deemed as not relevant for the case. According to the preparatory works, the arbitrators may direct the parties to definitively state all the legal facts and evidence to be presented within a certain time. This also includes the legal argumentation.[1130] A party may not on beforehand waive his right in this respect.[1131] On the request of one of the parties, an oral hearing shall be held with respect to the referred issue if the parties have not agreed otherwise. This unconditional right to an oral hearing is limited to the determination of the substantial issue.[1132] Thus, procedural issues are not included. The principle of communication, which is laid down in the same rule, means that a party shall be given an opportunity to review all documents and all other materials related to the dispute, which is supplied to the arbitrators by the opposing party or another person.[1133] If one of the parties, without valid reason, fails to appear at a hearing or otherwise fails to comply with an order of the arbitrators, the arbitrators may continue the proceedings and resolve the dispute on its merits.

819. Presentation of evidence is the responsibility of the parties. However, the arbitrators may appoint experts, unless both parties oppose it. An item of evidence that clearly is unnecessary may be rejected. In addition, evidence of relevance to the case may also be rejected if it is presented in a late stage of the proceedings. Only an ordinary court is entitled to decide about interim enforcement measures pursuant to Chapter 15 in the Procedural Code. The possibility the LSF in section 25 paragraph 3 gives the arbitrators to decide about interim measures does not have any sanction. Thus, if the party does not comply with the decision nothing will happen. This is why it has been said that the provision is unnecessary and that it might diminish the arbitrators' authority. The reason why the rule in question has been laid down in the LSF is to clarify what the arbitrators may do in this respect.[1134] In addition, the arbitrators may neither make orders on penalty of a fine nor use other means of compulsion, nor may they administer oaths or truth affirmations. Instead, where a party wishes a witness or an expert to testify under oath, or a party to be examined under truth affirmation, the party may, after obtaining the consent of the arbitrators, submit an application to such effect to the district court.[1135]

1130. Prop. 1998/99:35, p. 227.
1131. *Ibid.*
1132. Prop. 1998/99:35, p. 112.
1133. LSF s. 24.
1134. Prop. 1998/99:35, p. 74.
1135. LSF s. 26.

Chapter 5. The Arbitral Award

820. The notion arbitration award has been defined in the LSF.[1136] The reason why a legal definition has been laid down is mainly that it has been regarded as uncertain if the arbitrators may try their own competence as a preliminary issue.[1137] An arbitration award is always made when the arbitrators finally determine the substantial disputed issue by a final award, a part judgment or an intermediate judgment or confirm a settlement agreement between the parties.[1138] If the arbitrators dismiss the case this was previously also labelled as an award. After the revision of LSF dismissal is labelled as a decision. The mandate of the arbitrators shall be deemed to be completed when they have delivered a final award, unless otherwise provided in section 32 or 35 LSF.[1139] If a party withdraws a claim, the arbitrators shall dismiss that part of the dispute, unless the opposing party requests the arbitrators rule on the claim.[1140] A claim invoked as a defence by way of set-off shall be adjudicated in the same award as the main claim.

821. The old LSF required that all arbitrators participated in making the final award. In addition, the arbitration agreement ceased to exist if the majority of the arbitrators did not agree on the resolution of a question that had been referred to them. The new LSF is based on the idea that it is sufficient that an arbitrator has had the opportunity to participate in the examination of the disputed issues.[1141] Of course, the absent arbitrator must have attended hearings where parties and others have been heard and he must have taken part in all the documentation in the case. Furthermore, the opinion agreed upon by the majority of the arbitrators shall prevail. If no majority is attained, the opinion of the chairman shall prevail. This rule gives the chairperson a strong position, which is also pointed out in the preparatory works.[1142] In contrast to the Code, the arbitrators do not vote about the reasons for the conclusions. Instead, they vote separately about the conclusions.

822. In order to make it possible to enforce an arbitration award some minimum requirements have been laid down in section 31 in the LSF with respect to the shape and content of an award. An award shall be made in writing and signed by the arbitrators. It does not have to be signed by all arbitrators. It is sufficient that it is signed by a majority, provided that the reason why not all arbitrators have signed it is noted in the award. The parties may decide that the chairman of the tribunal alone shall sign the award. It is not a requirement that the arbitrators give reasons for the conclusions. Thus, it is sufficient if they state their conclusions. Of course, the parties may require the award to be motivated and dissenting opinions annexed to it. However, normally the arbitrators do give reasons without the parties have to ask for it.

1136. LSF s. 27.
1137. Prop. 1998/99:35, p. 124.
1138. With respect to separate judgments, *see* LSF s. 29.
1139. Section 32 provide about correction and supplementation of the arbitration award and s. 35 about resuming the arbitral proceedings in order to eliminate a ground for invalidity or setting aside.
1140. LSF s. 28.
1141. LSF s. 30.
1142. Prop. 1998/99:35, p. 128.

The award shall state the place of arbitration and the date when it is made and shall immediately be delivered to the parties. Section 33 provides that if an arbitration award is not in writing and not signed it is invalid.

823. Pursuant to section 32, an arbitration award can be corrected, supplemented or interpreted. The arbitrators may on their own motion correct any obvious inaccuracy within thirty days of the date of the announcement of the award. If the arbitrators by oversight failed to decide an issue which should have been dealt with in the award they may on their own motion supplement it within the same time limit. Interpretation may be done only with respect to the decision in the award. Thus, the arbitrators may not interpret the reasons for the decision. The arbitrators may also correct or supplement an award or interpret the decision in an award on the request of any of the parties within thirty days of receipt of the award by that party. If the arbitrators then decide to correct or interpret the award the measure must take place within thirty days from the date of receipt by the arbitrators of the party's request. Supplementation must take place within sixty days. The parties should be afforded an opportunity to express their view with respect to correction, supplementation and interpretation before any decision on the matter.

Chapter 6. Void and Challengeable Awards

824. As mentioned above, the LSF does not apply to an arbitration agreement, which provides for a right of appeal. This does not imply that it is impossible for a party to attack an arbitration award which he argues is incorrect, since the parties are regarded as having entered into the arbitration agreement on the understanding that the arbitration procedure will be carried out in an acceptable way. This is the reason why the LSF gives the parties certain limited options to set aside an arbitration award. However, an award can be set aside only if the procedure has been influenced by some serious defects. These defects are divided into two groups; the first makes the award void and the second challengeable. The borderline between these two groups has been drawn in such a way that, in one group, defects which justify the award not being accepted from a public point of view make it void, while the other group refers to circumstances which only relate to the party's interest.[1143]

825. Since the grounds, which can make an award void, have no time limits, they are very restricted. An award is pursuant to section 33 void if: (1) the arbitrators have rendered a decision on a question which, by law, cannot be submitted to arbitration; (2) the award, or the way in which it arose, is clearly incompatible with the basic principles of the Swedish legal system; or (3) the award was not put in writing and signed by the arbitrators in accordance with section 31, first paragraph. The invalidity may apply to a certain part of the award. In principal only indispositive issues cannot be submitted to arbitration, but there are exceptions, e.g., an arbitration award, which obligates someone to pay a debt, occurred in gambling would not – although it refers to a dispositive issue, comply either with point (1) or with public policy (*ordre public*) in p. 2. Thus, these provisions sometimes might overlap each other.[1144] As stated above the arbitrators may, e.g., not administer oaths or truth affirmations. Obviously, such questions cannot be submitted to arbitration. However, point (1) is not meant to be applied on procedural questions, but they can fall within the scope of point (2), although this provision is meant to have a narrow space of application. An arbitration award can be valid although an arbitrator does not sign it. It is, as mentioned before, sufficient that a majority of the arbitrators signs it, if the reason why not all of the arbitrators have signed the award is noted in the award.

826. At the request of a party, the award shall, according to section 34, be wholly or partially set aside by the court, if it may not be challenged in accordance with section 36, if (1) if it is not covered by a valid arbitration agreement between the parties, (2) if the arbitrators have given an award after the expiry of the period decided on by the parties, or where the arbitrators have gone beyond the matter submitted to them, (3) where the arbitrators have gone beyond the matter submitted to them which probably influenced the outcome of the case,[1145] (4) if the arbitrators have rendered an award on a case in which the arbitration proceedings according to

1143. Arbitration in Sweden, 83 et seq.
1144. Prop. 1998/99:35, p. 142.
1145. Influence on the outcome in (3) is new, *see* prop. 2017/18 p. 79.

section 47 should not have taken place in Sweden, (5) if an arbitrator has been appointed contrary to the agreement between the parties or the LSF, (6) if an arbitrator was unauthorized due to any circumstance set forth in section 7 or 8 LSF; or (7) if, through no fault of the party, any other irregularity of procedure has occurred which probably influenced the outcome of the case. An arbitration award can be challenged pursuant to point (1), e.g., where the parties have not made an arbitration agreement or the agreement later has become invalid. The assignment of the arbitrators is, in the first place, determined by the arbitration agreement and, second, by the request for arbitration, which must be made within the framework of the arbitration agreement. This is true for the most common situation where the arbitration agreement refers to future disputes.[1146] The claims presented by the party who has invoked the arbitration must also be within the framework of the request for arbitration, and, in addition, the award must coincide with the claims. Otherwise the arbitrators have gone beyond the subject submitted to them, alternatively point (1) will apply.[1147] Section 47 in the LSF state when arbitration may not take place in Sweden. It is unusual that arbitration awards are challenged on this ground. The provisions concerning disqualification of arbitrators and how to nominate arbitrators have been commented on above. If an arbitrator, pursuant to the parties' agreement that he shall be qualified in a certain way but is not, then this is regarded as a situation in which the disqualification rule in point (4) applies. If an arbitrator lacks competence, e.g., he is in bankruptcy point (5) will apply. The last-mentioned ground for challenging an award is similar to a general clause and is, therefore, frequently used when an award is challenged. Thus, it is not possible to enumerate all the situations where these ground can be applied. However, it is clear that it applies if the arbitrators have deviated from the few, but binding, rules in the LSF concerning the procedure or have not followed instructions given to them by the parties.[1148] It should be noted that the award will be set aside only if the fault is not caused by the party and, moreover, that it is probable that the fault influenced the outcome. Furthermore, a party may not rely on the existence of any irregularity if he takes part in the proceedings without objecting or otherwise is considered as having waived the irregularity. This provision is meant to prevent a party who knows that grounds for challenging exist from speculating on the outcome of the proceedings. Thus, a party shall not be given the opportunity to accept an award in his favour and to challenge a disadvantageous one.[1149]

827. An action against an award pursuant to section 33 or 34 shall be instituted in the Court of Appeal within the jurisdiction where the arbitral proceedings were

1146. If an arbitration agreement has been made because of an existing dispute, the agreement alone is normally decisive determining the extension of the arbitration agreement.

1147. Holmbäck, *Arbitration in Sweden*, 106. In order to decide if a determined issue lies within the framework of the arbitration agreement the latter must be interpreted. *See also* LSF s. 23.

1148. Examples of procedural errors are: where the arbitrators have exceeded a presented claim; where a circumstance not alleged by a party has formed the judgment; where the voting has not been performed correctly, and where a party has not been given the opportunity to give an answer to the other party. As far as precedent cases are concerned, *see, e.g.*, NJA 1953, p. 751; 1965, p. 384; 1973, p. 740 and 1975, p. 536.

1149. *See* NJA II 1929, p. 49.

held.[1150] An action must be instituted within two months from the date upon which the party received the award. If the award has been corrected, supplemented or interpreted in accordance with section 32, an action must be instituted within two months from the date when the party received the award in its final wording. The Court of Appeal may not examine the award in substance or amend it, but may only set it aside or not, and its determination may not be appealed. However, the Court of Appeal may grant review dispensation to the Supreme Court.

According to section 35, a court may stay proceedings with respect to the invalidity or setting aside an award for a certain period of time in order to give the arbitrators an opportunity to take some measure, which in their opinion will eliminate the ground for the invalidity or setting aside. The purpose of this provision is to give the arbitrators a possibility to cure defects in a simple way. Otherwise the only option would be to set aside the arbitration award. It should be noted that the arbitrators may not make a general re-examination of their previous determination.[1151]

1150. LSF s. 43.
1151. Prop. 1998/99:35, p. 236.

Chapter 7. The Costs of Arbitration

828. Concerning the costs of arbitration, one must distinguish between the arbitrators' right to be compensated by the parties and a party's right to get compensation from the other party. If the parties have not made an agreement about the costs, they shall pursuant to section 37 be jointly and severally liable to pay reasonable compensation to the arbitrators for work and expenses.[1152] The amount should be specified, and a division should be made between fee and other expenses. Interest can be included in the compensation. If the arbitrators would find that they lack jurisdiction to determine the dispute, normally the party that did not request arbitration shall not be liable to make payment. Since the arbitrators in the award can impose an obligation upon the parties to pay, where no agreement in that respect exists, they are guaranteed the requested compensation. However, an award may not be withheld pending payment.[1153] Since the arbitrators obviously decide in their own interest when determining their fees, a court must have the authority to examine the decision at issue. Consequently, the LSF provides that a party or an arbitrator who is dissatisfied with a decision by the arbitrators, with respect to the compensation payable to them, may bring the matter before the court. Pursuant to section 41, such an action must be brought within two months from the date upon which the party received the award, and in the case of an arbitrator, within the same period from the announcement of the award. According to the old LSF, an arbitrator was not allowed to accept compensation or demand compensation from one party, unless a similar benefit was due to him from the other party. In the present LSF, this prohibition only applies to agreements between an arbitrator and one of the parties. Thus, the parties may agree that their responsibility for the compensation to the arbitrators shall be different.

Pursuant to section 38, the arbitrators may request security for the compensation, and they may fix separate security for individual claims. Without support in an agreement between the parties a request for security should not be addressed to only one of the parties because of the risk that the arbitrators would be deemed to favour the other party. Where there is no agreement between the parties with respect to security, they should be requested to pay it in equal shares.[1154] If a party fails to provide its share within the period decided by the arbitrators, the opposing party may provide the entire security. Where the requested security is not provided, the arbitrators may terminate the proceedings, in whole or in part. It is stated in section 39 that the provisions in sections 38 and 39 are dispositive which *inter alia* means that the parties can agree that the compensation shall be determined by an arbitration institute.

829. As far as a party's right to be compensated by the other party, the arbitrators may, on request of either of the parties, determine this issue. Concerning arbitration costs (e.g., attorney's fees and costs for appearance), it is deemed natural that

1152. With respect to reasonable compensation, *see* NJA 1998, p. 574.
1153. LSF s. 40, Prop. 1998/99:35, p. 164.
1154. Prop. 1998/99:35, p. 164.

the arbitrators are guided by the provisions in Chapter 18 of the Code.[1155] With respect to the compensation of the arbitrators, the usual practice is that each party bears half of the costs, if the losing party had reasonable grounds for invoking the arbitration procedure.[1156]

1155. *Arbitration in Sweden*, 150.
1156. Cars, *supra*, 199.

Chapter 8. Forum and Time Limits

830. As stated above, an action against an award pursuant to sections 33, 34 and 36 shall be instituted by the Court of Appeal within the jurisdiction where the arbitral proceedings were held (seat of arbitration). An action regarding compensation to an arbitrator shall be considered by the district court at the seat of arbitration. If the arbitration award is silent with respect to the seat of arbitration, the action may be instituted before the Stockholm district court. Pursuant to section 44, an application to appoint or discharge an arbitrator shall be instituted by the district court at the place where one of the parties is domiciled, or by the district court at the seat of arbitration, or by the Stockholm district court. An application concerning the taking of evidence in accordance to section 26 shall be instituted by the district court determined by the arbitrators. If there is no such decision, the action shall be considered by the Stockholm district court. If the district court has granted an application to appoint or remove an arbitrator the decision may not appealed.

Chapter 9. International Matters

831. To begin with, something should be said about the Arbitration Institute of the SCC. The Arbitration Institute is an independent organ within SCC. Its activities are large and increasing, and it deals with both international and national arbitration. In order to meet new requirements from international business, the SCC Institute enacted new rules in 2017 (latest version) adjusted to international arbitration and, since 1981, has annually edited a yearbook, published in English every two years. In addition, it has contributed to the Establishment of the Scientific Institute for Arbitration at the University of Stockholm. According to its charters, the SCC Institute shall assist in the settlement of domestic and international disputes in accordance with the rules set forth in the charters and shall also assist in the settlement of disputes in accordance with other rules adopted by the Institute, in particular the conciliation rules and rules for procedure under the UNCITRAL Arbitration Rules. Furthermore, the SCC Institute seeks to assist, pursuant to its own decision on each case, in proceedings which take place in a manner that differs wholly or partly from that contemplated by the charter's rules and, finally, to provide information about arbitration matters. The SCC Institute has a board composed of three members who are appointed for a period of three years by the Executive Committee of the Chamber. The chairman shall be a judge experienced in business disputes, one member shall be a practising lawyer and the other member shall be a person who enjoys the confidence of the business community. The SCC Institute also has a secretariat composed of persons employed by the chamber. The secretariat is under the direction of a Secretary-General, who is a lawyer.

832. Sweden has ratified the Geneva Convention on enforcement of foreign arbitration awards. The ratification led to the enactment of the Act Concerning Foreign Arbitration Agreements and Awards (SFS 1929:147). This Act ceased to exist when the present LSF came into force in 1999. Provisions about foreign arbitration agreements and awards then became a part of the new Act. Sweden has also ratified the New York Convention on Recognition and Enforcement of Foreign Arbitration Awards from 1958, the scope of application of which is much broader than that of the Geneva Convention. Finally, it should be mentioned that Sweden has ratified the Convention of the World Bank, Concerning Settlement of Investment Disputes Between a State and a Citizen in Another State (1965). The Act on Recognition and Enforcement of Arbitration Awards Concerning Certain International Investment Disputes (SFS 1966:735) has been enacted as a result of Sweden's ratification of this Convention.

The issues which arise and must be regulated in international relations are mainly: (1) when may arbitration take place in Sweden, (2) which law should apply on the arbitration agreement, (3) which rules should apply with respect to recognition and enforcement, and (4) international arbitration agreements as a hinder for litigation.

833. Pursuant to section 46, the LSF applies to arbitral proceedings, which take place in Sweden regardless that the dispute has an international connection. Looking closely at this provision, the statement *in fine*, referring to 'an international connection' is unnecessary since the LSF applies to all arbitral proceedings that take place in Sweden. Nevertheless, the statement might have a pedagogical value since it clarifies the issue of jurisdiction. The implication of it is *inter alia* that the parties cannot make an arbitration agreement that sets aside the LSF. Thus, they may not agree that the procedure shall be in accordance with, e.g., German or French law.[1157] The parties may insert provisions from, e.g., German law in the arbitration agreement only as long as mandatory provisions in the LSF are not set aside. Arbitral proceedings in accordance with the LSF may, pursuant to section 47, be commenced in Sweden if the arbitration agreement provides it, or where the arbitrators or an arbitration institution in accordance with the agreement have determined that the proceedings shall have its seat in Sweden, or the opposing party otherwise consents thereto. Arbitration procedure may also be commenced in Sweden against a party, which is domiciled in Sweden or otherwise could be subject to jurisdiction in Sweden with regard to the matter in dispute, unless the arbitration agreement provides that the proceedings shall take place abroad.[1158] If an arbitration agreement has an international connection it shall, according to section 48, be governed by the law agreed upon by the parties.[1159] Where such an agreement does not exist, the law of the country in which, by virtue of the agreement, shall govern the arbitration agreement, the proceedings have taken place or shall take place. The notion 'international connection' is not defined in the LSF. Obviously, such a connection exists if one of the parties had his residence in a foreign country when the arbitration agreement was made. According to the preparatory works, a dispute can also be regarded as international if both parties have their residence in Sweden but the dispute has occurred in a foreign country.[1160]

834. The provision in LSF section 4 about an arbitration agreement as a hinder for litigation addresses domestic situations. In order to comply with Conventions signed by Sweden with regard to international arbitration agreements as hinder for litigation a provision has been laid down on this subject in LSF section 49. Thus, where foreign law is applicable to the arbitration agreement section 4 shall apply except when the agreement is invalid, inoperative or incapable to be performed in accordance with the applicable law, or arbitrators in accordance with Swedish law may not determine the dispute. If the arbitration procedure shall take place abroad and foreign law is applicable to the arbitration agreement it must be examined if the arbitration agreement is valid in accordance to the foreign law. Even if section 4 will apply arbitrators according to the foreign law or Swedish law may not determine the dispute.[1161]

1157. Prop. 1998/99:35, p. 244.
1158. The new LSF does not make a distinction between national and foreign arbitration agreements. This distinction has been deemed to be confusing and without substance.
1159. This provision is new.
1160. Prop. 1998/99:35, p. 244.
1161. Prop. 1998/99:35, pp. 196, 245.

If the proceedings are based upon an arbitration agreement and, pursuant to Swedish law, the issues may be resolved by arbitrators, the provisions of sections 26 and 44 shall apply with respect to the taking of evidence.

835. Pursuant to LSF section 51, parties who are not domiciled in Sweden nor have their place of business in Sweden may in a commercial relationship through an express written agreement exclude or limit the application of the grounds for setting aside an award as are set forth in section 34. Such an award shall be recognized and enforced in Sweden in accordance with the rules applicable to a foreign award. The limitation in the provision to foreign parties has been made because the New York Convention provides an examination when an international award shall be enforced. Thus, if the parties have inserted an exclusion or limitation clause in their agreement they avoid a double examination; one in the state where the proceedings took place and another in the state where enforcement is sought. A disadvantage with this regulation is that there will be no examination at all where the claims have been disapproved in the award or where the claim has been approved but the award is declaratory.[1162] Section 51 does not prevent a party to institute a declaratory action with a court with respect to the validity of the arbitration agreement.

1162. Prop. 1998/99:35, p. 157.

Chapter 10. Recognition and Enforcement of an Arbitration Award

§1. Swedish Awards

836. In contrast to a judgment rendered by a court, a Swedish arbitration award cannot be immediately enforced. The Enforcement Service must perform a summary review before the enforcement. However, the Enforcement Service shall only check that the arbitration agreement does not provide for a right to appeal and, if it does, that the time for appeal has expired and the award has not been appealed. In addition, the Enforcement Service shall check that the award complies with the requirements in LSF section 31, i.e., that the award is made in writing and signed by the arbitrators. The limited summary review means that a party who is not satisfied with the award must make a request to the court not to continue the enforcement. Obviously, such a request will not be made until the award has been challenged. The order made by the Enforcement Service that the award shall not be enforced may not be appealed. Before enforcement, the Enforcement Service must give the losing party an opportunity to state his opinion. As stated above, an arbitration agreement can be set aside as invalid because of public reasons. However, according to the LSF the Enforcement Service may not refuse enforcement even if it is obvious that the award is void. In such cases, the Enforcement Service shall direct the party to bring an action with respect to the validity of the award within a month after the order was served. The Enforcement that will follow such an order will be limited since the provisions on enforcement of revocable judgments will apply. Thus, the debtor can prevent enforcement by depositing a security. If a security is not deposited the attached property may not be sold without the consent of the debtor.

§2. Foreign Awards

837. The nationality of an arbitration award is pursuant to LSF section 52 determined in accordance with a territorial criterion based on where the award has been rendered. Thus, an award made abroad shall be deemed a foreign award. However, when the procedure has taken place in Sweden and the award has been signed abroad, the award will be Swedish since it shall be deemed to have been made in the country in which the place of arbitration is situated. Pursuant to section LSF section 53, a foreign award, which is based on an arbitration agreement, shall be recognized and enforced in Sweden. Some exceptions from this rule are laid down in sections 54–60. According to LSF section 54, a foreign award shall not be recognized and enforced in Sweden where the party against whom the award is invoked proves the existence of certain enumerated hinders. These hinders correspond to hinders laid down in the New York Convention on recognition and enforcement of foreign awards. Pursuant to LSF section 55, recognition and enforcement of a foreign award shall also be refused where a court finds that the arbitrators have determined an issue, which they may not decide in accordance with Swedish law, or where it is clear that the award is incompatible with the basic principles of the Swedish legal system. An application for the enforcement of a foreign award shall be made with the Svea Court of Appeal. The application may not be granted if the opposing party has not been given an opportunity to express his opinion upon the application (*see* sections 56 and 57).

If the opposing party objects that an arbitration agreement has been made, the applicant must submit the agreement in an original and certified copy or in some other way prove that an arbitration agreement was entered into. If the opposing party objects that a petition has been made to set aside the award or a motion for a stay of execution has been submitted the Court of Appeal may postpone its decision and order the opposing party to provide a reasonable security in default of which enforcement might otherwise be ordered. The court shall be restrictive to postpone a decision for a stay of enforcement.[1163] The examination in issue is discretionary and although only the applicant's interest is mentioned in the preparatory works there is no hinder to consider also the interest of the opposing party.[1164] According to the preparatory works, a stay of enforcement should be ordered only where the court finds that the action to set aside the award has not been made in order to delay the enforcement. The opposing party therefore must prove that his challenge of the award rests on substantial grounds.[1165] Pursuant to section 59, the award shall be enforced as a final judgment of a Swedish court if the Svea Court of Appeal grants the application. The Court of Appeal's decision can be appealed to the Supreme Court.

Where an arbitration award may be enforced in Sweden the court may grant a security measure in accordance with Chapter 15 of the RB also with respect to a claim which will be examined abroad.[1166] If a security measure has been granted the applicant must, pursuant to 15:7 in the Code, within a month institute an action with the court in order to secure its binding force. A request for arbitration abroad which might result in an award which is recognized and may be enforced in Sweden shall be equated with the commencement of such an action. The Court of Appeal shall examine a request for a security measure or a request to set aside such a decision.

1163. Prop. 1989/99:35, p. 202. *See also* NJA 1979, p. 527 and NJA 1992, p. 733.
1164. Prop. 1998/99:35, p. 202.
1165. Prop. 1998/99:35, p. 203.
1166. *See* NJA 1983, p. 814.

Chapter 11. Expedited Arbitration

838. The SCC adopted rules for expedited arbitration 1 January 2017. Expedited arbitration provides an alternative to the SCC's ordinary rules and to the provisions in the LSF. The parties can make their choice between the different set of rules when they insert an arbitration clause in their contract or, in a separate agreement, when a dispute has aroused. The disputed amount can be the determinant factor for the parties whether to use simplified arbitration. However, simplified arbitration can always be used instead of ordinary arbitration. In addition, the parties can let the SCC Institute decide which rules to apply taking into account the complexity of the case.

Salient features for expedited arbitration according to the rules issued by SCC is that: (1) the arbitration board shall always be composed by a sole arbitrator, (2) the parties may not – with the exception from the Statement of Claim and the Statement of Defence – submit more than one written statement each with regard to the disputed issue, including the evidence they wish to present. The documents must be brief and must be submitted within ten days. Oral hearings shall be held only on request of a party and if the Arbitrator deems it necessary, (3) the award must be rendered within three months. Only upon request of a party the award will be motivated, (4) the Arbitrator's fee and the SCC institute's compensation are based on the amount in dispute fixed in accordance with regulations issued by the SCC Institute. Thus, the parties can calculate their costs before the commencement of the proceedings.

Part XI. Mediation

Chapter 1. Introduction

839. To begin with, it should be underlined that the use of mediation to resolve disputes is not common in Sweden. Thus, there are few regulations, no court cases and few books and articles on mediation. However, because of the EU Directive on Mediation, an act on mediation came into force in 2011. The Swedish Act on Mediation in Certain Private Disputes (hereinafter 'the Mediation Act') implements the Directive of the European Parliament and the Council Directive 2008/52/EU of 21 May 2008, about certain aspects on mediation. The objective of the Directive is cross-border disputes, but the Mediation Act also applies to purely domestic extra-judicial mediation procedures.

840. Besides the Mediation Act and court-referred mediation, mediation is regulated with respect to certain labour law disputes between unions and employers according to provisions contained in the Act on Co-determination at Work, the Swedish Land Act for Leasehold and Tenancy Disputes and in the Copyright Act in relation to certain copyright disputes. Furthermore, the Funeral Act provides that mediation is the presumed way to resolve disputes with respect to funerals. Where it concerns family disputes, such as custody issues, the Social Welfare Board has, since 1970, arranged collaborative discussions between the parents, which is a form of mediation. In addition, through a reform implemented in 2006, mediation was introduced in the Children and Parents Code. However, the relatively new possibility for the courts to appoint a mediator in family cases does not seem to have been used often. Furthermore, the Code also provides the option of appointing a mediator at the enforcement stage of the judgment in family disputes. This situation, where a judgment has been rendered, but one of the parties does not wish to comply with it, is not unusual. Of course, the principle that mediation must be voluntary does not work in this situation; if the party does not collaborate the judgment will be enforced. Finally, the Act on Mediation in Criminal Cases, which focuses on juveniles, should be mentioned.

Chapter 2. The Mediation Act

841. The Mediation Act was preceded by a government investigation into Alternative Dispute Resolution (ADR). The tasks of the investigator were to elucidate the conditions for an alternative to court procedure in the first instance, in cases where the parties are allowed to settle the dispute through an agreement and to analyse the reasons why mediation is not so commonly used in Sweden.[1167] The findings of the investigation were subsequently published in the Swedish Government Official Reports Series, SOU 2007:26, 'Alternative Dispute Resolution'. In the Report, it was suggested that Sweden, like other Scandinavian countries, should introduce court-annexed mediation. Fast litigation and advance notifications were also proposed. However, these proposals were never realized.[1168]

842. Preparations for the existing Mediation Act were concluded thorough the Government Bill on Mediation and Court Settlement (prop. 2010/11:128). The proposition was a disappointment for those who had expected an act on court-annexed mediation, since it only, in principle, suggested a mere implementation of the Directive. According to the proposition, which also contains explanatory notes for the proposed act, the legislator rejected court-annexed mediation for the following reasons: First, because it would jeopardize the competition among mediators; second, because there are some major differences between court settlement and mediation, and, third, due to the clarity with respect to the role of the judge. As regards clarity, it was stated that, if the judge acts as a mediator one day and as a judge the next day, there is a risk that his or her role as a judge will become blurred and unclear, which could cause confusion.[1169]

843. The Mediation Act contains 12 sections. Sections 1 and 2 concern the scope of the Act, sections 3 and 4 contain definitions, section 5 is about confidentiality and section 6 regulates the effect of mediation on limitation periods and prescription. According to section 6 of the Mediation Act, a legal period assigned to institute an action in court stop running when a mediation procedure is initiated. The time starts running if the parties cannot agree and the mediation is terminated. Sections 7–12 concern the enforcement of an agreement resulting from mediation.

844. Pursuant to section 1 of the Mediation Act, the Act applies to private law disputes, if the parties are permitted to settle the dispute. However, the Act does not apply to mediation or settlement activity in cases that are already pending in a court, in front of another authority or in front of an arbitration tribunal. Nor does the Mediation Act apply to settlement activities in a foreign court. Thus, it applies only to private extrajudicial mediation. Furthermore, according to the preparatory works, mediation must concern an already existing dispute since it could otherwise deprive a party of its right to examination in court if enforcement is sought immediately

1167. *See* the Terms of Reference for the investigation, Dir. 2005:77.
1168. Cf. para. 107 *supra* about Dispute Resolution Boards.
1169. Prop. 2010/11:128, 12–13.

after an agreement is reached. Particularly in those cases where the parties use mediation to renegotiate an agreement this interpretation seems problematic and could be difficult to apply.

845. The term 'cross-border dispute' has no clear definition in Swedish procedural law. However, it normally means that one of the parties is domiciled in another jurisdiction. A Swedish court has competence to entertain such a dispute if there is a forum for it in the RB or in an international instrument. The main instrument in this respect is the Brussels-I Regulation. This regulation also provides some rules that give Swedish courts jurisdiction over certain cross-border disputes, e.g., insurance disputes.

846. Pursuant to section 3 of the Mediation Act, mediation is a structured procedure where two or more parties voluntarily try to resolve a dispute with the help of a mediator. A mediation agreement is defined as an agreement that presents the result of mediation and which imposes an obligation on one or more of the parties to the agreement. The definition of mediation, which the legislator more or less has taken from the Directive, is very open and broad. However, the Swedish Government's view is that a wide definition will create suitable conditions for the use of an easily accessible and low-cost procedure of high quality. It is assumed that a narrower definition would be more difficult to comply with. Furthermore, the Government believes that a more elaborate definition could cause objections and questioning of different kinds, e.g., that the agreement cannot be enforced since it is not a result of mediation but of some different procedure that is not governed by the Mediation Act. The Government's approach reflects the view that the result of the procedure is more important than the procedure in which the result is achieved.[1170] In this respect, it compares mediation with settlement in court, for which there are no explicit rules.

1170. *Ibid.*, 23–24.

Chapter 3. Court-Referred Mediation

847. In addition to the Mediation Act and the previously mentioned special regulations on mediation laid down in different laws, the general possibility for the district court to refer a case to a mediator in accordance with 42:17 of the Code has existed for many years in Sweden. An appellate court may also refer a case to mediation, but this option is more restricted. However, instead of referring the case to mediation the judge tries to make the parties settle the dispute. The judge is obligated to do so. In most cases, this leads to a settlement. In cases, which are governed by mandatory rules and the court acts on its own motion in order to secure public or other interests, the parties may not settle the dispute themselves through an agreement. Instead, such disputes require a judgment. Thus, in Sweden, mediation with some few exceptions, e.g., custody disputes, is restricted to dispositive disputes.

848. Pursuant to 42:17 in the Code, the district court may refer a dispositive case to special mediation if the parties agree. If the parties agree to mediation, the court shall order them to appear at a session in front of a mediator appointed by the court. In addition, the court shall give a deadline for the mediation to be concluded. The Code does not contain any additional information about mediation.

849. Simultaneously with the implementation of the Directive, amendments were made to the wording of 42:17 of the Code in order to underline the court's responsibility to make the parties settle their dispute. The court must act for a settlement between the parties or, if not, a settlement that the parties in some other way make a mutual agreement, unless it is considered inappropriate with respect to the nature of the case and other circumstances. Pursuant to paragraph 2 of the same section, the court may, if it is not inappropriate and with the consent of the parties, act for a decision about special mediation. Furthermore, according to explanatory notes contained in the proposition to the amendment of the paragraph it is recommended that the judges should consider special mediation more often and that it should be placed on an equal footing with settlement activities in court.[1171] In addition, no dispositive case should be excluded from court settlement or special mediation. The Government found that it complies with the Directive in its wording that the courts should encourage the parties to use mediation.[1172]

850. An important question is how to draw the line between cases that should be referred to mediation and cases that the judge shall try to settle. There is no simple answer to this question. The preparatory works to the Mediation Act indicate that if other legal relationships and non-legal factors tend to stand out more than rule-based criteria, mediation should be preferred.[1173]

1171. *Ibid.*, 28.
1172. *Ibid.*, 78.
1173. *Ibid.*, 28.

851. A connected problem associated with 42:17 in the Code is that the judge will consider him- or herself able to provide the parties with the same level of service as a mediator. If the judge fails to make the parties settle the dispute, the judge probably believes that a mediator would not be successful either. In the government proposal, there is quite a surprising statement, which confirms this view. The proposition states that if the court fails in its settlement attempts it is not probable that a mediator would be more successful.[1174] Such a statement will most likely make the courts reluctant to refer the parties to special mediation. In addition, legal insurance does not apply where it concerns extrajudicial mediation, while the settlement activities of the judge are free from charge. Furthermore, if the court refers a case to special mediation, legal insurance will normally cover the costs. Of course, extrajudicial mediation cannot under these conditions compete on equal terms with the courts.

1174. *Ibid.*

Chapter 4. Initiating Mediation

852. Mediation can be initiated mainly in two ways, privately by using the Mediation Act or through court referral. As stated in section 4 of the Mediation Act mediation will be considered initiated when: (1) the parties have agreed on mediation after a dispute has arisen, (2) an obligation to attend mediation has arisen by law or other statutes, (3) a foreign court has made a decision about mediation or urged the parties to attend mediation. However, court referral in accordance to 42:17 of the Code is the most common way to initiate mediation. The judge may, with the consent of the parties, refer their case to special mediation. A condition for this is that an action has been instituted at the court. To date, the provision on special mediation has not been frequently used. The main explanation for this can be found in the obligation of the judge to settle the dispute. A majority of dispositive cases, around 60%, are settled this way.[1175]

1175. SOU 1982:26, 32.

Chapter 5. Mediation Agreement

853. An agreement to mediate is made in the same way as other agreements, i.e. through an offer and an acceptance of that offer from the other party in accordance with the provisions in the Act on Agreement. As mentioned above, section 4 of the Mediation Act provides that mediation be initiated when the parties have agreed on mediation after a dispute has arisen. Thus, if the parties, when entering into a contract have agreed to mediate upcoming disputes in relation to that contract, they must make an additional agreement to mediate that dispute. The reason for this is the overall requirement that mediation in all stages must be voluntary.[1176] In the preparatory works to the Mediation Act, the issue of whether or not a mediation clause, in the same way as an arbitration clause, should be regarded as a procedural hinder, is discussed. In the proposition to the Mediation Act the Government maintained that a mediation clause is not a procedural hinder, since mediation is a purely voluntary procedure. However, to prevent a party from instituting a court action, a deterrent fine for doing so can be put into the mediation contract. Furthermore, a mediation clause is not enforceable according to Swedish law.[1177] However, multi-tiered dispute resolution clauses have become more common in business contracts in Sweden.[1178] Usually, such clauses provide for a mechanism whereby the parties agree to settle their dispute through mediation and, if this fails, move on to arbitration or court litigation.

1176. D. Engström, *Lag om medling i vissa privaträttsliga tvister* 31 (2011).
1177. Prop. 2010/11:28, 43.
1178. C. Söderlind, *Multimodala tvistlösningsklausuler*, 187 et seq. Juridisk tidsskrift 2005-06, Stockholm.

Chapter 6. Confidentiality

854. In order to safeguard the rule on confidentiality for mediators the provision on secrecy in 35:5 of the Code was amended at the same time as the Mediation Act was introduced with a provision stating that a mediator or an assistant mediator may not be called as a witness. A mediator or an assistant can be heard only if the parties waive their right to confidentiality or where there is a provision in the law that the mediator must testify in court. Revealing confidential information protected by the law is a crime. By contrast, an arbitrator may be called as a witness since arbitrators are not listed in 35:5 of the Code as persons who may not be called as witnesses.

Chapter 7. Persons Who Can Act as Mediator

855. There are no official rules on the accreditation of mediators in Sweden. Thus, anyone with legal capacity may call him- or herself mediator and also act as a mediator. It appears clear that the intention of the Government is to use no regulation in order to enhance or strengthen the profession of mediators. Thus, it is a task for private actors to enhance the use of mediation.

Chapter 8. Mediated Outcomes and Enforceability

856. Section 2 of the Mediation Act provides that a mediation agreement which is made abroad is only valid if, at the same time mediation was initiated: (1) all parties had their domicile or habitual residence in Sweden or (2) one of the parties had its domicile or habitual residence in a different Member State of the EU than any of the other parties, and if none of the parties had their domicile or habitual residence in Denmark. Domicile pursuant to these rules shall be interpreted in accordance with Articles 59 and 60 of the Council's Regulation EG No. 44/2001 of 22, 2000 on Judicial Authorization and Enforcement of Private Law Judgments.

857. In Chapter 3 section 1 of the UB, valid titles of execution are enumerated. In 2011, in conjunction with the enactment of the Mediation Act, a provision stating that mediation agreements are enforceable was inserted into the Code of Execution. The rules on enforcement in the Mediation Act, which make a cross-border mediated agreement enforceable according to the Brussels-I Regulation, are of great importance. The prerequisites for enforcement in the Mediation Act are rather restrictive and could be regarded as discriminatory. However, according to the preparatory works, the legislator meant that it was important to avoid the risk for forum shopping. The present rules are considered to balance different interests in a reasonable way.

858. A separate agreement must be made if the other party applies for an enforcement declaration. Such an application shall be made in writing at the district court where any of the parties have their residence.[1179] Regardless of when the agreement to enforcement was made, the party may withdraw the consent as long as the court has not made an enforcement declaration.[1180] However, if the agreement is made in the mediation agreement, the party risks having to pay damage for breach of contract.

859. If a case has been referred to special mediation pursuant to 42:17 of the Code, and the parties have made a settlement agreement which the court has confirmed through a judgment, it will be enforceable as an ordinary judgment in accordance with the Code of Execution.

1179. Section 8, The Mediation Act.
1180. Prop. 2010/11:28, 47–49.

Selected Bibliography

Among older literature should be mentioned E. Kallenberg, *Svensk Civilprocessrätt*, Lund 1923–1939. This commentary on civil procedure is, in spite of its age, in some respects of interest. Most known and generally respected is a series of five books by P.O. Ekelöf, *Rättegång* 1–5 (C.E. Fritzes, Stockholm). These books which today are edited by Prof. H. Edelstam are frequently used in teaching and also by practitioners. They consist of a comprehensive and analytical study of the courts and the procedural system in both civil and criminal cases.

Andersson, T. *Dispositionsprincipen och EG:s konkurrensregler. En studie i snittet av EG-rätten och den svenska processrätten.* Uppsala: Iustus Förlag, 1999. An analysis of the principle of judicial passivity and EC competition law.

Andersson, T. *Rättsskyddsprincipen. EG-rätt och nationell sanktions-och processrätt ur ett svenskt civilprocessuellt perspektiv.* Uppsala: Iustus Förlag, 1997. A study of the protection of individual community rights.

Bellander, H., Om kostnadsbördan i dispositiva tvistemål (Uppsala 2017).

Bergholtz, G. *Ratio et auctoritas.* Juristförlaget i Lund, 1987. A survey of motivation of judgments.[1181]

Bolding, P.O. *Bevisbördan och den juridiska tekniken.* Uppsala, 1951. A study of burden of proof principles and their application in judicial proceedings.

Boman, R. *Om åberopande och åberopsbörda i dispositiva tvistemål.* Stockholm, 1964. An investigation of the basic rule in 17:3, p. 2 of the Code that a judgment in a dispositive case must not be based on a circumstance that has not been alleged by the party.

Bylander, E. *Muntlighetsprincipen. En rättsvetenskaplig studie av processuella handläggningsformer i svensk rätt.* Uppsala: Iustus Förlag, 2006. An analysis of the principle of orality and different ways to entertain a case in Swedish procedural law.

Diesen, C. *Lekman som domare.* Stockholm: Norstedts Juridik AB, 1996. An analysis of the function of lay judges.

Diesen, C. *Bevis 1-9.* Stockholm: Norstedts Juridik AB, 1998–2012. Nine books about the evaluation of evidence and the burden of proof in different areas of substantive law.

1181. It should be mentioned that the publisher is named only with respect to titles available in the bookshops.

Selected Bibliography

Edelstam, H. *Offentlighet och sekretess i rättegång. Principen om förhandlingsoffentlighet*. Stockholm: Norstedts Juridik AB, 2001. A comprehensive study on publicity and confidentiality in litigation.

Edelstam, H. *Sakkunnigbeviset. En studie rörande användningen av experter inom rättsväsendet*. Uppsala: Iustus Förlag, 1991. A study of the use of experts in the judicial system.

Eklund, H. Inhibition. *Om verkställighetsförbud m.m. i judiciell process, inom förvaltningsrätten och i utsökningsförfarandet*. Uppsala: Iustus Förlag, 1998. A study on stay of execution: on the prohibition of implementation of judgments and decisions in the general courts, in administrative law and execution law.

Fridén, H. *Beneficium vid löneexekution*. Uppsala: Faculty of Law, 1992. The book analysis the minimum figure of earnings a debtor is entitled to retain when the rest of his income is subject to attachment.

Gullnäs, I., et al. *Rättegångsbalken I, II och III* (Stockholm: C.E. Fritzes, 1984). This is a modern commentary to the Code, used as a handbook. It consists of three separate parts in a loose-leaf system and contains more than 3,000 pages.

Heuman, L. *Current Issues in Swedish Arbitration* (Stockholm: C.E. Fritzes, 1990).

Heuman, L. *Skiljemannrätt*. Stockholm: Norstedt Juridik, 1999. A comprehensive book on arbitration.

Jacobsson, U. *Parts kostnad i civilprocess*. Stockholm, 1964. A survey of the rules concerning legal costs in RB, treated mostly from an ideological and historical perspective.

Larsson, S. *Förlikning i tvistemål*. Uppsala, 1958. A treatise on private settlement in civil cases.

Lehrberg, E. *Processgemenskap*. Stockholm: Norstedt Juridik, 2000. An analysis of joinder of parties in Swedish procedural law.

Lindblom, P.H. *Miljöprocess I*. Uppsala: Iustus Förlag, 2001, och *Miljöprocess II*. Uppsala: Iustus Förlag, 2002. Environmental Procedure. Two extensive books on i.e., standing, res judicata and burden of proof in environmental litigation.

Lindblom, P.H. *Grupptalan i Sverige*. Stockholm: Norstedts Juridik, 2008. A commentary on class-action in Sweden.

Lindblom, P.H. *Studier i processrätt*. Stockholm: C.E. Fritzes, 1993. The book contains essays on different procedural issues.

Lindell, B. *Sakfrågor och rättsfrågor*. Uppsala: Iustus Förlag, 1987. An analysis of the relations between questions of facts and questions of law.

Lindell, B. *Processuell preklusion – av nya omständigheter eller bevis rörande saken*. Stockholm: C.E. Fritzes AB, 1993. A study of the rules of preclusion.

Lindell, B. *Civilprocessen* (4th ed.). (Uppsala: Iustus Förlag, 2017). Civil Procedure. A comprehensive and extensive study on civil procedure.

Lindell, B. *Alternativ tvistlösning – särskilt medling och skiljeförfarande*. Uppsala: Iustus Förlag, 2000. A study on alternative dispute resolution, in particular mediation and arbitration.

Lindell, B. *Alternativ rättskipning eller alternativ till rättskipning*. Uppsala, 2006. This book addresses the question of whether there are any differences between ADR (Alternative Dispute Resolution) and alternative administration of justice.

Nordh, R. *Talerätt i miljömål*. Uppsala: Iustus Förlag, 1999. Standing in environmental litigation. A comprehensive study on the subject.

Nordback, K. *Interimistiska åtgärder i EG-rättsliga mål. Om gemenskapsrättens inverkan på det provisoriska rättsskyddet i svensk civil och förvaltningsprocess.* Uppsala, 2005. An analysis of interim measures in EU law.

Olivecrona, K. *Rätt och dom*, 2nd edn. (Stockholm, 1966). This book, partly out of date, primarily concerns the relationship between substantive and procedural law.

Renfors, C. & E. Sverne Arvill. Rättshjälpslagen och annan lagstiftning om rättsligt bistånd. En kommentar. 2:a uppl. Stockholm 2006.

Storskrubb, E., *Civil Procedure and EU-Law: A Policy Area Uncovered* (Oxford, 2008).

Sverne Arvill, E. & Renfors, C., Rättshjälpslagen och annan lagstiftning om rättsligt bistånd. En kommentar. 3:e uppl. Stockholm, 2012.

Walin, G., T. Gregow & P. Löfmarck. *Utsökningsbalken*, 4th edn. Stockholm: C.E. Fritzes AB, 2009. A comprehensive commentary on the Execution Code.

Welamson, L. & J. Munck. *Processen i hovrätt och Högsta domstolen*, 4:e uppl. Stockholm: Norstedts Juridik, 2011.

Westberg, P. *Anskaffning av bevisning i dispositiva tvistemål*. Stockholm: Norstedts Juridik, 2010. A comprehensive study about the gathering of evidence in dispositive civil cases.

Westberg, P. *Det provisoriska rättsskyddet i tvistemål*, bok 1-4. Lund: Juristförlaget, 2004. A comprehensive study about interim measures in civil cases.

Westberg, P. *Domstols officialprövning* (Juristförlaget i Lund, 1989. In this extensive book, the rule in 17:3, p. 1 is analysed. This rule states that a judgment may not grant different or more extensive relief than has been properly demanded by a party.

In recent years, a number of *Festschrifts* have been published in procedural law, containing several Articles on different procedural topics: *Festskrift till Lars Welamson*. Stockholm: C.E. Fritzes AB, 1988; *Festskrift till Per Olof Bolding*. Stockholm: Juristförlaget, 1992; *Vänbok till Robert Boman*. Uppsala: Iustus Förlag, 1990 and *Festskrift till Ulla Jacobson*. Stockholm: C.E. Fritzes, 1991.

Literature in English. There is a comprehensive study from 1965 by R.A. Ginsburg, & A. Bruzelius. *Civil Procedure in Sweden*. The Hague, 1965. However, much has happened since 1965. In addition, there is a chapter about Swedish procedure written by P.H. Lindblom in *Scandinavian Studies in Law*. Stockholm, 1988. From the same author: 'The Privatization of Justice: Some Aspects of Recent Developments in American and Swedish Procedural Law'. In *Law and Reality*. Essays on National and International Procedural Law in Honour of Cornelis Carel Albert Voskuil. Martinus Nijhoff Publishers, 1992, 192 et seq.; Complex Litigation – A Comparative Perspective. In *Civil Justice Quarterly*, 33 et seq. *See also* the report on the procedure in the Scandinavian countries made by P.O. Ekelöf, *International Encyclopedia of Comparative Law*, Volume XVI, edited by M. Cappelletti. Boston, London: The Hague, 1984. In addition, *see* U. Jacobsson, 'General Procedural Law, Criminal Procedure, Civil Procedure and Enforcement', in *Swedish Law, A Survey* (Stockholm: Juristförlaget, 1995), 448 et seq. Concerning arbitration, the Swedish Chamber of Commerce edits a book in English every other year concerning issues in the arbitration area. They also have published a comprehensive study on the subject: *Arbitration in Sweden*. Stockholm, 1984.

Selected Bibliography

See also T. Andersson (ed.). *Parallel and Conflicting Enforcement of Law*. Stockholm: Norstedt Juridik, 2005; M. Berglund. *Cross-Border Enforcement of Claims in the EU*. Stockholm, 2009. K. Hobér. *International Commercial Arbitration in Sweden*. Oxford University Press, 2011 and B. Lindell. *Alternative Dispute Resolution and the Administration of Justice – Basic Principles*, volume 51 (Stockholm: Scandinavian Studies in-Law. Procedural Law. Court Administrations, 2007), 311 et. seq.

Index

The numbers here refer to paragraph numbers.

Index